Essays on
Sri Aurobindo

Essays on Sri Aurobindo

Edited by
Aparajita Mukhopadhyay

Centre for Sri Aurobindo Studies
Deparment of Philosophy
Jadavpur University

Suryodaya Books

Cataloging in Publication Data — DK
[Courtesy: D.K. Agencies (P) Ltd. <docinfo@dkagencies.com>]

Essays on Sri Aurobindo / edited by Aparajita Mukhopadhyay.
pages cm
Includes bibliographical references.
ISBN: 9788192570280

1. Ghose, Aurobindo, 1872-1950. 2. Philosophy, Indic. I. Mukhopadhyay, Aparajita, editor.

DDC 181.4 23

ISBN: 978-81-925702-8-0
First published in India in 2015

Published by:
Centre for Sri Aurobindo Studies
Jadavpur University
Kolkata (West Bengal)

and

Suryodaya Books
"*Suryodaya*", D-36A/1, Mohan Garden
Najafgarh Road, New Delhi – 110 059
Phone: (011) 2535 3435

Distributed by:
D.K. Printworld (P) Ltd.
Regd. Office: "Vedaśrī", F-395, Sudarshan Park
(Metro Station: Ramesh Nagar), New Delhi – 110 015
Phones: (011) 2545 3975, 2546 6019; *Fax*: (011) 2546 5926
e-mail: indology@dkprintworld.com
Website: www.dkprintworld.com

Printed by: Suryodaya Books, New Delhi

Contents

Introduction

Aparajita Mukhopadhyay

Sri Aurobindo, one of the distinguished philosophers of twentieth century, provides a unique, integral metaphysical system, which makes a bridge between science and spirituality, West and East. The integrality of his philosophy lies in his attempt to combine physical, vital and mental elements into one single reality which is called the *Saccidānanda Brahman*. Sri Aurobindo, the philosopher, *yogī* and the poet, has spent the later stage of his life in search of spiritual truth. His idea of spirituality is not limited to the scope of any religious framework; he believes in the attitude of sacrifice to a transcendental authority. His concept of divinity and spirituality inspires us to transcend ourselves to a superior level where the materialistic demands cannot mar our mental purity. Sri Aurobindo's belief in the metaphysical existence of one ultimate reality reminds us of his affinity with the Advaita Vedānta. At the same time his attitude of not considering world as *māyā* and his reliance on the process of evolution and involution reflects his difference from the philosophy of Advaita Vedānta. A kind of mysticism is present in the philosophy of Sri Aurobindo as he counts the supreme consciousness as the ultimate source of the material world. His perspective differs from the purely scientific one as he felt, its extreme materialistic explanation cannot prove the existence of consciousness and similarly he realized that divinity only cannot justify the worldly experiences. Sri Aurobindo's comprehensive and systematic exposition of integral system provides a logical justification to his concept of creation of the world. His acceptance of Supermind as the conscious force of *Brahman* gives his explanation a spiritual flavour. He has explained his metaphysics as the relation between one and many. His philosophy encourages us not to act mechanically, rather creates the sense of morality and spirituality in us. Such positive attitude towards life ensures us about our potentiality to illuminate ourselves through manifestation to the higher mind. The aim of this book is to understand the integral philosophy of Sri Aurobindo from his spiritual, religious, humanistic, rationalistic and moral perspectives. Uniqueness of this book is that though the papers included in this book focus on the metaphysical approach of Sri Aurobindo, they have discussed the issue from different standpoints. Some writers are concentrating on Sri Aurobindo's *The Life Divine* to understand the proper meaning of divine life; to justify the necessity to accept the existence of evil and suffering for the manifestation of life; the essentiality to accept the different mental levels to know the true reality. Some writers are focusing on Sri Aurobindo's poetic expressions to understand the meaning of life, the humanistic and moral attitude of life. The linguistic expressions used in Sri Aurobindo's *Sāvitrī* and other works are discussed in this book.

Ramesh Chandra Pradhan in his paper "Sri Aurobindo's Integral Metaphysics: Problems and Prospects" thinks that Sri Aurobindo has offered an integral metaphysical system to establish a harmony among those things which are considered as opposites according to the traditional view. Sri Aurobindo realized the need to bridge the gap between one and many, spirit and matter, infinite and finite, perfect and imperfect, and between God and man. His integral metaphysics accepts both the celestial and terrestrial levels of existence and at the same time unity and diversity of Reality. Thus Pradhan thinks Sri Aurobindo's attempt to integrate the scientific spirit of the West with the spirituality of the East matches with the thought of Hegel. Sri Aurobindo's metaphysical exposition shows how a limited man who is capable to apply his reason, analyse the situation, act with the awareness of the consequences aspires for spiritual enlightenment. His integral metaphysics dismisses the monistic approach. Pradhan comments that Sri Aurobindo denies the materialistic approach which admits the primacy of matter and disregard spirit because he thinks if we deny the reality of mind or consciousness then knowledge of the material universe will be impossible. Similarly we cannot ignore the reality of matter when we are interested in explaining the nature of the universe. We cannot describe the Infinite Reality by any finite way. *Brahman*, as the non-dual Ultimate Reality includes in it everything and so any attempt to draw any division between things actually misleads us to capture the truth about the reality. To cope with the Reality, Mind must be evolved into Supermind which is free from all kinds of limitations. Pradhan thinks, Sri Aurobindo's ascending unity suggests that there are two levels of integration — one is in ontological level and another in epistemic level. Pradhan very clearly explains the difference between Aurobindo's monism and Śaṅkara's monism. Sri Aurobindo's acceptance of matter as Real is the proof for his rejection of Śaṅkara's pure monism which accepts *Brahman* alone as real. In this respect Pradhan has introduced Sri Aurobindo's view about both mind and matter.

Though Sri Aurobindo accepts the reality of this perceptible world, it is impossible for a finite being to know the creation of this world by his limited perspective. Realizing this Ulrich Mohrhoff in his paper "Spiritual Physics" has compared two different views about world creation — one is from the standpoint of quantum mechanics which understands objects as measurable and believes that objects exist in a particular space–time framework and the second one is the spiritual explanation which understands *Brahman*, the Ultimate Reality as a timeless, unlimited entity. We normally differentiate scientific explanation from spiritual one as scientific proofs are based on empirical data whereas spiritual exposition cannot provide any factual evidence. But Ulrich Mohrhoff has taken an attempt to show that though there is a difference in their approach, still we see that modern physics does not differ from the Upaniṣadic explanation. He rather suggests that their difference arises not because they differ about the nature of truth, but because they are trying to know the reality from different mental levels. Spiritual explanation understands the truth from Supramental level. As scientific explanation is confined in the mental level it fails to answer properly why the ultimate building blocks combine with each other to create the world. Their finite explanation of reality from the bottom up is incomplete as it is the outcome of the mind.

Quantum mechanics has proved that the atoms, the ultimate indivisible parts of physical objects, are formless. From these formless atoms all the objects of the physical world are created. Ulrich applies this theory to the Upaniṣadic process of creation where the formless Ultimate Reality *Brahman* constitutes, contains and originates all worldly objects. In terms of quantum mechanics he expresses it as: *Brahman enters into spatial relations with itself.* Ulrich finds an affinity between science and Upaniṣad regarding the nature of space. Kant thinks that space is essentially one, though we accept space as manifold only to understand the division of the material objects. But modern physicists do not consider space as the condition for perception and imagination; on the contrary they think that spatial multiplicity divides surface. But our conceptual partition of the world does not reflect the actual state of the world. Similarly Sri Aurobindo accepts that spatial multiplicity is the outcome of our mental level. Supermind, the conscious force of *Brahman* is primarily qualitative and infinite. But secondarily in the mental level it is quantitative and finite.

So the goal of mankind must be the dynamic elevation towards the fully conscious state through self-knowledge, self-recovery and creative evolution. To prove this S.E. Bhelke has concentrated on Sri Aurobindo's *The Life Divine.* His aim is to understand Sri Aurobindo's view regarding the spiritual goal of mankind which is described as a state of perfection and divine delight. Bhelke clarifies in his paper "Remarks on the Foundations of *The Life Divine*" that there is no difference between being and becoming, or between the present limited life and the manifested illuminated state of life. He makes us conscious that the task of our life is to transform our divine life to life divine. The transformation of life is not a mechanical, but a creative process as the conscious desire directs us towards a thoughtful, vertical and hierarchical destination. In the primary level of manifestation incompleteness is completed as potentialities are actualized. In the higher level of manifestation fully manifested Being manifests not for any incompleteness, but to reveal a novel form. Bhelke has emphasized on Sri Aurobindo's attempt to use the logic of negation to develop his philosophy about reality. It is not possible to know by our limited capacity the nature of infinite reality which is evolving continuously and dynamically due to a Universal Force. But at least we must know that the apparent oppositions are essential integral parts of the same homogeneous reality. Sri Aurobindo has accepted four categories — matter, life, mind and consciousness — in his philosophy. The Vedānta concepts of *māyā, ātman, Brahman* and *Saccidānanda* are utlized in his thought to account for his integral Advaita Vedāntic standpoint. Bhelke in his paper has uniquely described how the metaphysical system of Sri Aurobindo differs from the system of Advaita Vedānta, specially regarding the ontological status of *māyā* and the world.

To prove the inevitability of divine life Sri Aurobindo in his *The Life Divine* has admitted the metaphysical existence of two incompatible things — one is the *Saccidānanda Brahman* and the other one is evil. Stephen Phillips in his paper "God's Last World: Sri Aurobindo's Argument for Divine Life" has raised a very relevant question about the justification for the existence of evil in this God-created world. Existence of evil actually expresses doubt about the omnipotent and benevolent nature of God. To understand this problem of evil from the standpoint of Indian philosophy Phillips has discussed the philosophy of Sri Aurobindo along with that of Śaṅkara. In Śaṅkara's *Brahma-Sūtras* we find *Īśvara* or *Saguṇa-Brahman* creates this world out of Himself. But if the world comes out of *Brahman* then how could the evil exist in this world which is just the opposite in nature of *Brahman*? How does the perfect God allow evil (*avidyā*) in his own creation? Here Phillips is especially concerned about natural evils and not about the moral evils, because moral evils are the consequences of human actions and not included in the realm of God's activity. But it seems that natural evils are different in nature as mankind is not responsible for the natural evils like disease, old age and death though these are unavoidable and obvious consequences of their lives. Phillips has proved that natural evils are also the result of our deeds. In accordance to the classical Indian philosophy we face the natural evils in our worldly life due to our rebirth. The reason for rebirth is our evil performances in the past life. Thus natural evils are also the result of our *karma*. Someone may ask how the God could allow us to perform evil actions which are the cause of suffering and pain. In response to this Śaṅkara introduces his theory of *māyā*. Sri Aurobindo thinks that we are getting such a life as *Brahman* is giving us the opportunity to develop. We are responsible for our inner tendencies and so we should be rewarded or punished for those actions which we perform out of these tendencies. Through this method justice is actually established in this God's world. According to Sri Aurobindo evil has an instrumental value to the development of divine life. He considers positive value as end and negative value as means. Negative values though not the part of divine life, are helpful to transform our life to a divine life. Sri Aurobindo in his *The Life Divine* explains *Brahman* or *Saccidānanda* as *ānanda* who for his intrinsic value forcing the 'divine life'. We realize *ānanda* when we realize the value of becoming, *ānanda* is the accompaniment with the achievement of higher life.

Phillips considers this world as the 'last world', because though it is not the best among all possible worlds, it is different as 'I' exist in this world. This world may not be the best world but we should not overlook the good things, the bliss of God which is showered on us in this world. In *The Life Divine* Sri Aurobindo has given different explanations regarding *Brahman*'s motivation for the creation of the world. Sometimes we believe that the reason for the creation of the world is to liberate (*mukti*) people. But Sri Aurobindo does not accept such view because then the process of manifestation will turn to a meaningless process. So *mukti* cannot motivate *Brahman* to create the world as *mukti* means end of the cosmic process and return to a native state. Rather Sri Aurobindo accepts the view which suggests God's *līlā* as the reason for the creation. He agrees that *Brahman*'s delight in creation is his motivation. But Phillips expresses his doubt about its justification. In his opinion if *Brahman* is supposed to be intrinsically blissful then self-manifestation cannot be considered as essential to be delighted. Phillips thinks that to consider delight as a motivational force Sri Aurobindo has to admit that the delight of *Brahman* in the process of manifestation must be a different kind of delight than the delight which is present intrinsically in *Brahman*.

Indrani Sanyal in her paper "Does the Delightful Absolute Provide for Evils?" has also discussed about the difficulty to define the notion of evil and to determine its scope. Western culture views evil as a metaphysical entity which exists as a contrary notion of perfectly good God. Sanyal very lucidly shows that Sri Aurobindo, going against the Indian traditional explanation of Śaṅkara, accepts the reality of evil. But Sri Aurobindo thinks that its occurrence is not accidental one, it appears due to the interaction between the different forms of consciousness. Unlike Western concept he considers the perfect God as the source of all evils, sufferings and falsehood, though denies the fundamentality or eternity of it. Sanyal with her nice expressions clarifies Sri Aurobindo's view about the origination of evil. Ignorance, which is called by Sri Aurobindo half-light and half-shadow, is the cause of evil and is a self-limiting separative knowledge. Sanyal suggests understanding evil from three standpoints — transcendental, universal and individual — which are considered by Sri Aurobindo as the three aspects of one existence. Evil which is caused by ignorance has no absolute existence because his integral system accepts one Being as Real which has the above-mentioned three interrelated aspects. So evil is not any fundamental aspect of the Being as it is caused by ignorance. Sri Aurobindo as a Satkāryavādin thinks that ignorance cannot be totally devoid of consciousness as it arises from *Brahman* as a by-product of the cosmic manifestation of consciousness. This state of ignorance has to be accepted to understand the evolutionary process. Sanyal thinks that the world-being is the individuating consciousness which is the cause of all self-experiences and world-experiences. The world-being as the individuating consciousness has the power to transcend himself through his self-experience. This transcendence, the evolutionary process needs an intermediate stage which is a stage of part knowledge and part ignorance. To understand the manifestation of Supramental it is necessary to understand the imperfection.

To understand the divinity of life Raghunath Ghosh in his paper "'Sāvitrī' as a Religio-Literary Composition" has focused on Sri Aurobindo's poetic art form expressed specially in his book *Sāvitrī*. In his poetic sense we find the influence of European literature as well as the impact of Sanskrit literature. To Sri Aurobindo poetry reflects the Truth and so the poet is considered as *ṛṣi*. Ghosh has reminded us about the power of poetic language which is not present in prose. Though the language of prose has the ability to denote objects, it fails to arouse the aesthetic impact as it cannot go beyond the words. Aesthetic value of *Sāvitrī* lies in its poetic expressions which go beyond the informative senses of words and touch the senses of words. Ghosh thinks that Sri Aurobindo's 'overhead poetry' goes beyond the creative intelligence as his use of words and rhythms creates a harmony between the ultimate one and the cosmic divergent. By his poetic expressions he gives the message that like the glorious lady Sāvitrī one can reach the plane of divinity through the means of knowledge, love, emotion, power and *yoga*. His aesthetic approach is conducive to conquer Death through realizing the connection with the Supramental consciousness. This sense of deathlessness helps to enter in an immortal, blissful, sufferingless state even in this world.

Ghosh's intention is to discover the aesthetic beauty which is woven harmoniously with religious truth in the book *Sāvitrī*. He points out that Sri Aurobindo has glorified the character of Sāvitrī with the virtues of love, courage, devotion to prove that through the power of all these virtues one can make a bridge between man and God. He describes the way through which Sāvitrī connects herself with this ignorant world to explain her absolute manifestation. Sri Aurobindo explains how does self-consciousness revealed from the unconscious; how does Divine Mother, Sāvitrī prepares the mortal, ignorant world to accept the glimpses of divinity to understand the absolute manifestation of Supramental consciousness. Thus in Ghosh's opinion *Sāvitrī* breaks the barrier of creative intelligence and spreads its religious truth through its aesthetic fragrance. Sāvitrī is painted by Sri Aurobindo as a symbol of ideal woman who is devoted to her husband. Her devotion is expressed in her love, in her protective nature as she becomes successful to snatch her husband from the God of Death, Yama, after a long argumentation and dialogue. It makes clear that Sāvitrī is also wise as to save her husband she is not creating any emotional pressure on Yama, but she is giving intellectual arguments. Sāvitrī is called Divine Mother because like Divine Mother she is able to resist Death and helps man to reach the level of immortality. Ghosh also mentions that Sri Aurobindo gives value to *yoga* and devotion as the methods of reaching the celestial plane. Through *yoga*, Sāvitrī comes to know her own self, her own spirit which provides her the confidence to compel Yama to change her destiny. Yoga gives her supremacy, turns her to Mighty Mother. Devotion not only empowers a devotee and helps him to cross the limited boundary of the physical and mental world through self illumination, but at the same time ensures bliss for the whole world. Thus the character of Sāvitrī gives some messages, depicts some religious truths for us.

Dilip Kumar Roy, in his paper "Sri Aurobindo's Observations on Heraclitus, an Aphoristic Philosopher", has discussed in a very lucid way the similarities in the thought of Sri Aurobindo and the great Greek thinker Heraclitus though they belong to two different cultures. Roy thinks that Sri Aurobindo's uniqueness lies in his attempt to understand philosophy of Heraclitus in the light of classical Indian philosophy. Sri Aurobindo thinks Heraclitus possesses intellectual stimulation and at the same time he has a psychic and intuitive vision. But Sri Aurobindo is interested to explore the mysticism which is present in Heraclitus's style of philosophizing. In his view Heraclitus's mysticism reflects from his linguistic expressions. Sri Aurobindo thinks that we may fail to cope up the actual sense of an expression used by Heraclitus if we do not interpret it from the mystic viewpoint. According to Sri Aurobindo, apart from his aphoristic and epigrammatic style, Heraclitus has followed cryptic style which is the source of his mysticism. Roy has rightly identified that obscurity and symbolic expression, the two characteristics of mystic language, are prominently present in Heraclitus's language. Heraclitus puts emphasis in uncovering the universal reality by explaining the relation of one with many. He believes both in unity and multiplicity as in his view same matter takes the form of multiple bodies. In a similar way it can be claimed that there is one Mind, but there are several mental beings. Heraclitus has realized that we cannot deny the eternal coexistence of one and its multiplicity. He acknowledges 'the ever-living fire' as one eternal which is called as the stuff of the universe. The eternal one which is called by Heraclitus as 'the ever-living fire' cannot be considered simply as the physical stuff of the universe. Sri Aurobindo claims that the mystic interpretation clarifies that this stuff is not any physical substance or energy, but it is actually the will which insists the one to create many and the same will is the cause of the transformation of many to one. This continuous process of eternal change is the foundation of Heraclitus's philosophical thought. Roy considers this upward and downward movement as the justification of Heraclitus's theory of the creation of the world from fire. In Sri Aurobindo's view Heraclitus is successful to provide a logical exposition of his system. But he criticizes Heraclitus for overlooking delight which is important for the realization of divine love and joy.

Bijayananda Kar in his paper "Sri Aurobindo and Spiritual Humanism" has given a critical exposition to Sri Aurobindo's concept of spiritual humanism. Kar thinks Sri Aurobindo's philosophy is an intellectual search for truth and to him religion is the realization of truth in our soul. So his 'spiritual religion of humanity' though founded on spirituality, is not decoupled from the humanitarian goal. His humanism does not lead to transcendentalism, but encourages transforming ourselves by the feeling of oneness with others and helps us to realize the universal spirit within us by breaking the barrier of our individual mind and body. In this respect the writer of the paper has taken an attempt to understand the actual nature of Sri Aurobindo's personified religion which aims to make philosophic truth dynamic in the soul of man. He thinks that Sri Aurobindo's such fusionist attitude has helped him to overcome the rigidity of Indian classical tradition and on the other hand to refuse the materialist trend which underestimates the spiritual element of life. But Kar thinks that in spite of adopting intellect as a method, Sri Aurobindo believes that divinity of life is ensured by the realization of human unity through spiritual oneness and this realization can be possible only through mystic experience, not by intellect or justification. He is raising an objection against Sri Aurobindo for keeping reliance on mystic experience rather than rational justification. Kar thinks that the validity of self experience cannot be considered as a proof for the reality of the content of the experience. The reality of existence can be proved by the method of public verification. But such method cannot be considered as a plausible method in case of mystic experience. So Kar is not ready to accept Sri Aurobindo's mystic experience of divineness as it is not founded on rationality.

Kar in his paper has very nicely entered into a discussion on the meaning of 'fundamental truth of things' to clarify Sri Aurobindo's unusual interpretation of philosophy. Kar's discussion of the 'fundamental truth of things' centres on two issues: first, what does exactly mean by fundamental truth? Is it relative due to the subjective perspectives of the observers? Second, what is the nature of things which are denoted by 'all'? 'All' can be intelligible if we understand by limiting it within a boundary or 'all' may indicate a generalized concept like 'man'. Now if we presuppose that things are essentially one and that is the fundamental truth then Kar argues that establishment of both fundamentality and truth will go in vain. Kar thinks that Sri Aurobindo understands existence as absolute real or as the only real which is neither based on any factual evidence nor rests on any justification. He has also expressed his doubt about Sri Aurobindo's idea of humanity. By the use of this word, he thinks, we indicate some good qualities which help us to deal with other human and non-human beings and humanity is not at all connected with God. But the notion humanity also encompasses good gestures towards other, i.e. having a good will to feel concern for other beings. Thus the concept includes honesty and soberness as its essential components. In this sense humanity turns to spiritual humanism. Kar thinks, perhaps Sri Aurobindo reformulated humanity in this manner. But there are several strong views according to which humanism should be separated from religious viewpoint to maintain its objectivity.

Asok Kumar Mukhopadhyay in his paper "Political Theory of Sri Aurobindo: A Critical Appreciation" has focused on the pre-Pondicherry life of Sri Aurobindo, especially on his views about the political attitude and activities at the time of India's nationalist movement. The uniqueness of his political thought lies in the fact that it is based on spirituality. But his spiritualism does not preconceive any personified deity, but it is the feeling of fraternity, realization of humanity. His intention was to understand the relation between nation and individual in terms of personal relation like that of a mother and her son. This humanity can be achieved through human development, through the upward movement towards larger entity. Sri Aurobindo criticizes the attitude of the moderate

Congressmen who failed to show their sincerity and wholeheartedness to connect them to the common people. To him nationalism is an emergent emotion which associates men on the basis of their common interests and feeling of passion. His anti-individualistic and anti-materialistic attitudes encourage him to dismiss Capitalism and Imperialism as these systems ignore the interests of people by encouraging some personal vices. His aim was to revive India's spiritual tradition refuting the tendency of imitating Western style. He was interested to connect the intellectualism of the West with the spirituality of the East. Mukhopadhyay thinks that Sri Aurobindo has rightly identified the problem of present era where the ideal of the ruling class is forcefully imposed on the common people. But any such attempts should be strongly resisted as the traditional Indian culture does not allow such tendencies. Sri Aurobindo thinks that the unity of mankind can be achieved when our soul will be able to discover its spiritual character through the upward transformation of life from *tamas* to *sattva*, through the realization of freedom or self-fulfilment. Like Karl Marx he never thinks that the unity of mankind can be achieved through the equality of material property or power. He refutes the party-oriented concept of politics, but his sole aim was the evolution of humanity which is reflected through the fraternity. For this Sri Aurobindo introduces his concept of "Sanātan Dharma". His interpretation puts emphasis on the harmony of non-physical aspects going beyond the material needs.

Susmita Bhattacharya in her paper "A Perspective on Inter-personal Relation: A Journey from Jean-Paul Sartre to Sri Aurobindo" has focused on the peculiar nature of interpersonal relation of man as she thinks it is the result of both subject-oriented desires and collective impulses. To get a clear picture of human relation she has included in her writing several approaches both from the Western and Indian cultures. We find that Sartre considers human relation as complicated due to the conflicting human nature. Both the attitudes of possessiveness and collective impulses are present in man. Sartre realized that a continuous tension persists in human relation due to the contradictory attitude of human nature. Man's fear to lose freedom insists him not to tolerate others, but at the same time he realizes that for the possession of a relation presence of other beings is necessary. In the view of Sartre relation among primitive men was founded on their acceptance of a single totem. Totem as a genetic origin of a group is the source of the feeling of brotherhood among the people of that particular group. Sartre thus takes the help of a myth to prove that a feeling of bonding among people succeeds to overthrow this attitude of tension in human relation. But Bhattacharya mentions that myth cannot provide us the logical ground for a stable relation. She points out that Sri Aurobindo is giving a complete explanation of the relation between people. Sri Aurobindo also accepts that man possesses an egoistic attitude at first. But to fulfil his self-interest he realizes the necessity of other people in his life. But in the higher stage of manifestation man can identify him with other and such realization dissolves the self–other distinction. Sri Aurobindo thinks due to an ethical impulse man realizes the supreme oneness which is the cause of his feeling of identity with others. Realization of true self means understanding oneself as a part of the collective existence.

Anirban Ganguly in his paper "An Educationist in a Princely State: Sri Aurobindo and His Early Thoughts on Education" has described how the wholehearted attempt of Sri Aurobindo to establish National Education brought a systematic change in Indian educational framework. Sri Aurobindo was critical about the British education system imparted to Indian people to make them intellectually dull and to spoil them by injecting some narrow mechanical bad habits. To him education is not just to gather information and memorization of that, but education is cultivation of the power of reasoning, the capacity to compare and differentiate things, the capability to express it in own words, which are already present in man. He realized that mere accumulation of knowledge is not enough, we must give more emphasis on the capacity to use that knowledge.

Most of the articles included in this anthology were published in some journals. "God's Last World: Sri Aurobindo's Argument for Divine Life" and "Sri Aurobindo's Integral Metaphysics: Problems and Prospects" were published in the *Jadavpur Journal of Philosophy*, Jadavpur University, in the volume 18, number 2 in 2008.

The paper "Spiritual Physics" was published in the same journal in the volume 19, number 1, in 2009. "Sri Aurobindo and Spiritual Humanism", 'Sāvitrī' as a Religio-Literary Composition" and "A Perspective on Inter-Personal Relation: A Journey from Jean-Paul Sartre to Sri Aurobindo" were also published in the *Jadavpur Journal of Philosophy*, Jadavpur University, volume 22, number 1, in 2012. I express my heartiest thanks to the editor of the journal for giving me permission to include these scholarly papers in this anthology. The paper "Does the Delightful Absolute Provide for Evils?" was published in *Sraddhā*, volume 5, number 3, Sri Aurobindo Bhavan, Kolkata, in 2014 and "Sri Aurobindo's Observations on Heraclitus, an Aphoristic Philosopher" was published originally in *Sri Aurobindo Mandir*, Annual of Sri Aurobindo Pāthamandir, Kolkata in 2014. I am also thankful to the editors of these two journals for allowing me to publish these papers. The present paper "Political Theory of Sri Aurubindo: A Critical Appreciation" is a written version of Professor Asok Kumar Mukhopadhyay's lecture delivered by him in the 29th Annual Sri Aurobindo Memorial Lecture organized by Jadavpur University and Centre for Sri Aurobindo Studies, Department of Philosophy, on the auspicious occasion of Sri Aurobindo's birth anniversary. Professor S.E. Bhelke was invited to the Centre for Sri Aurobindo Studies as a visiting faculty and "Remarks on the Foundations of *The Life Divine*" is a written version of his all those valuable lectures delivered by him in the Centre. "An Educationist in a Princely State: Sri Aurobindo and His Early Thoughts on Education" is a part of Dr Anirban Ganguly's PhD thesis "Sri Aurobindo and the Quest for a Philosophy of National Education". I am grateful to all the contributors of this volume for their heartiest cooperation to publish this anthology. I am thankful to Jadavpur University for providing warm assistance to run the academic activities of the Centre. I also express my thanks to University Grants Commission for giving us approval for the continuation of the Centre and for providing financial assistance for this publication. I am also thankful to Professor Indrani Sanyal, the former Coordinator of the Centre for Sri Aurobindo Studies, Department of Philosophy, Jadavpur University for providing her active cooperation and valuable suggestions to publish this book.

1

Sri Aurobindo's Integral Metaphysics
Problems and Prospects*

R.C. Pradhan

SRI Aurobindo is one of the metaphysicians of the world having a system of his own which can match that of Hegel in the breadth of its scope and depth. He is an Advaitin being loyal to the Vedāntic tradition[1] and is yet at the same time an integralist like Hegel in the West. He combines the scientific spirit of the West with the spiritual bent of mind of the East. As a metaphysician, he sees no contradiction between materialism and spiritualism, and relativism and absolutism. He evolves a grand synthesis of all apparently contradicting metaphysical systems. That is why he is aptly an integral metaphysician who sees no unbridgeable gulf between matter and spirit and between the lowest and the highest in the scheme of things.

I

The Need of Integral Metaphysics

Sri Aurobindo is well aware of the deep need of a metaphysics that can integrate rather than disintegrate the diverse aspects of Reality. That is, he is well on the way to reject the traditionally demarcated binary categories[2] such as one and many, matter and spirit, finite

* The present essay incorporates under three major sections of deliberations of mine during my stay in September 2007 at Jadavpur University, Kolkata, as a visiting faculty to the Centre for Sri Aurobindo Studies.

1 Sri Aurobindo's integral philosophy is steeped in the Vedāntic tradition derived from the Vedas and the Upaniṣads, through which he also derives inspiration of the tradition of Tantra.

2 The binary categories like mind–matter, truth–falsity and perfection–imperfection are part of the logic of the finite, according to Sri Aurobindo. The logic of the finite is the logic shaped by the finite mind.

and infinite, perfect and imperfect, man and God and so on. He is inspired by the fact that the binary categories divide reality into absolutely divergent blocks that can never be harmonized. His main aim is to dismantle the walls created between the different blocks of reality such as matter and spirit, and finite and infinite. According to him, metaphysics has been divided between the two mental blocks, one of complete spiritual negation of matter and the other of the complete denial of the spirit by the materialists. Our civilization has been divided over these two negations[3] which have spelt doom so far as our total spiritual growth is concerned.

According to Sri Aurobindo, the greatest problem of metaphysics is the problem of harmony and integration of the divergent viewpoints and the elimination of the discord which arises from this divergence. Discord may be a natural state of affairs in the imperfect world in which we live, but that is not the ideal state of affairs which the spiritual man can conceive of. Sri Aurobindo writes:

> For all problems of existence are essentially problems of harmony. They arise from the perception of an uresolved discord and the instinct of an undiscovered agreement or unity. To rest content with an unsolved discord is possible for the practical and more animal part of man, but impossible for his fully awakened mind. . . .[4]

That is, the earthly man suffers necessarily from discord and disharmony but that is not the final state of human existence. There is a more developed state of the human mind that is one of harmony and integration. The spiritually illumined mind is the mind of harmony.

For Sri Aurobindo, metaphysics as an intellectual and reflective discipline aims at furthering the cause of the Nature which is itself a process of integration of matter, life and mind in various complex stages of evolution. Metaphysics reflects the intellectual aspiration to provide a conceptual map regarding how Nature itself is marching towards the final elimination of discord and the differences. Thus

---

3 See *The Life Divine*, Pondicherry: Sri Aurobindo Ashram, 1973, Book One, chaps. II and III.

4 Ibid., p. 2.

there is the necessity of an integral metaphysics that truly codifies the inner movement of Nature. In Sri Aurobindo there is the convergence of the integral processes of reality and the metaphysical effort to reach harmony at the highest spiritual level. He writes:

> If it be true that Spirit is involved in Matter and apparent Nature is secret God, then the manifestation of the divine in himself and the realization of God within and without are the highest and the most legitimate aims possible to man on earth.[5]

Metaphysics thus intellectuallly sorts out the divine plan of existence and makes it clear how the human mind aspires for spiritual enlightenment while embedded in the earthly existence.

"The Two Negations" and the Binary Categories

Sri Aurobindo's *The Life Divine* aims at eliminating the "two negations" which constitute the two poles of metaphysics that led to a deep discord in human thought. These two negations are those of the materialist denial and the refusal of the ascetic[6] which have been part of the metaphysical and moral traditions of the East and the West. In both these traditions, the materialist thinkers have rejected the existence of anything spiritual and supernatural, because they believe that the only reality that we can accept is that of matter and the material bodies. On the contrary, the spiritualist philosophers have denied the existence of matter because they believe that spirit and its manifestations are alone real. Thus metaphysical traditions have come into existence representing two different negations.

The materialist denial consists in the stark refusal to recognize anything spiritual because of the positive affirmation that matter alone is real. Characterizing the materialist position, Sri Aurobindo writes:

> The materialist has an easier field; it is possible for him by denying Spirit to arrive at a more readily convincing simplicity of statement, a real Monism, the Monism of Matter or else of Force.[7]

---

5 See *The Life Divine*, p. 4.

6 Cf. Ibid., pp. 6-17.

7 See *The Life Divine*, p. 7.

This monistic metaphysics is one-sided because it denies the reality of the mind, consciousness and spirit in its urge to affirm the supremacy of the material or the physical universe. Materialist monism reduces every form of existence into that of the material bodies and their ultimate constituents. It makes effort to provide an ontology of the material or the physical forces that are the known sources of all reality.[8]

But Sri Aurobindo wonders how there can be denial of the mind and consciousness when these are the grounds of our knowledge of the material universe. In the universe there are not only material bodies but also mental beings so that prima facie there is not one reality called matter. At least minds exist side by side matter and life. Sri Aurobindo finds it entirely unacceptable that there is only matter everywhere. He finds that the mind has a great role to play in the universe, especially in the evolutionary scheme of things. "As soon as we begin to investigate the operations of mind and supermind", says Sri Aurobindo, "in themselves and without prejudgement that is determined from the beginning to see in them only a subordinate term of matter, we come ino contact with a mass of phenomena which escape entirely from the rigid hold, the limiting dogmatism of the materialist formula."[9] These phenomena are those of mind and supermind to satisfy our reason in explaining the universe because it cannot explain the very basis of our reasoning about the universe. The universe is itself intelligible only to the mind and therefore any doctrine that denies the mind must be an incomplete and inconsistent doctrine.

The refusal of the ascetic is equally vulnerable to the charge that it denies the existence of matter while explaining the universe. The spiritualist holds that the universe is out and out spiritual and that the universe of matter is a sheer illusion. The spiritual theory in its extreme form advocates that matter does not exist at all because all reality is mental and spiritual by nature. Matter is a superimposition[10] on the Spirit, as the Advaitins believe. This theory

---

8 Cf. J. Poland, 1994, *Physicalism*, Oxford: Clarendon Press, chap. 1.

9 Sri Aurobindo, *The Life Divine*, p. 10.

10 Cf. Ibid., chap. III.

is monistic in its metaphysical approach and thus takes everything that is material as unreal. For this theory everything is essentially spiritual.

According to Sri Aurobindo, the spiritual monism like materialist monism does not fare well in explaining the universe because it fails to recognize the fact that there are material bodies like the mighty heavens which are as much real as our minds and spirits. That is, there is a whole level of terrestrial existence that is made of matter which cannot be missed in our investigation into the nature of Reality. Matter exists even if ultimately the universe is spiritual in essence.

For Sri Aurobindo, the old controversy between the spiritualist and the materialist monism is out of place because Reality is something different from what each doctrine propounds it to be. Reality is both matter and spirit in the sense that there is a totality of Being in which matter and spirit have their respective places. Reality is all-comprehensive and so has the infinite capacity to include in a unique whole all that is physically real as well as all that is real beyond the world of physics. Sri Aurobindo writes:

> And still there is a beyond.
>
> For on the other side of the cosmic consciousness there is, attainable to us, a consciousness yet more transcendent — transcendent not only of the ego, but of the Cosmos itself, — against which the universe seems to hand out like a petty picture against an immeasurable background.[11]

This transcendent consciousness is the vast reality of which our universe is only a fraction, a drop in the vast ocean. Seen from this point of view, both matter and mind are only parts of this Infinite Reality and so cannot claim to be real on their own. Therefore the binary categories of matter and spirit must be jettisoned in order to make room for a holistic view of Reality.

The Infinite Reality

Reality is infinite because there is no limit to what is ultimately real. That is, there is no finite way we can describe Reality. Hence the

---

[11] Sri Aurobindo, *The Life Divine*, p. 17.

binary categories devised by our finite mind cannot capture the essence of Reality. It is in this sense that Sri Aurobindo talks about the Ultimate Reality being beyond all our finite and limited mind and language. The Reality which is of the nature of Truth–Consciousness–Bliss is the Infinite Reality. The Infinite Reality is all-inclusive as it includes all forms of existence, both material and non-material in its totality. Reality does not exclude anything because it stands for what is real and is true. Therefore there is no reason to divide Reality into matter and Spirit as the dualists do. Both matter and Spirit are the two ways the Infinite Reality has manifested itself. Truth lies in the harmony and the reconciliation between matter and Spirit and not in the schism between the two. Sri Aurobindo writes:

> The real Monism, the true Advaita, is that which admits all things as the one Brahman and does not seek to bisect Its existence into two incompatible entities, an eternal Truth and an eternal Falsehood, Brahman and not-Brahman, Self and not-Self, a real Self and an unreal and yet perpetual Māyā.[12]

That is to say that Reality which is always non-dual (*advaita*) knows no division within it and so does not harbour any discord within its existence.

Sri Aurobindo's chief concern is to do away with all superficial depictions of Reality in one-sided binary terms which exclude rather than include and which deny rather than affirm. For him, Reality is the principle that unifies all and brings all beings under the singlemost all-inclusive category of Being. It is the one Brahman, one God and the one Absolute Spirit. The Infinite Reality is the all affirming Existence and is the true ground of all that passes as real including the so-called appearances. The apparently negative existence is also the manifestation of the Infinite Existence. Sri Aurobindo writes:

> Thus, after reconciling Spirit and Matter in the cosmic consciousness, we perceive the reconciliation, in the transcendental consciousness, of the final assertion of all and its negations. We discover that all affirmations are assertions of status or activity in the Unknowable; all the corresponding negations

[12] Sri Aurobindo, *The Life Divine*, p. 31.

> are assertions of Its freedom both from and in that status or activity.[13]

That is, even the negations are assertions of freedom of the Spirit in all its unlimited existential manifestations. Existence can have no limit because even the so-called non-existent or non-being has some form of Being. The Absolute Non-Being is another name for the Absolute Being because ultimately Being and Non-Being merge into one another.

Sri Aurobindo rejects the Buddhist view that the Ultimate Reality is a Void or Nihil (*śūnya*), because he thinks that such a view denies the very nature of Reality in characterizing it in only negative terms. The Being is a positive Reality and it includes everything and so it cannot be described as an emptiness.[14] The Non-Being is in essence the Being, since, "when we examine closely the Nihil of certain philosophies, we begin to perceive that it is a zero which is All or an indefinable Infinite which appears to the mind as blank, because mind grasps only finite constructions, but is in fact the only true Existence".[15] Therefore it is absolutely wrong to say that everything is Void at the ultimate level of existence.

The Infinite Reality is taken to be "Pure Existent"[16] because it includes everything that is real. It includes not only the Known but also the Unknown; it is both Being and Becoming. It is not only the phenomenon but also the noumenon. Brahman is *sat, cit* and *ānanda* in the all-inclusive sense.

> We have, therefore, two fundamental facts of pure existence and of world-existence, a fact of Being, a fact of Becoming. To deny one or the other is easy; to recognize the facts of consciousness and find out their relation is the true and fruitful wisdom.[17]

Brahman encompasses the cosmic as well as the supracosmic Reality. For Sri Aurobindo, the Pure Existent is the foundation of all Reality

---

13 Sri Aurobindo , *The Life Divine*, p. 30.

14 Cf. Ibid., pp. 28-30.

15 Ibid., p. 28.

16 Cf. Ibid., pp. 71-79.

17 Sri Aurobindo, *The Life Divine*, p. 78.

both in the eternal time and beyond. It is the Absolute Existence beyond change and temporal succession and is also beyond the unity and multiplicity of things in the universe.

Reality as Consciousness Force

Sri Aurobindo takes the Ultimate Reality, Brahman, as a Conscious Force[18] because of the fact that Brahman is a dynamic existence which is the ground of all existence. If Reality would have been static, then it would be difficult to explain changes in the universe. The world that we perceive is itself a dynamic process of events in Time and so the Reality which is the ground of this world cannot be without being dynamic. Activity is the very essence of all existence. In that sense the Supreme Reality, Brahman, cannot be without dynamism. Hence the Brahman is characterized as the embodiment of Force.

Sri Aurobindo accepts that the world is real and is caused by Brahman because there is no other way by which the world can come into existence except through the creative force of Brahman. Unlike Śaṅkara who is a Māyāvādin, Sri Aurobindo admits the real causation of the world by Brahman. This leads him to admit the causal dynamism of Brahman. He argues that the Supreme Reality of Brahman includes Force (*śakti*) and Consciousness (*cit*), so that it can explain how the world has come into being from Brahman, the Saccidānanda. Sri Aurobindo writes:

> . . . that which has thrown itself out into forms is a triune Existence–Consciousness–Bliss, Saccidānanda, whose consciousness is in its nature a creative or rather a self-expressive Force capable of infinite variation in phenomenon and form of its self-conscious being and endlessly enjoying the delight of that variation. It follows that all things that exist are what they are as terms of existence, terms of that conscious force, terms of that delight of being.[19]

That is, all existence is a manifestation of the Supreme Existence in that there is no gap between Brahman, the Conscious Force, and its creation, the world which is Brahman in its material manifestation.

---

[18] Sri Aurobindo, *The Life Divine*, pp. 80-90.

[19] Cf. Ibid., p. 92.

For Sri Aurobindo, Brahman is the Consciousness in its supreme manifestation and thus is the source of all forms of consciousness in the universe. As the Supreme Conscious Being, it gives rise to all forms of consciousness from the most primitive forms as found in the plant and the animal world to the human consciousness and beyond. Consciousness is the real nature of Brahman because it is of the nature of the supreme intelligence that accounts for the world. The world with its infinite variety is the embodiment of consciousness in so far as Brahman is involved in the world. That is, Brahman has willingly involved itself in the world for its own delight. The world is the field of the conscious activity of Brahman, and hence it bears close affinity with Brahman. In fact, everything is Brahman as each thing in the world manifests Brahman.

The Supramental Consciousness

Sri Aurobindo's theory of evolution presents a new world-picture in which the world itself progressively evolves towards the supramental consciousness. From matter which constitutes the physical world, there arise life and mind in an emergent fashion, and from the mind there arise the overmind and the supermind. The supermind embodies the highest form of consciousness and is the creative matrix of the world. It is through the supermind that the world has come into being and it is through it that the world is evolving towards the Saccidānanda.

According to Sri Aurobindo, the evolution of the human race as a mental race so far is due to the evolutionary urge in the universe to manifest a greater force than that of matter. Mind has struggled to come out of life in its infinite variety and power. Mind is, however, limited and is still steeped in ignorance. This can be removed only if the mind evolves into supermind as the latter is free from all limitations.

> The fundamental error of the Mind is, then, this fall from self-knowledge by which the individual soul conceives of its individuality as a separate fact instead of a form of Oneness and makes itself the centre of its own universe instead of knowing itself as one concentration of the universal.[20]

---

[20] Sri Aurobindo, *The Life Divine*, p. 171.

This error is removed at the supramental stage because at this stage the supermind restores the self-knowledge of the human soul. The soul realizes its oneness with Brahman, the Supreme Reality. The supermind is Truth Consciousness itself and is therefore free from ignorance and limitations.

The nature of the supramental consciousness is such that it arrives at the real integration of the universe and man in the grand harmony of the universal existence. The universal existence includes the human existence as well such that there is no more divide between the cosmic existence and the human world. The human world shares with the cosmic existence the same divine nature manifesting itself in various degrees at different levels of existence. Man is not the centre of the cosmos but rather the cosmos along with man belongs to the Universal Self. The supracosmic being is the centre of everything including the human beings. Thus supermind raises us to the supercosmic being by an incessant process of evolution. Sri Aurobindo writes:

> Mind cannot possess the infinite, it can only suffer it or be possessed by it: it can only lie blissfully helpless under the luminous shadow of the Real cast down on it from the planes of existence beyond its reach. The possession of the infinite cannot come except by an ascent to those supramental planes, nor the knowledge of it except by an inert submission of Mind to the descending messages of the Truth-Conscious Reality.[21]

Thus the supermind overcomes the barriers of the mind and establishes the divine life in the human race. The human race is divinized by the descent of the supermind to the plane of the mind and life by its creative force.

The Ascending Unity

In Sri Aurobindo's integral picture of the universe, there is an ascending unity culminating in the supramental plane of existence. The supramentalization of the world ensures the existence of the divine life in the world. In this process there is a definite progress towards a unification of all existence, divine and human, human

---

[21] Sri Aurobindo, *The Life Divine*, p. 163.

and animal, life and matter. This great unification is the very nature of Reality, according to Sri Aurobindo.

There are two ways in which the unification or integration takes place. First, all planes of existence from the material to the supramental are centred on the Divine Being which is the source of all existence. This may be called the ontological unification of existence. Second, the unification takes place in the consciousness of the human being on the epistemological level. There is a progressive realization of the unity of all existence taking place in the human consciousness. The epistemological unification is inevitable because the spirit of unification working in the universe is also taking place in the human consciousness. The spiritual unification characteristic of the divine life in man is the same as the spiritual unification of the universe. Man and the universe are connected by the unifying thread of the Divine Being. Sri Aurobindo writes:

> The universe and the individual are necessary to each other in their ascent. Always indeed they exist for each other and profit by each other. Universe is a diffusion of the divine All in infinite Space and Time, the individual its concentration within limits of Space and Time.[22]

The divine unity is the ultimate unity of all existence and so the universe and the individual are united in their progressive realization of the self-unity or self-identity.

The process of descent of the Divine Being into matter is followed by its ascent from matter to the Saccidānanda. Both these processes are unifying processes so that at every level of existence there is already a unifying background that secures the intended unification. The process of involution and evolution are the two ways in which the Divine Being acts on the universe and man. The universe itself is the play of the Divine Being and it shows the fact that the universe is God in the making.

> Therefore it creates in itself a self-conscious concentration of the All through which it can aspire. In the conscious individual *Prakṛti* turns back to perceive *Puruṣa,* World seeks after Self; God having

---

[22] Sri Aurobindo, *The Life Divine,* p. 45.

> entirely become Nature, Nature seeks to become progressively God.[23]

The process of unification is eternal, taking place in the infinite time and space. That is why there is no abrupt discontinuity in this process. Both Nature and man are God's two streams of this process of ascent.

From Monism to Integralism

Sri Aurobindo rejects the pure monism of Śaṅkara because of the fact that monism of the Advaitic type does not do justice to the world. The Advaitic monism treats the world as illusory because, if Brahman is alone real, the world cannot be real in the same ultimate sense. Sri Aurobindo disagrees with Śaṅkara on the status of the world because, according to him, the world is real in the sense that it is a manifestation of the Brahman in space and time. From Sri Aurobindo's point of view, the world is a form of Brahman and is real in the sense in which Brahman is also real.

Sri Aurobindo realizes that monism as such cannot solve the problem of the existence of the world because it reduces all reality into one single reality by denying the diversity of the phenomenal world. The plurality of the world is denied for the sake of the monistic principle. Hence he opts for an integral approach to Reality by emphasizing the fact that both the unity and the diversity of Reality must be preserved in a higher synthesis. This synthetic whole can be taken as the Total Reality comprising all the phenomena from the lower matter to the highest consciousness. The lower matter is as much a part of Reality as the higher forms of consciousness and so Reality itself does not exclude any part of it. Sri Aurobindo writes:

> The view I am presenting goes farther in idealism; it sees the creative idea as Real-Idea, that is to say, a power of Conscious Force expressive of real being, born out of real being and partaking of its nature and neither a child of the Void nor a weaver of fictions. It is conscious Reality throwing itself into mutable forms of its own imperishable and immutable substance.[24]

---

[23] Sri Aurobindo, *The Life Divine*, p. 45.

[24] Ibid., p. 117.

Thus though there is one imperishable Reality, there are many perishable forms of it which constitute the totality of Reality. This system of Reality is an integral system.

In an integral system the things or the objects in it do not stand disconnected from one another. They are so connected that they cross-refer to one another. In Sri Aurobindo's system, material bodies and minds do not stand apart ontologically because they are involved in each other. Mind is involved in matter as matter is involved in mind in the sense that if we talk about matter we also necessarily talk about mind. There is no question of one being real at the expense of the other. That is the typical monistic position. In integralism the whole situation is reversed in that both the so-called opposite entities are taken as real parts of a whole. In this case Brahman alone is real of which mind and matter are parts. That is, the reality of Brahman is the total existence in which matter and mind are situated.

Sri Aurobindo takes the Infinite Consciousness as the One and Infinite Reality which includes all objects which are real parts of the Infinite Reality. Nothing in this vast Reality is real independently; everything is contained within it. Brahman encompasses all. From the lower level of entities to the higher level of conscious beings, there is a continuous process of integration culminating in the higher-order reality of the Brahman. From the temporal to the non-temporal, from the transient to the eternal and from the sub-rational to the supra-rational, there is a process of integration and unification that abolishes all dualities and opposites. This is Sri Aurobindo's theory of integration as opposed to the monistic theory of reduction. He writes:

> Above, the formula of the One eternally stable and immutable; below, the formula of the Many which, eternally mutable, seeks but hardly finds in the flux of things a firm and immutable starting point; between, the seat of all trinities, of all that is biune, of all that becomes Many-in-One and yet remains One-in-Many, because it was originally one that is always potentially Many. This intermediary term is therefore the beginning and end of all creation and arrangement, the Alpha and Omega, the starting point of all differentiation, the instrument of all unification, originative,

> executive and consummative of all realized or realizable harmonies.[25]

The complex process of harmonization of the one and the many is the hallmark of the metaphysics of integration.

The Secret of Existence

Sri Aurobindo's main objective is to provide an ontology that makes room for the existence of both material universe and the conscious beings like the human beings. It is the physical universe which has thrown a challenge to metaphysics. His problem is: how can there be a physical universe in a predominantly spiritual reality of Brahman? That Brahman is real is taken as axiomatically true and is taken for granted as true without proof. However, the existence of the world needs proof because it has no reality in the sense of Brahman but yet has reality for all practical purposes. Sri Aurobindo is inclined to believe that the physical world is caused by Brahman for its own manifestation and its own concretization. The world is therefore real in Brahman itself and has no existence out of it. Brahman is the secret of all existence including that of the world and therefore there is reason to believe that Brahman has created the world with the instrumentality of the supermind or the cosmic *māyā*. In Sri Aurobindo's words:

> A Consciousness-force, everywhere inherent in Existence, acting even when concealed, is the creator of the worlds, the occult secret of Nature. But in our material world and in our own being consciousness has a double aspect; there is a force of Knowledge, there is a force of Ignorance. In the infinite consciousness of a self-aware Infinite Existence knowledge must be everywhere implicit or operative in the very grain of its action. . . .[26]

The all-prevading Consciousness-Force is the creative matrix from which everything has issued forth as a matter of the creative urge of the Supreme Reality. The creative force through its cosmic *māyā* beings into existence all the multiplicities in the universe.

The cosmic energy manifested in the material universe is a form

[25] Sri Aurobindo, *The Life Divine*, pp. 125-26.

[26] Ibid., p. 295.

of the Consciousness-Force in the sense that there is ultimately one energy and that is divine by nature. This Ultimate Divine Energy is the underlying reality of all existence, material and spiritual.

> On that hypothesis, there must be behind the action of the material Energy a secret involved Consciousness, cosmic, infinite, building up through the action of that frontal Energy its means of an evolutionary manifestation, a creation out of itself in the boundless finite of the material universe.[27]

This Ultimate Creative Force which is of the nature of consciousness unifies all forms of existence. It integrates them together into a unified whole thus making room for everything in it. The integral metaphysics thus allows for all forms of being united in the Ultimate Being, Brahman.

Reason, Intuition and Truth

Sri Aurobindo explores the limits of human reason in order to venture into the realm of the supramental Reality which he thinks is more real than the mental realm. The sphere of the human reason is the sphere of the finite reality — the reality of the limited world or worlds and also the limited human life. Human life is centred on the terrestrial existence of matter and its various manifestations. That is why Sri Aurobindo finds in it the reign of the nescience or ignorance which obstructs the emergence of light and knowledge in this region.

For Sri Aurobindo, as for the ancient Upaniṣadic *ṛṣis*, the realm of the mind is finite, limited and surrounded by the nescience. Mind is therefore steeped in the depth of ignorance regarding the ultimate nature of Reality. Brahman is only vaguely recognized by the mind. As Sri Aurobindo observes:

> Mind is not sufficient to explain existence in the universe. Infinite Consciousness must first translate itself into infinite faculty of Knowledge or, as we call it from our point of view, omniscience. But Mind is not a faculty of knowledge nor an instrument of omniscience. . . . Even when it finds, it does not possess; it ony keeps a certain fund of the current coin of Truth — not Truth itself

[27] Sri Aurobindo, *The Life Divine*, p. 303.

> — in the bank of memory to draw upon according to its needs. For Mind is that which does not know, which tries to know and which never knows except in a glass darkly. It is the power which interprets truth of universal existence for the practical uses of certain order of things. . . .[28]

Thus the mind is limited in its cognitive capacity and therefore cannot get hold of the Truth that lies far beyond its conceptual powers. It remains mid-way between matter and the supermind or the Infinite Mind. Hence the mental beings are transitional beings.

The Infinite Mind is the higher mind that penetrates into Reality and Truth in a more decisive manner. Sri Aurobindo emphasizes this point. The higher mind has the power of intuition by which it can have direct access to Truth. The supermind is the creative power of Brahman which brings into existence the manifold universe and its multiple worlds. It is the great power that makes a total sweep of all existence and time and thus presents total view of Reality at a glance as the omniscient Being.

> Supermind is the vast self-extension of Brahman that contains and develops. By the Idea it develops the triune principle of existence, consciousness and bliss out of their indivisible unity. It differentiates them, but does not divide. It establishes a Trinity, not arriving like the Mind from the three to the One, but manifesting the three out of the One — for it manifests and develops — and yet maintaining them in the unity — for it knows and contains.[29]

Thus there is unfolded to the supermind a vast realm of Reality that is unknown to the mind. The creative matrix that it is, it creates all the manifold possibilities within the realm of Reality. At this level knowledge and Reality coincide because what is known to be real is the self-knowledge of Brahman.

> In Supermind being, consciousness of knowledge and consciousness of will are not divided as they seem to be in our mental operations; they are a trinity, one movement with three effective aspects.[30]

---

28 Sri Aurobindo, *The Life Divine*, p. 118.

29 Ibid., p. 128.

30 Ibid., p. 130.

This unity of being and knowledge of being is possible because the creative power of the supermind.

For Sri Aurobindo, Truth is the knowledge aspect of the metaphysical reality of Brahman. Truth-Consciousness is the Consciousness that constitutes Reality itself. Truth, in this sense, does not stand apart from Reality, it is the way Reality reveals itself. Truth and Being are one in this metaphysical system. Sri Aurobindo writes:

> The Truth-Consciousness is everywhere present in the universe as an ordering self-knowledge by which the One manifests the harmonies of its infinite operational multiplicity.[31]

That is, Truth and Being pervade every aspect of existence and thus are centred in all beings which are the manifestations of the one Truth and Being.

The Truth-Consciousness cannot, however, be grasped through the reason or the finite mind because the latter is limited in its cognitive powers. Therefore, Sri Aurobindo proposes a higher faculty called the supermind which can have direct access to the Truth-Consciousness. This he calls the knowledge by identity[32] which means that in this case the knower and the known become identical. This knowledge is different from knowledge which presupposes a duality of subject and object. Sri Aurobindo says:

> We arrive at the conception and the knowledge of the divine existence by exceeding the evidence of the senses and piercing beyond the walls of the physical mind. So long as we confine ourselves to sense-evidence and the physical consciousness, we can conceive nothing and know nothing except the material world and its phenomena.[33]

Thus we are led from the level of reason to that of intuition in search of the divine Truth which lies beyond the realm of the mental consciousness. The rational faculty "is incapable of knowing what is, it only knows what appears to be",[34] so that we have to exceed it

31 Sri Aurobindo, *The Life Divine*, p. 132.

32 Cf. ibid., pp. 524-52.

33 Ibid., p. 60.

34 Ibid.

to have the knowledge by identity. In the words of Sri Aurobindo:

> But the cosmic consciousness of things is founded upon knowledge by identity; for the universal Spirit knows itself as the self of all, knows all as itself and in itself, knows all nature as part of its nature.[35]

Knowledge by identity overrules all separative knowledge because the latter can never give the knowledge of Truth. It is in essence the intuitive knowledge that facilitates our access to the Ultimate Truth.

To conclude: integral metaphysics is based on integral knowledge of the Supreme Reality. Metaphysics brings together the totality of existence into one harmonious unity, and thus overthrows all dualistic metaphysics of matter and mind. The unified picture of the universe is the quintessential result of integral metaphysics which incidentally is also the goal of modern science. The fusion of science and metaphysics is the end result of integral metaphysics which has taken shape for the first time in Sri Aurobindo's system of philosophy.

II

From Physics to Metaphysics: Sri Aurobindo on the Realm of the Supraphysical

The relation between physics and metaphysics has been a matter of philosophical debate over the centuries. It has been contended by many that metaphysics falls outside the domain of physics precisely because it deals with the realm of Reality that far exceeds the domain physics.[36] Those who accept this view hold that metaphysics transcends the realm of the physical reality which is the subject matter of physics. However, the contrary view that metaphysics and physics deal with the same reality, though from different standpoints, has been equally strong, if not stronger. There is no doubt that metaphysics deals with the world which physics deals with, but the fact remains that metaphysics deals with many aspects of Reality which are not within the purview of physics. Those aspects

---

35 Sri Aurobindo, *The Life Divine*, p. 542.

36 See Aristotle, *Metaphysics*, tr. H. Trendennick.

of Reality which are specifically dealt with by metaphysics are the non-physical or the supraphysical aspects.

Sri Aurobindo has highlighted the metaphysics of the supraphysical in his account of Reality. In this section an attempt will be made to examine the legitimacy of the metaphysics of the supraphysical. My argument is that the supraphysical realm is as much real as the realm of the physical, because the very nature of the physical reality suggests the possibility of the supraphysical reality.

The Physical vs. the Supraphysical

The most common view of physics is that it deals with the nature of the physical world and brings out the physical laws that regulate the physical world. That the physical laws are supreme in the physical world has been the general contention of the physicists. That these laws are not supervenient on any law other than the physical goes without saying, according to the physicists. But metaphysics brings a new dimension into the world picture by suggesting that even the so-called physical reality needs a supraphysical realm in order to be coherently explained. That is to say, in other words, that the physical world presupposes the mental world which gives rise to the ideas or conceptual frameworks within which the physical world is understood. The ideational schemes provided by physics regarding the world hint at the realm of the mind which demands the recognition of the metaphysicians as well as the scientists.

Sri Aurobindo argues for the reality of the mind which lies beyond the realm of matter. He holds that mind with all its higher functions leading to the idea of overmind and supermind contains such possibilities which cannot be mapped by a mere physical theory of the world. He provides a new world picture in which mind is taken to be prior to matter in the sense that mind is already involved in matter. He says:

> In fact, life, mind, Supermind are present in the atom, are at work there, but invisible, occult, latent in a subconscious or apparently unconscious action of the Energy; there is an informing Spirit, but the outer force and figure of being, what we might call the formal

> or form existence as distinguished from the immanent or secretly governing consciousness is lost in the physical action, is so absorbed into it as to be fixed in a stereotyped self-oblivion unaware of what it is and what it is doing. The electron and atom are in this view eternal somnambulists; each material object contains an outer or form consciousness involved, absorbed in the form, asleep, seeming to be an unconsciousness driven by an unknown and unfelt inner Existence. . . .[37]

Sri Aurobindo thus argues that the so-called material object is already a sleeping consciousness as the latter is already latent in it. There is the involution of the mind in the matter because it is the mind which descends into the material plane for its own future evolution.

Sri Aurobindo's argument leads to the following conclusions: (i) that matter is not the last word in the evolutionary scheme of things, (ii) that mind is a higher reality than matter, and (iii) that the higher mind is already potentially in matter. Each conclusion is grounded in a metaphysical insight that has no apparent empirical justification. None the less, each is a far-reaching and bold metaphysical proposition.

Against physics, metaphysics holds that matter is only a tiny fraction of reality and in fact, it is, in Sri Aurobindo's view, the first level of reality of the universe giving rise to many more levels of reality culminating in the Spirit. From matter arise life, mind, overmind, supermind and so on culminating in the Ultimate Reality, Brahman. Thereby, metaphysics unfolds the vast panorama of Reality lying beyond the material universe.

That mind is higher than matter is proved by the fact that mind has consciousness in it which is not in matter except in the latent form. Besides, mind contains the awareness of the supermind and so is higher than matter, since matter is unaware of consciousness and is steeped in inconscience[38] or ignorance. For Sri Aurobindo, mind is not causally dependent on matter because mind is already involved in matter and is thus ontologically prior to it. Matter is only the outer form of consciousness which is embedded in the

---

[37] Sri Aurobindo, *The Life Divine*, p. 711.

[38] Ibid., p. 704.

matter in the latent or involved form. Sri Aurobindo puts it:

> Here the evolution takes place in the material universe; the foundation, the original substance, the first established all-conditioning status of things is Matter. Mind and Life are evolved in Matter. . . .[39]

From this, of course, it does not follow that life and mind are caused by matter; rather matter is only a shadow of life and mind in that evolutionary order.

The idea of involution is the idea of a descent of mind and supermind into matter. Involution is a logical way of explaining how matter itself comes into being. The metaphor of descent must be taken in the sense of accepting the ontological priority of mind to matter. If mind would not have been already in matter, then it would not have been possible to explain how life and mind would come into existence. If matter would have been ontologically closed within the physical laws, then under no circumstances we can show how mind comes into existence in a purely material universe.[40] This difficulty is removed by Sri Aurobindo by bringing in the idea of involution. Since mind is already there in matter, it is possible for mind to evolve from matter. Otherwise, mind would be impossible in the universe.

The Supremacy of Mind in the Evolutionary Process

For Sri Aurobindo, mind and its higher form supermind dominate the world process on the ground that the mental and the spiritual planes of existence are ontologically prior to the physical universe. The physical universe is only a manifestation of the supramental Consciousness-Force. Therefore, there is no way the physical universe can be supreme in its existence and power. Sri Aurobindo, writes:

> Mind in its turn, when it emerges, becomes dominant; it uses Life and Matter as means of its expression, a field for its own growth and sovereignty, and it begins to work as if it were a true reality and the creator even as it is the witness of existence. But Mind also

39 Sri Aurobindo, *The Life Divine*, p. 704.

40 See David Chalmers, *The Conscious Mind: In Search of a Fundamental Theory*, 1996.

> is a limited and derivative power; it is an outcome of Overmind or it is here a luminous shadow thrown by the divine Supermind. . . .[41]

Thus mind with its higher source in the overmind and the supermind dominates the world scene because what we call the world — the physical world — is a manifestation of the higher consciousness.

Sri Aurobindo is aware of the enormous difficulties in presenting this thesis of the ontological priority of the mind over matter. Modern science presupposes that it is matter which is prior to mind and all its ramifications. But Sri Aurobindo argues that modern science might be wrong in having this presupposition. To accept that the physical universe is the only reality and that the only experience is the sense-experience, according to Sri Aurobindo, is a dogma of modern science.[42] This has emboldened him to accept experiences other than the physical to account for the supraphysical world beyond the world of matter. According to him, it is the supraphysical world which is the foundation on which the physical world is based. Sri Aurobindo writes:

> It is the pressure of the supramental and the spiritual worlds which is preparing to develop here the manifest power of the Spirit and by it open our being on the physical plane into the freedom and infinity of the superconscient Divine; that contact, that pressure can alone liberate from the apparent Inconscience, which was our starting point, the all-conscient Godhead concealed in us.[43]

The supramental or the supraphysical thus holds the key to the unfolding of the physical universe in the sense that only within the broad parameters of the supraphysical, the physical reality can be understood.

Sri Aurobindo's argument is this: if the supraphysical were not the source of the physical reality, we cannot account for the reality of the physical world. If we say that the physical world is self-sufficient and it needs no source beyond matter, then we have to show how the physical universe came into existence at all. If we say

---

41 Sri Aurobindo, *The Life Divine*, p. 665.

42 Ibid., pp. 789-90.

43 Ibid., p. 781.

that it came ino existence because of its inherent physical force, we have still to show why the universe developed the way it has developed. If the universe has no purposes for its existence and if it is the result of the fortuitous conglomeration of the material forces and elements, then we are robbing the universe of its meaning and thus condemning it into the limbo of darkness. Therefore Sri Aurobindo comes forward with a bold assertion that the universe has a luminous aspect which needs to be highlighted by linking it with the higher reality of the supermind. Without a supramental direction and guidance the physical world cannot be found to be meaningful and intelligible.

Sri Aurobindo develops his theory of spiritual evolution of the physical universe into the supermind and the Saccidānanda in order to show that the physical universe itself is not physically closed and that it is progressing towards a brighter spiritual future culminating in the supramental manifestation on earth. In Sri Aurobindo's words:

> It is the pressure of the Mind-world which evolves and develops mind here and helps to find a leverage for our mental self-uplifting and expansion, so that we may hope to enlarge continually our self of intelligence and even to break the prison walls of our matter-bound physical mentality.[44]

The notion of evolution goes hand in hand with that of involution for the reason that evolution from matter to mind and beyond cannot be a mere arbitrary phenomenon. The prison walls of the physical world can be broken because matter itself has the potentiality of becoming mental by virtue of the involution of the supraphysical.

The Integration of Matter and Mind

Sri Aurobindo has developed an integral picture of reality by showing that ultimately matter and mind converge on the supramental reality and therefore there is no conflict between the material world and the supraphysical world of the mind and the supermind. Integration stands for unification and harmonization and therefore on this evolutionary principle mind and matter are harmonized in the Spirit, the Ultimate Divine Reality. The Divine

---

[44] Sri Aurobindo, *The Life Divine*, p. 781.

Reality is the One Supreme Reality and hence it contains everything including the so-called physical reality.

The dualistic metaphysics initiated by Descartes and purused by modern science is overcome by Sri Aurobindo's integral metaphysics by emphasizing the fact that matter and mind are not two binary realities confronting each other thus dividing Reality right in the middle. This leads not only to a mechanistic world-view propounded by modern science and the scientific metaphysics of the West, but also it leads to the philosophies of world-negation which emphasize the spiritual to the exclusion of the physical reality in the East. These two negations[45] have been opposed to the integral picture of Reality. There, Sri Aurobindo, says:

> The affirmation of a divine life on earth and an immortal sense in mortal existence can have no base unless we recognize not only the eternal Spirit as the inhabitant of this bodily mansion, the wearer of this mutable robe, but accept Matter of which it is made, as a fit and noble material out of which He weaves constantly His garbs, builds recurrently the unending series of His mansions.[46]

This shows that there is a definite purpose in the physical universe for manifesting the divine life on earth, which goes to prove that there is always a higher reality beyond the physical world. What is more important is that both the higher reality of the Spirit and the lower reality of the physical world are connected by an invisible thread such that the Spirit descends into matter and matter ascends to the Spirit. This two-way process goes on incessantly in the realm of the supraphysical obeying its own laws.

Now the question may arise, how is it the case that the material universe which lacks mentality and intelligence can evolve into the supramental and the supraconscient? For many philosophers, it may look puzzling that Sri Aurobindo demands a higher evolution from the gross physical world into the realm of the supramental consciousness. But the fact of the matter is that Sri Aurobindo has taken into account the puzzle of the ordinary mind in understanding the higher truth of integral evolution. According to him, the puzzle

---

45 Sri Aurobindo, *The Life Divine*, pp. 6-24.

46 Ibid., p. 6.

arises precisely because we are at the common level of the material mind in raising this question. If we look beyond our ordinary mind and take a higher point of view, it becomes obvious that the physical level is not the whole of reality and that there is a vast realm of existence beyond the material world.

Our ordinary mind gets puzzled because we accept that there is a contradiction between mind and matter and that there is an unbridgeable gulf between the two. This is because our conceptions of matter and mind are narrow and unenlightened. But the mind has a tendency to rise beyond this narrowness and see the reality holistically. Hence mind has to evolve further in order to understand the dynamics of the spiritual evolution. Says Sri Aurobindo, "in these barren contradictions the human mind cannot rest satisfied. It must seek always a complete affirmation; it can find it only by a luminous reconciliation."[47] This reconciliation is possible by rising to the supramental level of experience. The supramental experience brings the message of the harmony of all existence, the unity and oneness of the Spirit.

Sri Aurobindo rejects both the materialist and spiritualist monism in favour of spiritual integralism. He builds up the case for integralism on the foundation of the Vedāntic notion of Saccidānanda, the Existence–Consciousness–Bliss as the Ultimate Reality. In this reality he finds a reconciliation of matter and Spirit in the graded development of reality from matter, life and mind to supermind and Saccidānanda. In this process of evolution, no plane of existence is left out and everything is taken into the grand fold of the Spirit which is the infinite all-inclusive consciousness.

Logic of the Infinite

Sri Aurobindo has proposed the idea of a logic of the Infinite as distinguished from that of the logic of the finite. His idea is that the evolution theory that he propounds is understandable only from the standpoint of the Infinite Spirit and not from the standpoint of the finite mind. That is, the question why the spirit descends into matter and then rise from matter to reach its self-identity can be

---

47 Sri Aurobindo, *The Life Divine*, p. 7.

answered only if we station ourselves on the plane of the Infinite Reality. The logic of the Infinite is really the God's point of view which transcends the finite human categories. Human mind is admittedly the finite mind with its limited categories. Therefore to demand from it God's point of view is to ask for the impossible. Hence it is justifiable to talk of the logic of the Infinite.

The hallmark of the logic of the Infinite is its integral point of view and its principle of reconciliation. This principle reconciles the Being with Non-Being, the Finite Being with the Infinite Being and the matter with the Spirit. This dissolution of the binary categories is the basic function of the logic of the Infinite. The logic of the finite is a binary logic with determinate categories of Being and its opposite thus committed to the laws of the logic which we take for granted in our understanding of Reality. But the logic of the Infinite transcends it and makes room for the reconciliation of the opposites thus breaking down the law of Excluded Middle. Thus it brings about a revision in our understanding of the world. The physical wold is no more viewed as a material world as opposed to a supraphysical world. We are forced to recognize the limitless possibility of worlds that are not bound by the logic of the finite mind. The laws of logic as we know them are true of the possible worlds within the confines of the logic of the finite mind, but there are other possible worlds which are infinitely conceivable within the logic of the Infinite. Such words are the worlds of the overmind and supermind that go beyond all our known and intelligible categories.

One may ask here, if the logic of the Infinite is completely divorced from the logic of the finite. In answer to the question it can be said that the logic of the Infinite is not opposed to the logic of the finite, but it overcomes the limits of the latter. Even the logic of the finite has the notion of Infinite, so the logic of the Infinite can accommodate the notion of the finite. But what the logic of the Infinite can do is abolish the so-called binary opposites and place these categories in the totality of the scheme of things. Sri Aurobindo demands that the logic of the Infinite makes room for the emergence of the supramental consciousness from the finite level of matter and mind. The finite existence must yield to the infinite existence and prepare the ground for the future evolution of the spiritual man with infinite knowledge. The spiritual or the Gnostic being is the epitome of the logic of the Infinite in his or her supramental infinite knowledge.

The infinite reality is the same as the infinite knowledge and the infinite consciousness because reality is the same as the conscious being in its complete manifestation. That is why there is no difference between the logic of the Infinite and the metaphysics of the Infinite, as there is a progressive development from the logical idea of the infinity to the reality of the Infinite existence. Sri Aurobindo writes:

> In the same movement, by the very awakening into the spirit, there is dissolution of the cosmic ignorance; for we have the knowledge of ourselves as our timeless immutable self possessing itself in cosmos and beyond cosmos: this knowledge becomes the basis of the Divine Play in time, reconciles the one and the many, the eternal unity and the eternal multiplicity, unites the soul with God and discovers the Divine in the universe.[48]

Thus in the scheme of the logic of the Infinite we can have the map of the reality that disowns all conflicting categories and makes room for the infinite fusion of things and horizons. The Infinite asserts itself over everything. That is the supramental reality which the physical world is meant to manifest within its bosom.

The Reversal of Consciousness

The idea of the logic of the Infinite is linked with the idea of the reversal of consciousness which amounts to the reversal of our ordinary world-view. The world-view we are endowed with is the one embedded in our upbringing in the physical world. We tend to take the physical world as our home and ultimate destiny. This is because we are led to believe by both common sense and science that we are the children of the material gods and that we are not destined to look beyond these gods. Sri Aurobindo has tried to break these prison walls with his supraphysical and supramental world-view.

The reversal of consciousness amounts to a transformation and

---

[48] Sri Aurobindo, *The Life Divine*, pp. 740-41.

conversion of consciousness in the sense that a supramental change takes place with the descent of the Truth-Consciousness of the supermind into the earthly plane. This change takes place in the very plane of the human mind such that it undergoes a category-reversal of a very radical sort. As a result our thinking guided by ordinary logic or the logic of the finite undergoes a profound change so that we appreciate the possibility of a higher logic with infinity at the centre. As Sri Aurobindo puts it:

> This transformation would be the natural completion of the upward process of Nature as it heightens the forces of consciousness from principle to higher principle until the highest, the spiritual principle, becomes expressed and dominant in her, takes up cosmic and individual existence on the lower planes into its truth and transforms all into a conscious manifestation of the Spirit.[49]

This shows that the upward movement of mind and consciousness culminates in a higher plane of existence and makes room for higher forms of knowledge.

The cognitive changes that are ushered in as a result of the reversal of consciousness amount to bringing into existence the Gnostic Beings who are endowed with a higher faculty of knowledge which is knowledge by identity.[50] This knowledge breaks the barriers of narrowness and separateness and awakens the spirit of oneness. Sri Aurobindo says:

> The being breaks out of its imprisonment in a separated individuality, becomes universal, assumes cosmic consciousness in which it identifies itself with the self and spirit, the life, the mind, the body of all beings. Or it breaks out upward into a supreme pinnacle and infinity and eternity of self-existence independent of its cosmic or its individual existence.[51]

Thus there takes place a radical upward movement of consciousness and makes the supramental reality a fact of the universe. The universe

---

[49] Sri Aurobindo, *The Life Divine*, p. 741.

[50] Ibid., pp. 982-83.

[51] Ibid., p. 740.

or the cosmos stands itself reversed from the physical to the supraphysical.

To conclude, Sri Aurobindo's theory of the supraphysical and the supramental is a standing testimony to his new vision of Reality that comprehends everything in one sweep of the supramental consciousness. That brings about a radical change to our so-called scientific world-view.

III

From Man to Superman: Sri Aurobindo's Evolution Strategy and Its Implications

In this section I will discuss Sri Aurobindo's theory of evolution of superman as a part of his general theory of evolution of consciousness. It is well known that Sri Aurobindo has proposed a new theory of spiritual evolution which emphasizes the centrality of the Spirit in the process of evolution culminating in the supramental manifestation of the Spirit on earth. The chief characteristic of this theory of evolution is its integral character which implies that there is a gradual but all-comprehensive transformation of the lower level of existence into a higher level leading to the evolution of the Superman.

I will argue that Sri Aurobindo's theory of evolution surpasses the Western theories of evolution by emphasizing the fact that evolution is a priori dependent on involution and that what evolves, namely, the Spirit, is already involved in the material world. In fact, evolution is not teleological as in Aristotle and Hegel, but is more like the unfoldment of what is potentially contained in the material world. Sri Aurobindo's is a theory of progressive unfoldment of the Spirit rather than of its evolution in the Western sense of the term.

Sri Aurobindo's theory of evolution is meant to explain the possibility of the evolutionary transformation of man into superman. It is in this context that the theory of spiritual evolution is central to the understanding of the future of mankind.

The Idea of Evolution and Its Metaphysical Significance

The word evolution etymologically means to evolve, to grow or to develop in power and capacity on the part of any organism or any individual or a collection of individuals. There is evolution of man and society as there is evolution of the whole universe. Thus evolution can be a phenomenon in any aspect of reality. An evolutionary state of things is generally contrasted with a static state of things. In a static state of affairs, there is no movement, no becoming in reality. Things stand fixed and immutable in such a state of reality. The idea of evolution brings dynamism into reality and thus injects the idea of purpose and goal into Nature.

The idea of evolution of Nature was first introduced by Aristotle[52] in metaphysics by showing that the things in Nature are in constant struggle to realize more and more forms and thus to attain complete substancehood. From the primary matter to the state of complete substancehood there is evolution. It is a process of becoming from potentiality to actuality and from non-substantiality to substantiality. Thus Aristotle gave us the picture of the universe with a certain teleology according to which the universe itself has a purpose which is otherwise called the final cause[53] in his metaphysics. It was later on fine-tuned by Hegel[54] who provided a dialectical map for the evolutionary process of the universe. In Hegel, the universe moves forward within the circle of reason or thought till it realizes the Absolute Idea or the Spirit.[55] The Hegelian evolution theory was a major metaphysical advance over Aristotle's theory because it injected more dynamism into the universe under the control of the universal reason.

However, in the nineteenth century, the metaphysics of

---

52 Aristotle had the notion of evolution in his theory of final causes. It explained his teleological view of the universe as outlined in his physics. See D.J. Allan, *The Philosophy of Aristotle*, Oxford: University Press, 1963.

53 See D.J. Allan, 1963, op. cit.

54 Hegel developed the Aristotelian notion of becoming in his dialectical scheme which foreshadows the later theories of evolution. See G.R.G. Mure, *The Philosophy of Hegel*, London: Oxford University Press, 1965.

55 *The Philosophy of Hegel*, London: Oxford University Press, 1965.

evolution[56] took a serious turn because of the rise of evolutionary biology founded by Darwin and Lamarck. Evolutionary sciences had a major impact on the metaphysical theories of evolution in the twentieth century, especially those of Bergson, Alexander and Morgan Llyod, and Whitehead in different dimensions. While Bergson talked of creative evolution, Alexander and Morgan talked about emergent evolution and Whitehead about organistic evolution. However, Herbert Spencer had already laid the foundations of a theory of evolution of the physical universe and its complex physical processes. His theory was largely devoted to the explanation of the phenomena of life and mind in the universe in terms of the physical laws of integration and disintegration.[57]

The cosmological goal of the theories of evolution was to show that the whole universe is a process of becoming in which eternal objects called forms are concretized as Whitehead[58] has claimed. The idea of an organic whole of the universe is very much a Whiteheadian idea which brings dynamism into the universe. The fixed universe of the early nineteenth century gives way to the dynamic universe of the early twentieth century thus making room for the emergence of higher forms of Reality because of the evolutionary drive of the universe. The emergence of Deity[59] or God in the process of the universe was the distinct goal of the evolutionary theories. The transformation of the species and the emergence of the rational man on the scene of the world are some of the highlights of the cosmic evolution.

However, a deeper theory of spiritual evolution was anticipated in the metaphysics of the Upaniṣads.[60] According to this theory, the

56 See S. Radhakrishnan, *An Idealist View of Life,* London: Unwin Books, 1932; second impression 1964, chap. VIII.

57 For a discussion on Spencer's theory of evolution see H.M. Bhattacharya, *The Principles of Philosophy,* Calcutta: University of Calcutta, 1959, pp. 245-48.

58 Ibid.

59 See A.N. Whitehead, *Process and Reality: An Essay in Cosmology,* New York: The Free Press, 1978; first published 1929, part I, chap. III.

60 The Upaniṣadic view of the evolution is reflected in the idea of the manifestation of the world with the multiple names and forms from Brahman. See R.D. Ranade, *A Constructive Survey of the Upanishadic Philosophy,* Bombay: Bharatiya Vidya Bhavan, 1968, chap. II.

universe was taken to have evolved from Brahman which is the Ultimate Reality. That is how a theory of evolution of the universe from the basic stuff of consciousness was established in the pre-Greek thought in India much before the Western mind attempted a scientific theory of evolution.

Limitations of the Physicalist Theory of Evolution

Sri Aurobindo brings us back to the Upaniṣadic theory in order to explain the nature of cosmos as well as man because it is in the understanding of man and cosmos that there is the possibility of a comprehensive theory of evolution. Sri Aurobindo's theory is not only cosmological but also spiritual because it attempts to explain the evolution of the spiritual consciousness. It is in this context that he develops a comprehensive critique of the Western materialist theory of evolution.

The Western theory of evolution based on the scientific findings since Darwin has been largely materialistic precisely because it emphasizes the mere physical facts regarding the existence of man and the universe. For Darwin the existence of the human species was the main object of scientific explanation. His attempt was to show how there is biological evolution of the human species from the lower species of animals. However, there is no cosmological theory underlying Darwin's theory of evolution. It is Herbert Spencer who brings the whole cosmos under the evolutionary scheme by suggesting that the universe evolves from matter through a process of integration and disintegration. He could provide a comprehensive theory of the universe in terms of matter and force thus conforming to the scientific findings about the universe. However, man's existence is not a crucial issue in this theory as it subsumes human existence under the physical facts. Therefore, it seems so radically different from Sri Aurobindo's theory of spiritual evolution in which man's place is central.

Sri Aurobindo brings out the following limitations of the materialist theory of cosmological evolution:

1. That matter is not the sole reality which can explain the whole of universe, because the universe is ultimately spiritual by nature.

2. That man's evolution into the superman is the aim of evolution because the cosmic evolution is incomplete without the development of superhuman consciousness.
3. That the spiritual evolution of man is facilitated by the Divine intervention in the world process which a mute cosmic evolution cannot accomplish.

Sri Aurobindo argues that the cosmic evolution is not an accidental event at all, because it is the culmination of the Spirit or Brahman's choice to manifest in the universe. The Spirit is so dynamic that it naturally manifests itself in the material unfoldment of the universe. Brahman spontaneously becomes the universe with its multiple processes at all levels.[61]

The biological evolution does not explain, according to Sri Aurobindo, how man, the intelligent creature on earth, arrived in the cosmic process because it only explains the biological features which are transmitted from generation to generation. It does not touch the evolution of the human mind at all except indirectly by showing that the biological complexities include the mental behaviour of mankind. But Sri Aurobindo has a comprehensive account of the evolution of mind from life and matter. He writes:

> A spiritual evolution, an evolution of consciousness in Matter in a constant developing self-formation till the form can reveal the indwelling Spirit, is the keynote, the central significant motive of the terrestrial existence.[62]

Thus the evolutionary process in the world is the process of revealing the indwelling Spirit. This is a very peculiar kind of evolution because it does not talk of a linear development of matter in its complexity as suggested by Spencer. Rather, the indwelling Spirit is expected to manifest itself in matter, life and mind such that mind is not a mere evolute of matter and life. Mind is, in fact, the underlying reality of matter and life. Such a proposal goes against

---

[61] For a discussion on the emergent evolution, see D.M. Datta, *The Chief Currents of Contemporary Philosophy*, Calcutta: University of Calcutta, 1950; 3rd edn. 1970, chap. VIII.

[62] Sri Aurobindo, 1972, *The Life Divine*, Pondicherry: Sri Aurobindo Ashram, p. 824.

the Western theory of evolution on the materialist lines. Therefore "a theory of evolution is not identical with a scientific theory of form-evolution and physical life-evolution; it must stand on its own inherent justification. . . ."[63] Its inherent justification lies in the fact that the Spirit itself undergoes this transformation out of its inner necessity. It is not matter which evolves into life and mind as is suggested in the scientific theory of evolution, but the Spirit which compels matter to come into existence as the pre-condition of life and mind.

Sri Aurobindo characterizes the spiritual evolution as the "evolution of Consciousness, a progression of the souls' manifestation in material existence"[64] such that there is a gradual development of the mental out of the material and the biological. He recognizes that there is no sudden appearance of matter, life and mind out of nothing because it is evident that only gradually matter has developed into life and life into mind. For Sri Aurobindo, the self-evident conclusion is that "there is a graduated necessary succession in the evolution, first the evolution of matter, next the evolution of life in matter, then the evolution of mind in living matter, and in this last stage an animal evolution followed by human evolution".[65] That is to say, the evolutionary process running through matter, life and mind is real even though it is the Spirit which initiates this process culminating in the evolution of the human race.

The following are the bold ontological commitments regarding the evolution of man in Nature:

1. That Nature is the Spirit in its unconcealed form. Nature is not material in its inner structure, since it is the Spirit in the material form.
2. That matter is itself a dynamic process of transformation which gives rise to mind and consciousness.
3. That evolution is a self-movement of matter in its upward rise towards consciousness.

---

63 Sri Aurobindo, 1972, *The Life Divine*, p. 835.

64 Ibid., pp. 835-36.

65 Sri Aurobindo, 1972, *The Life Divine*, Pondicherry: Sri Aurobindo Ashram, p. 836.

These ontological commitments are part of the evolution strategy of Sri Aurobindo which makes the theory of spiritual evolution completely different from the materialist theory.

Involution of the Spirit in Matter

Sri Aurobindo's theory of evolution is complementary to the theory of involution which acts as the mediating link between the source of evolution and the effects of evolution. According to him, no evolution is possible if it is not preceded by a reverse process of involution in which the ultimate stage of evolution is already implicit in the initial stage of evolution. That is, in this case, the Spirit is already involved in matter in the sense that matter already embodies the spiritual force which initiates the evolutionary process.

The process of involution, for Sri Aurobindo, is the process of the Spirit manifesting itself in the lower order of matter. This takes place in the way opposite to the process of evolving in an ascending order. Involution is the order of descent, while evolution is the order of ascent. But the question may arise: Why does the Spirit enter into the lower level of matter at all? That is, why is there involution of the Spirit in matter, when the Spirit and matter are so disparate from each other? To this Sri Aurobindo's answer is that matter and Spirit are not different from each other and that they share a common nature, though varied in degrees. The Spirit in its purest form is free from matter, but matter in purest form is not free from the Spirit. In fact, matter is a crude form of the Spirit. It is because the Spirit is veiled in matter due to ignorance. Sri Aurobindo writes:

> This significance is concealed at the outset by the involution of the Spirit, the Divine reality, in a dense material Inconscience; a veil of Inconscience, a veil of insensibility of Matter hides the universal Consciousness-Force which works within it, so that the Energy, which is the first form the Force of creation assumes in the physical universe, appears to be inconscient and yet does the works of a vast occult Intelligence.[66]

The Spirit's concealing of itself under the veil of ignorance is the

---

66 Sri Aurobindo, *The Life Divine*, p. 824.

involution. It is undertaken by the Spirit vountarily, i.e. out of its own will. In fact, that is its natural state of affairs. Involution is as much natural for the Spirit as its evolution. The veiled Spirit rises spontaneously by tearing the veil of Ignorance and by

> delivering the secret consciousness out of its thick and tenebrous prison; but she delivers it slowly, little by little, in minute infinitesimal drops, in thin jets, in small vibrant concretions of energy and substance, of life, of mind, as if that were all she could get through the crass obstacle, the dull reluctant medium of an inconscient stuff of existence.[67]

The Spirit's involution in matter is a momentous ontological moment which is called the *līlā* (sport) of the Divine. It is because of this willing appearance in the form of matter that the Divine Spirit emerges out of matter by an inner necessity. The Spirit rises out of the veil of ignorance by its inner force. Hence it is called the Consciousness-Force that is dynamic and vibrant in its activity. Evolution is the process of the emergence of the Divine Spirit from out of the material existence. Therefore we have a gradual ascent from matter to Spirit that is guided by the Spirit itself.

The Spiritual Ascent

Sri Aurobindo characterizes the ascent of the Spirit from its own self-oblivion as the gradual process of evolution. It is a case of self-awakening of the Spirit out of the deep and thick materiality which binds the Spirit to the lower world of matter. The Spirit moves in a timeless path by creating moments of its blissful existence at different stages in a hierarchy. This is expressed in an ascending order from matter to the Spirit. Thus evolution is really a process of manifestation or of unfoldment. It is not evolution in the temporal sense accepted by the Western evolution theorists. Sri Aurobindo overturns the evolution project of the West by just taking away time from the process. Time itself is a creation of the Spirit just as the material world is. Hence there is nothing that can evolve in time to be called the emergence of something new in the cosmic process. The so-called new form of existence is really a case of manifestation.

67 Sri Aurobindo, *The Life Divine*, p. 825.

Therefore Sri Aurobindo rejects both the mechanical and the teleological theories of evolution on the ground that there is no purpose or lack of it in the creation. He writes:

> There is no teleological purpose in creation and there cannot be, for all is there in the Infinite: the Divine has nothing that he needs to gain or that he has not; if there is creation and manifestation, it is the delight of creation, of manifestation, not for any purpose. There is then no reason for an evolutionary movement with a culmination to be reached or an aim to be worked out and effectuated or a drive towards ultimate perfection.[68]

This shows that the concept of teleology is misplaced in the theory of spiritual evolution because the Spirit itself, which does the manifestation, has no purpose other than its delight. The Infinite Spirit is self-complete and self-contained.

But the question is: If there is no purpose in the evolutionary process, then does it not lapse into a mere chaos and an ultimate blunder? That is, can the Spirit act so arbitrarily in its own self-manifestation? The answer is that the Spirit has its own purpose and its own goal. It is just manifesting itself ceaselessly by its inner freedom. That is all that there is in the cosmic process. It is an eternal flow of blissful existence in the cosmic process. It is an eternal process of self-manifestation and eternal flow of existence, consciousness and bliss. What is thus found is that the Spirit is at work on its own eternally and timelessly.

One may wonder if there is anything called evolution in Western sense in Sri Aurobindo's philosophy if everything is a self-manifestation of the Spirit? In self-manifestation, there is no requirement of time and so there is absence of any temporal movement. Hence one cannot but think that Sri Aurobindo has no concept of evolution in the usual sense of the term. None the less, he speaks of spiritual evolution and the transformation of consciousness from the lower level to the higher level. This process of becoming from matter to life and from life to mind is called evolution by him. All that he means by this is that things change in the universe and they change according to a divine plan. Matter,

---

[68] Sri Aurobindo, *The Life Divine*, p. 827.

life and mind are really the different phases in which the original Consciousness-Force has manifested itself. The ascent from the lower level of material existence to the higher level of mental existence is real. Sri Aurobindo writes:

> If it be asked, how then did all these various gradations and types of being come into existence, it can be answered that, fundamentally, they were manifested in Matter by the Consciousness-Force in it, by the power of the Real-Idea building its own significant forms and types for the indwelling Spirit's cosmic existence. . . .[69]

That is, the Spirit's cosmic existence is the real divine manifestation at various levels and therefore there is a gradual process in which things have happened. So a cosmic timescale is built into this cosmic manifestation of the Divine Being. The material, the biological and the mental phenomena in their own spheres have been the result of a complex organization of the Consciousness-Force. That is the evidence of the fact that there have been evolutionary changes in the cosmic process because of, or due to, the conscious intervention of the Spirit in the world process.

Sri Aurobindo does not deny the validity of the scientific theory of evolution both in the animal and the material world. He does admit that there have been cosmic changes in a progressive way from the material world to the biological and the mental worlds where Consciousness has been manifested in a more organized way. But he differs from the scientific theory of evolution by suggesting that the whole evolutionary machine is driven by the Divine Spirit itself. That is to say, it is the evolution of the Spirit from its primitive forms to its more complex forms in man. This theory of spiritual evolution is something unique which is totally alien to the Western concept of evolution.

Temporality and the Emergence of Higher Forms of Consciousness

Sri Aurobindo's treatment of time and temporality is very different from that of the Western thinkers like Bergson, Alexander and

---

[69] Sri Aurobindo, *The Life Divine*, p. 829.

Morgan who have accepted time as an important category. For Bergson, time is duration[70] and the creative evolution of the life forms takes place within a temporal process. The creative flow of the divergent life forms is due to the life force underlying it. For Bergson, even the existence of matter is dependent on the life force. For the emergentist thinkers, time is a significant factor in the evolution from matter to life and mind. The emergence of higher forms of life and mind is due to the temporality of the sequential order in the universe.[71]

Sri Aurobindo does not accept the centrality of time in the cosmic order. For him, time is as much a creation as anything else in time because time is the form the Spirit takes in its creative manifestation. For Sri Aurobindo, the divine creation does not take place in a pre-existing temporal order. The divine manifestation is an atemporal process, though it takes the form of time for us, who are placed in the world order, and it is the divine order from the point of view of the Spirit, but from the human point of view, the divine order is temporal and sequential. Thus time is basically a human idea imposed on the timeless divine order of things.

However, the temporality and the historicality of the process of the cosmic evolution are real and cannot be taken as subjective phenomena. It is due to the divine intervention that the human consciousness gets its present form and therefore what is real for man is real in the universe. But from the ultimate point of view, time itself transcends its own form and becomes timeless. The interplay between the time and the timeless is a matter of special importance to Sri Aurobindo because he does not believe that time can explain anything without the timeless.

The higher forms of consciousness emerge from the lower order of matter, not because of any material necessity or causal force, but because of the fact that the Consciousness-Force itself is already pre-existing in matter. It is only because of the force of the Consciousness that new forms of consciousness emerge. So emergence is not a completely new event in the cosmic process; it is only an unfoldment

---

70 See D.M. Datta, op. cit.

71 Ibid.

of what is already there. The Western theory of emergence is incomplete because it cannot explain how consciousness can come out of, emerge from, matter which is itself unconscious. If matter can give rise to consciousness, then it is really an arbitrary phenomenon which has no reason or rhyme for its occurrence. There is no reason why there can be the emergence of higher consciousness from the lower mental plane. Therefore, Sri Aurobindo rejects the Western concept of emergence and shows that from consciousness only new forms of consciousness can arise. There is emergence of new forms of consciousness but only from the conscious matrix and not from matter. Even matter, for him, is a form of consciousness.

The higher forms of consciousness are part of the order of the cosmos because the whole cosmos itself has the signature of consciousness. The lower order of consciousness by its nature moves on to the higher order, but it takes its own rhythm for its execution of the inherent project. There is some amount of inevitability about the cosmic order. Sri Aurobindo holds that beyond the human evolution there is the further possibility of the order of the superman who will embody consciousness in a new form. The possibility of supramental consciousness is written into the structure of the divine plan. Sri Aurobindo writes:

> If a supramental being is to appear in the terrestrial creation, it must be a new and independent manifestation; just as Life and Mind have manifested in Matter, so Supermind must manifest there and the secret Conscious-Energy must create the necessary pattern for this new grade of its potencies.[72]

That is, though the evolution of the supermind is already implicit in the cosmic order, it is not an automatic emergence; the conscious intervention of the Spirit is necessary for this purpose. This is because all higher forms of consciousness are inevitably due to the conscious decisions of the Spirit involved in the cosmic process.

The higher order of the supermen is due in the cosmic order because of the fact that there is no more any physical constraint in the evolution of consciousness. The new transformation is within

---

[72] Sri Aurobindo, *The Life Divine*, p. 831.

consciousness and can be undertaken by the Consciousness-Force itself. This is purely a matter of inner freedom and can be taken as self-evolution. Sri Aurobindo writes:

> But in man a reversal is possible, indeed inevitable; for it is through his consciousness, through its transmutation and no longer through a new bodily organism as a first instrumentation that the evolution can and must be effected.[73]

The reversal of consciousness takes place under the supervision of the Spirit and so there is no inner compulsion for the change. Change takes place freely and out of joy. That is why Sri Aurobindo makes the inner evolution of consciousness a matter of self-effort.

The Superman and the Last Point in the Evolutionary Journey

Sri Aurobindo introduces the concept of superman in order to give a final destination to the evolution of man's consciousness. It is logically the case that the higher we reach in our evolutionary ladder, we reach a stage which ensures the stability of consciousness at a supramental stage. That is the stage of the superman or the spiritual man who commands the height of perfection.

The superman is not a biologically changed man with a different set of physical capacities. He is rather the new man with a new consciousness which is "reversed" inwardly and which is free from the limitations of the mental plane. This sounds to be consistent with Sri Aurobindo's doctrine that supermind is the next stage of the human mental development. The superman is identical with the man with a supermind. The superman is truly the spiritual man who has evolved into supermanhood by means of an inward transformation.

> Man's urge towards spirituality is the inner driving of the spirit within him towards emergence, the insistence of the Consciousness-Force of the being towards the next step of its manifestation.[74]

---

[73] Sri Aurobindo, *The Life Divine*, p. 844.

[74] Ibid., p. 846.

The next step after man is the superman who carries the inner dynamism of the Spirit. Man in no case is the last step in the evolution of consciousness. He is the intermediary between the brute and the superman. Sri Aurobindo writes:

> If a spiritual unfolding on earth is the hidden truth of our birth in Matter, if it is fundamentally an evolution of consciousness that has been taking place in Nature, then man as he is cannot be the last term of that evolution: he is too imperfect an expression of the Spirit, Mind itself a too limited form and instrumentation; Mind is only a middle term of consciousness, the mental being can only be a transitional being.[75]

That is to say that man is only a half-finished being who has a greater future before him. Had he been the last link in the chain of being, then he would have been self-complete. But that is not the case. Man is still an imperfect being who is vulnerable to the tantrums of Nature. In order to get rid of limitation of the biological and mental nature, man has to go beyond his present condition.

The idea of superman is the idea of the spiritually, perfect man who can be the ideal limit of our evolution. The superman is the ideal limit of evolution because that is the end point of our reversal of our consciousness. It is not the case that the superman ceases to be man and becomes a God. He remains man but changes inwardly towards spiritual perfection, such that he becomes "the spiritual man, the fully conscious being, man exceeding his first material self and discoverer of his true self and highest nature".[76] The spiritual man is the fully developed consciousness that defies any limitation of the physical kind. It is not the case that the superman does not belong to the physical world, but he remains above it for the reason that he is not bound by the laws of the mental plane. He defies the limitations of the mental being and carries further the banner of the Spirit into the higher order of consciousness. Sri Aurobindo describes the situation of the superman in the following way:

> The last or highest emergence is the liberated man who has realized the Self and Spirit within him, entered into the cosmic

[75] Sri Aurobindo, *The Life Divine*, pp. 846-47.

[76] Ibid., p. 851.

> consciousness, passed into union with Eternal and, so far as he still accepts life and action, acts by the light and energy of the Power within him . . .[77]

The spiritual man is the divine man who has entered the highest region of the Divine Consciousness.

> Beyond this height and largeness there opens only the supramental ascent or the incommunicable Transcendence.[78]

That is the last point in our evolutionary journey because here we can find the culmination of the path of perfection.

Sri Aurobindo's theory of supramental evolution is based on the fact that man is already potentially a spiritual being who can perfect his nature further by making self-effort. It is genuinely a spiritual evolution because it aims at the perfection of man. But the question arises: Can man attain this stage with the limited capacities that he has? That is, can the earthly man become the superman? The answer to these questions lies in that man has shown sign of evolution in his present stage of culture and mental life. He has already given indication of the fact that he has urge for higher consciousness and that he can attain a state of consciousness that is higher than the present state of consciousness. Thus as a possibility one cannot deny that man is not yet fully spiritual and so a higher man is awaiting to be born.

The Future of History: The Possibility of the Supramental Age

The major implication of Sri Aurobindo's theory of evolution is the new interpretation of the history of man and society. His theory of history is derived from his theory of the cosmic evolution. The history of man is a divine drama written in human terms. It is the human beings who are the players in the divine drama. The cosmic chain of events makes up the whole history in which human beings constitute a society and establish a civilization. The historical process is marked by the divine urge to bring about more integration at

---

77 Sri Aurobindo, *The Life Divine*, p. 882.

78 Ibid.

very stage. The ultimate aim of the historical process is the arrival of the supramental race, i.e. the race of the supermen.

The following are the implications for the mankind as a whole which we can derive from Sri Aurobindo's theory of evolution:

1. That mankind is to be organized into one spiritual unity so that the whole of mankind can function within one civilizational set-up.
2. That man's sole agenda is not his material progress but the spiritual progress that leads to better forms of civilization.
3. That spiritual life is the free life of the human beings who can make their spiritual perfection possible by the practice of *yoga*.

It is the human–divine integration that is the target of the theory of spiritual evolution. It takes the human to the level of the divine and brings the divine into the fold of the human. As Sri Aurobindo puts it:

> The supramental *yoga* is at once an ascent towards God and a descent of Godhead into the embodied nature.[79]

The goal of human existence is to accomplish this ascent towards Godhead and bring back the Godhead to transform the earthly existence. This is the gigantic task that mankind has to accomplish in history. The great future of mankind is waiting to be inaugurated by man through his supramental effort. Sri Aurobindo writes:

> The subhuman was once here supreme in her, the human replacing it walks now in the form of Time, but still, aim and goal of the future, there awaits the supramental, the superman, an unborn glory yet unachieved before her.[80]

The future of mankind thus is waiting to arrive and it is the collective yogic effort which can make it realizable in the history of man's cosmic existence.

To conclude, the age of the supramental race is the goal of the cosmic evolution enunciated by Sri Aurobindo. This goal is no doubt a distant dream at the present stage of mankind, but it is not an

[79] Sri Aurobindo, *The Hour of God*, p. 106.

[80] Ibid., p. 105.

impossibility, if we look at the history of man on earth from the earliest faint glimmer of civilization. The march of human civilization so far indicates that if mankind survives, then it can do so only the ground that it goes beyond its present existence and aspires for the supramental consciousness.

References

Allan, D.J., 1963, *The Philosophy of Aristotle*, Oxford: Oxford University Press.

Aurobindo Sri, 1972, *The Life Divine*, Pondicherry: Sri Aurobindo Ashram.

———, 1998, *The Hour of God*, Pondicherry: Sri Aurobindo Ashram, first published in 1959.

Bhattacharya, H.M., 1959, *The Principles of Philosophy*, Calcutta: University of Calcutta.

Datta, D.M., 1950, *The Chief Currents of Contemporary Philosophy*, Calcutta: University of Calcutta, 3rd edn. 1970.

Mure, G.R.G., 1965, *The Philosophy of Hegel*, London: Oxford University Press.

Radhakrishnan, S., 1932, *An Idealist View of Life*, London: Unwin Books, second impression, 1964.

Ranade, R.D., 1968, *A Constructive Survey of the Upanishadic Philosophy*, Bombay: Bharatiya Vidya Bhavan.

Whitehead, A.N., 1978, *Process and Reality: An Essay in Cosmology*, New York: The Free Press, first published 1929.

2

Spiritual Physics

Ulrich Mohrhoff

> I think it is safe to say that no one understands quantum mechanics.
> — Richard Feynman*

> The theory has, indeed, two powerful bodies of fact in its favour, and only one thing against it. First, in its favour are all the marvellous agreements that the theory has had with every experimental result to date. Second, it is a theory of astonishing and profound mathematical beauty. The one thing that can be said against it is that it makes absolutely no sense!
> — Sir Roger Penrose**

QUANTUM mechanics (QM, also known as quantum physics and quantum theory) is the fundamental theoretical framework of contemporary physics. What does it tell us about the physical world? The answer depends on your metaphysical presuppositions.

Science operates within an interpretative framework that formulates questions and interprets answers. This interpretative framework is not testable by scientific methods. The "bare" empirical data are consistent with a variety of such frameworks. (The scare quotes serve as a reminder that there really is no such thing as a bare, uninterpreted datum.)

The mathematical formalism of QM is a collection of algorithms (computational tools). You may think of these algorithms as machines with inputs and outputs. You insert . . .

- a mathematical representation of a measurement M that you intend to make,

---

* Theortical physcist; ** Mathematical physcist.

- the time of *M*, and
- mathematical representations of some or all of the relevant measurement outcomes previously obtained,

. . . and out pop the probabilities of the possible outcomes of *M*. Barring technicalities that are irrelevant for the purpose of this lecture, this is all there is to it! The rest is metaphysical embroidery.

Why is the fundamental theoretical framework of physics concerned with *measurements* of physical quantities, like position or energy, rather than the physical quantities themselves? Why does it let us predict the *probabilities* of the possible outcomes of a measurement but not the actual outcome? Few physicists or philosophers of science believe that they have the answers, and fewer still believe in the answers that have been proposed. This state of affairs is reflected in the statements by two eminent physicists quoted above.

Equally disconcerting are the probabilities that QM assigns to the possible outcomes of measurements. As our first example, we will consider the following scattering experiment. Initially we have one particle (N) heading in a direction we call "northward" and one particle (S) heading southward. The next thing we know is that we have again two particles, one (E) heading eastward and one (W) heading westward. Which outgoing particle is identical with which incoming particle?

If the particles carry "identity tags" — for instance, if they are of different types and no "type swapping" takes place — then obviously there is an answer: either E is the same as S and W is the same as N, or E is the same as N and W is the same as S:

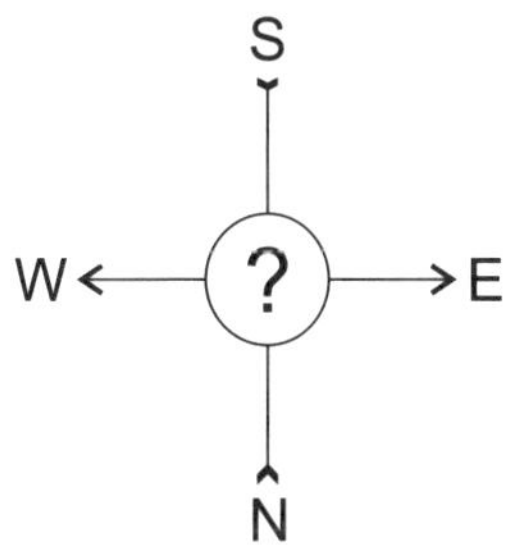

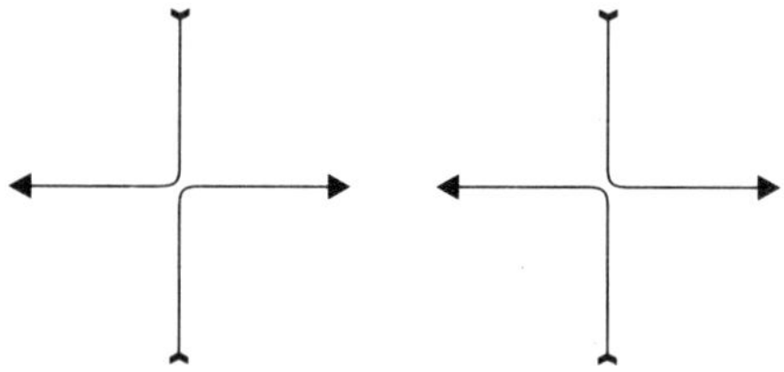

But if the particles lack "identity tags" — i.e. if they lack properties by which they could be distinguished — then there is *no answer*. The reason for this is that the very asssumption that what *really* happens corresponds to either of the above diagrams, is at odds with what QM predicts. The question — which incoming particle is identical with which outgoing particle? — is meaningless.

Here as elsewhere, the challenge is to think in ways that do not lead to meaningless questions. Meaningless questions arise from false assumptions, in this case the assumptions that

- initially there are *two* things, one moving northward and one moving southward, and
- in the end there are *two* things, one moving eastward and one moving westward.

"Obvious" though they may be, if we make these assumptions, we are led to ask the meaningless question: which outgoing particle is identical with which incoming one? If, on the other hand, we assume that

- initially there is *one* thing moving *both* northward *and* southward, and
- in the end there is *one* thing moving *both* eastward *and* westward,

then the meaningless question — Which is which? — does not arise. If these are the correct assumptions — and there are other experimental scenarios and aspects of QM that support this conclusion — then ultimately there is only one "thing". By taking on distinct properties, such as being in different places or moving in different directions, this appears to be — or manifests itself as — a multitude of things, but the underlying substance — what ultimately exists — is *one*.

While the above scenario bears on the concept of *substance,* the following experiment throws light on the nature of *space.* An electron is launched in front of a plate with two slits. The next thing we know is that it is detected at the backdrop at a particular horizontal position x.

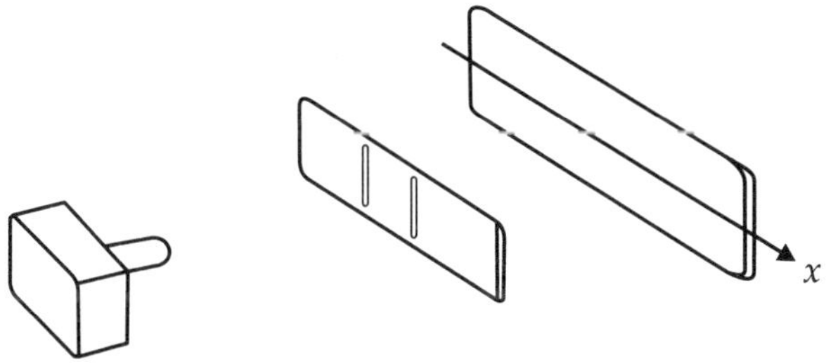

Here the million-dollar question is: through which slit did the electron go? If there is *anything* — any event or state of affairs — from which the answer can be inferred, then obviously there is an answer. But if there is no such event or state of affairs, then there also is *no answer*. Once again we are asking a meaningless question. This time it involves the false assumption that the electron necessarily goes *either* through the left slit *or* through the right slit.

To see why this assumption is wrong, let us contemplate the following images.

Each of these eight images "shows" the fuzzy position of the electron relative to the nucleus — a proton — in a stationary state of atomic hydrogen. (Neither the proton nor the electron is shown; all you see is fuzzy relative positions.)

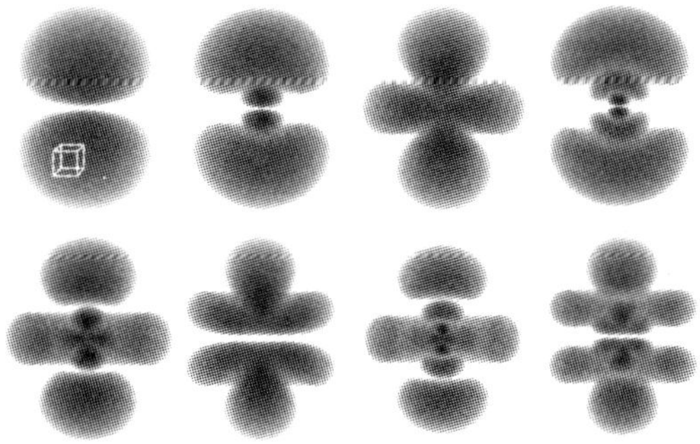

Explanation: A (quantum) *state* is one of the aforementioned probability algorithms. As you will remember, every quantum-mechanical probability algorithm depends on the outcomes of previous measurements. In this case three quantities were measured: the atom's energy, its total angular momentum and the vertical component of its angular momentum. The outcome of the latter quantity was zero in each case. In the first row, the total angular momentum (in suitable units) was found equal to 1, 1, 2 and 1, respectively; in the second row, it was found equal to 2, 3, 2 and 3. A (quantum) state is *stationary* if the probabilities it assign to the possible outcomes of any future measurement do not depend on the time at which this is performed. In a stationary state, the possible outcomes of an energy measurement form a discrete sequence; they can therefore be labelled by the "principal" quantum numbers N = 0, 1, 2, ... In the first row, the values of N were found to be 2, 3, 3 and 4; in the second row, they were found to be 4, 4, 5 and 5.

The images themselves represent something that (i) has a rotational symmetry about the vertical axis, and (ii) can obviously be described as "fuzzy". But in what sense can a *relative position* be described as fuzzy? And how can a fuzzy relative position be defined in quantitative terms?

Embedded in the first fuzzy image is a small cube. If the image represented the variable water density (mass of water per unit volume) of an actual cloud, integrating it over the cube would yield the total mass of the water contained in the cube. What the image actually represents is a variable "probability density": integrating it over the cube yields the probability of finding the electron inside the cube, provided that the appropriate measurement is made. The proper definition (as well as description) of the fuzzy position of a particle thus is an algorithm that yields the probability of finding the particle in any given region (again, provided that the appropriate measurement is made).

Now take a look at this image:

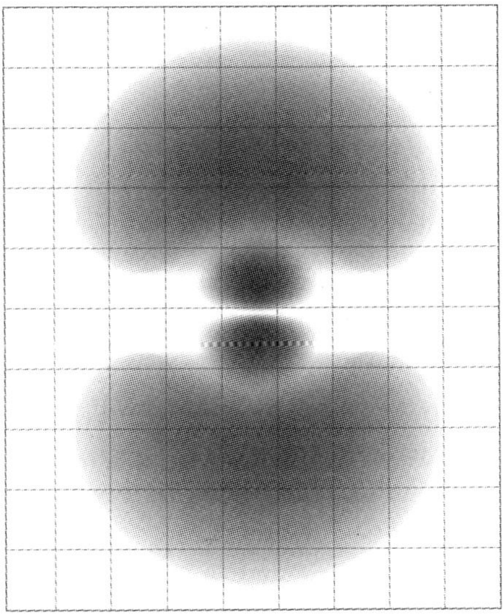

If we conceptually divide the space "occupied" by this probability "cloud" into different regions — for simplicity's sake we here ignore one spatial dimension and represent these regions as rectangles — then different parts of the electron's fuzzy position are contained in different parts of space. But surely this doesn't make sense. A position isn't the kind of thing that has parts. We can divide a *material* object and attribute a position to each of its parts, but we cannot divide a position and attribute a position to each part!

Hence space cannot be something that has intrinsic (in-built) parts, for if it were such a thing, the existence of its parts would imply that positions have parts. If we think of space as a 3-dimensional expanse, we must think of it as an *undivided* expanse. Paradoxically yet to the point, we may say that ultimately there is only one place, and this is everywhere.

Returning to our question about the two-slit experiment, is there an objective, physical difference between (i) "the electron went through *L*", and (ii) "the electron went through *R*"? Because space — considered as a self-existent (substantial) expanse — is undivided, "parts of space" only exist in our imagination, and so do points, paths and surfaces. The answer, therefore, is negative: there isn't any objective differencce between (i) and (ii), unless something —

some actual event or state of affairs — indicates which of the two possibilities actually took place. Otherwise the question "Through which slit did the electron go?" is meaningless. It then involves a false assumption, namely that the distinction we make between "going through L" and "going through R" corresponds to something in the actual, physical world.

If space (qua expanse) is intrinsically undivided, what gives rise to the spatial (or synchronic) multiplicity of the world? What makes "here" different from "there"?

To thinkers from Aristotle to Kant and Gauss it appeared self-evident that space wasn't composed of parts. They considered space an expanse that makes it possible to divide *material* objects. "Space is essentially one," Kant wrote, "the manifold in it . . . arises entirely from the introduction of limits." Today physicists no longer reflect on space as a condition of perception and imagination, but they still hold (more or less implicitly) that spatial multiplicity rests on limits — bounding or dividing surfaces. This way of thinking — and perceiving — is inherent to mental (as against supramental) consciousness. It is one of its defining characteristics:

> Mind in its essence is a consciousness which measures, limits, cuts out forms of things from the indivisible whole and contains them as if each were a separate integer. . . . It conceives, perceives, senses things as if rigidly cut out from a background or a mass and employs them as fixed units of the material given to it for creation or possession. — Sri Aurobindo 2005: 173-74

There is also considerable neuropsychological evidence that the brain processes sensory information in such a way that the result — the perceived world — is a world of objects whose shapes are first and foremost bounding surfaces (Mohrhoff 2001, 2007). This appears to support the current view that the working of the mind is determined by the working of the brain, but let us keep in mind that, according to Sri Aurobindo (2005: 270),

> the physical sense-organs are not the creators of sense-perceptions, but themselves the creation, the instruments and here a necessary convenience of the cosmic sense; . . . the brain is not the creator of

> thought, but itself the creation, the instrument and here a necessary convenience of the cosmic Mind.

Mind, however, is not the original creative principle. That, according to Sri Aurobindo, is the supermind. So we have no reason to expect that the synchronic multiplicity of the world rests on dividing or bounding surfaces. And in fact it doesn't. What our analysis of QM leads us to conclude is that spatial multiplicity rests on fuzzy relative positions. Consequently, the shapes of things are not boundaries but sets of fuzzy relative positions.

Remember the ancient conundrum about the divisibility of matter? If the synchronic multiplicity of the world rested on surfaces that carve up things much as cookie cutters carve up rolled-out pastry, then things ought to be divisible ad infinitum. If on the other hand, we want to understand matter in the manner which has been paradigmatic for some 25 centuries — i.e. in terms of the composition and interaction of parts — then there have to be ultimate, not further divisible parts. But why then are these parts not further divisible? Thanks to QM, we know now why the modern "atoms" — quarks and leptons — are not further divisible. The reason they are not further divisible is that they are *formless*. The shapes of things resolve themselves into sets of fuzzy relative positions (or spatial relations) between formless objects.

If now you recall that ultimately there is only one "thing" and that this is or constitutes everything, you will conclude that the shapes of things resolve themselves into the *self-relations* of a single formless "something". Taking our cue from the Upaniṣads, we might as well call it Brahman. Brahman is said

- to be without form,
- to constitute all things,
- to contain all things,
- to originate all things.

Here is a nutshell account, based on QM, of how formless Brahman originates and comes to contain and constitute all things: Brahman *enters into spatial relations with itself.* As a result,

- there are things that have shapes (sets of spatial relations),

- there is space — Brahman as the one place that contains them all,
- there is matter — Brahman as the apparent multitude of relata ("apparent" because the relations are self-relations) and as the one thing that constitutes them all.

Can you think of a more concise creation story or a more economical way to manifest a world?

But why are the positions of Brahman relative to Brahman *fuzzy*? The answer is that this appears to be the only way to manifest "ordinary" objects. By this I mean objects that

- "occupy" space,
- are made of a large but finite number of objects that do not "occupy" space,
- are stable — they neither collapse nor explode as soon as they are formed.

The existence of such objects requires that the entire theoretical framework of contemporary physics has exactly the form that it does! If you want "ordinary" objects, you need QM. You also need Einstein's two theories of relativity as well as the rest of the Standard Model: electroweak theory and quantum chromodynamics, at least as effective theories (Mohrhoff 2002, 2009).

Explanation: The general theory of relativity (Einstein's theory of gravity) and the so-called Standard Model (which is based on quantum theory and the special theory of relativity) comprise all well-tested physical theories. The electroweak theory is a unified theory of the electric force and the so-called "weak" nuclear force. Quantum chromodynamics is our theory of the so-called "strong" nuclear force. An effective theory is a theory that is valid on some but not all scales of length.

And you need *spin* — a property that has no classical analogue. It therefore can only be defined in quantum-probabilistic terms. Formally, it resembles a vector in that it has components. Measuring any spin component associated with any one of the "building blocks" of "ordinary" matter — a proton, a neutron, an electron, or a quark — yields either of two outcomes: +1 or –1 (in appropriate units).

Moreover, it is impossible, on both theoretical and experimental grounds, to measure more than one component of the spin of any given particle at any given time.

Because of its small number of possible outcomes, experiments involving particle spins are ideal for demonstrating some of the common sense-defying features of QM. For example, it is possible to prepare three particles A, B, C in a state that has the following properties:

- whenever the *x* components of their spins are measured, the product of the outcomes equals –1;
- whenever the *x* component of the spin of one particle and the *y* components of the spins of the two other particles are measured, the product of the outcomes equals +1.

Another million dollar question: is it possible for the spin components of the particles to have values even if they are not measured? If this *is* possible, then the following four equations hold:

$$X_A X_B X_C = -1 \quad X_A Y_B Y_C = 1 \quad Y_A X_B Y_C = 1 \quad Y_A Y_B X_C = 1.$$

Can they all hold with the same values of the spin components X_A, X_B, X_C, Y_A, Y_B and Y_C?

To find out, let us multiply the last three equations (both the left-hand sides and the right-hand sides). This yields

$$X_A Y_B Y_C Y_A X_B Y_C Y_A Y_B X_C = 1.$$

Since the *Y* factors appear twice, which is to say squared, and since their squares are equal to 1 (because their values are either –1 or +1), this boils down to $X_A X_B X_C = 1$. But this obviously cannot hold if the first equation $X_A X_B X_C = -1$ holds. Those four equations therefore cannot be satisfied by *any* given set of values X_A, X_B, X_C, Y_A, Y_B, X_C.

And so it is *not* possible for the spin components to have values if they are not actually measured! Many other experimental arrangements lead to the same conclusion: for any physical property and any physical value, to *be* is to be *measured*.

This means that the values of the spin components are created as and when they are measured. Which raises another conundrum: on the basis of any two outcomes, the third outcome can be predicted.

If, for instance, we measure the x components of particles A and B and thus know X_A and X_B, the equation $X_AX_BX_C = -1$ allows us to predict the outcome of a measurement of the x component of particle C. How is this possible, considering that the relative timing of the three measurements is irrelevant, and that in principle the three particles can be light years apart? How do the first two measurements influence the outcome of the third measurement? What kind of mechanism is at work? *You understand this as much as anybody else!*

The laws of QM are about correlations between measurement outcomes. The correlations are of two kinds: synchronic and diachronic. The former concern the outcomes of measurements that in some reference frames are simultaneous; the latter concern the outcomes of measurements that happen at different times regardless of the reference frame that is used to describe them. (Think of a reference frame as part of the physicist's language. As you can say the same thing in different languages, so you can describe the same experiment using different reference frames.)

Where the *synchronic* correlations are concerned, most physicists readily admit that they have no idea — in fact, cannot imagine — "how nature does it". One is therefore left to wonder how it is that there has been no dearth of attempts to explain the *diachronic* correlations.

One possible reason is this: we experience time as an ever-changing present. This suggests that we can describe the physical world by means of a time-dependent state: we thus have *kinematics*, which is concerned with the description (state) of a physical system at any one time, and we have *dynamics*, which is concerned with how a state changes with time (evolves).

The advent of the special theory of relativity made it clear that this view was fundamentally flawed, for it implies that one can always pick three events A, B, C in such a way that

- A is objectively (i.e. regardless of the reference frame used) earlier than B,
- C is simultaneous with A if a certain class of reference frames is used,

- C is simultaneous with B if a different class of reference frames is used.

In other words, it is up to us how we conceptually decompose the four-dimensional "block" of space–time into three-dimensional "slices" containing simultaneous events. Only the "block" as a four-dimensional whole does not depend on the language we chose to describe the physical world. The physical description of the world is therefore at odds with our experience of time as an ever-changing present.

Tellingly, while physics here is again at odds with mental experience, it is once more in agreement with an aspect of supramental experience:

> The supramental consciousness . . . can either take its station in the time consciousness and keep the timeless infinite as its background of supreme and original being from which it receives all its organising knowledge, will and action, or it can, centred in its essential being, live in the timeless but live too in a manifestation in time which it feels and sees as infinite and as the same Infinite, and can bring out, sustain and develop in the one what it holds supernally in the other. Its time consciousness therefore will be different from that of the mental being, not swept helplessly on the stream of the moments and clutching at each moment as a stay and a swiftly disappearing standpoint, but founded first on its eternal identity beyond the changes of time, secondly, on a simultaneous eternity of Time in which past, present and future exist together for ever in the self-knowledge and self-power of the Eternal, thirdly, in a total view of the three times as one movement singly and indivisibly seen even in their succession of stages, periods, cycles, last — and that only in the instrumental consciousness — in the step by step evolution of the moments.
>
> — Sri Aurobindo 1999: 886

Heedless of the lesson of special relativity, physicists have persisted in the "division of labour" between kinematics and dynamics. Specifically, they continue to think of quantum states as descriptions of physical systems that change with time. To understand their mistake, you need to recall that the mathematical formalism of QM is a collection of "computing machines". What you insert is a measurement to be made, the time of this measurement, and some relevant measurement outcomes previously obtained; what pops out is the probabilities of the possible outcomes of this measurement. The mistake is to transmogrify (i) this computing machine into an evolving physical state, and (ii) the time of a measurement (which was to be inserted into the computing machine) into the time-dependence of this state. This sleight-of-hand has engendered a host of pseudo-problems and a whole industry dedicated to solving them. Chances are that if you pick a popular book on QM, it will regale you with some of these pseudo-problems and some of their (spurious) solutions. Meanwhile the question as to "how nature does it" has remained as elusive as ever.

To see why actually this should be so, look at it this way: in the quantum world everything is possible. To be precise: every conceivable measurement outcome has a probability greater than zero *unless* it violates a conservation law. Physics, therefore, *never* explains *how* something is possible, let alone "how nature does it". It only explains — via its conservation laws — why certain things *won't* happen.

But this is exactly what one would expect if the force at work in the world were an *omnipotent* force operating under self-imposed constraints. There would then be no reason to be surprised by the apparent impossibility of explaining the quantum-mechanical correlations laws — to account for them in terms of mechanisms or processes — for it would be self-contradictory to explain the working of an omnipotent force. What needs to be explained is why this force works under self-imposed constraints, and why under this particular set of constraints.

As we have seen, the purpose of this particular set of constraints is to allow for the existence of stable objects that "occupy space" even though they are made of finite numbers of objects that do not "occupy space".

But why are objects that "occupy space" made of finite numbers of objects that do not "occupy space"? One possible answer is, to set the stage for the adventure of evolution. According to Sri Aurobindo, evolution presupposes involution, and the final outcome of the process of involution is the creation of a universe in which objects that "occupy space" are made of a finite number of formless objects and obey the well-established physical laws, at least initially. We shall look into this process in the next lecture.

Right now, another mystery calls for attention. As indicated earlier, physical properties — the values of physical quantities — are possessed only if, only when, and only to the extent that they are measured (i.e. indicated by or inferable from an actual event or state of affairs). Why? Because a macroscopic apparatus is needed to realize (make real) attributable properties. A detector, for instance, not only serves to indicate the presence of something in its sensitive region *R* but also, and in the first place, to realize the property of being in *R*, to make it available for attribution. By the same token, an apparatus for measuring the spin of a particle is needed not only to indicate an outcome but, in the first place, to realize the axis with respect to which the spin is measured. (This is the experimental reason why the spin components of a particle can be measured only one at a time.)

It follows that the so-called microworld is what it is because of what happens or is the case in the macroworld, rather than the other way around, as we are wont to think. This too runs counter to the twenty-five year-old paradigm which asks: what are the ultimate building blocks, and how do they interact and combine? The right question to ask is: how does Brahman manifest the world — or manifest itself *as* the world? It is no longer appropriate to model physical reality "from the bottom up", by assembling pre-existent building blocks, or by constructing a model of reality on the foundation of an intrinsically differentiated space or space–time. Molecules, atoms, and subatomic particles are instrumental in the manifestation of the macroworld, rather than being its constituent parts or structures, or forming an "underlying" microworld. QM affords us a glimpse "behind" the manifested world, at what is instrumental in its manifestation, but it does not let us describe what we see except in terms of the finished product — the manifested world.

If we conceptually partition the world into smaller and smaller regions, we reach a point at which the distinctions we make between regions no longer correspond to anything in the actual world. And if we keep dividing a material object, its so-called "constituents" lose both their form and their individuality. We reach an omnipresent point and an all-constituting substance. If we follow the opposite direction, starting at formless Brahman, we obtain insight into the coming into being of form. Begin by adding self-relations to this all-constituting substance, which owe their quality of spatial extension to that omnipresent point. This yields composite objects such as protons and atoms. These objects cannot be visualized "as they are". They can only be described abstractly, in terms of correlations between measurement outcomes. The smallest objects with an aspect that can be visualized "as it is" are molecules. This aspect corresponds to the sticks in the chemist's balls-and-sticks model of a molecule. Forms thus arise by a self-differentiation of Brahman that results in a multitude of fuzzy spatial relations, which serve to manifest the shapes of things. As it was said in *Ṛgveda*, the foundation is above.

The self-differentiation of Brahman, moreover, does not go "all the way down" since beyond a certain point we return to the undifferentiated unity both of space and of substance. Nor could it go all the way down, for if it did, the spatial relations between Brahman and Brahman could not be fuzzy, and ordinary objects as previously defined could not exist.

The creations of the supermind — the conscious force by which Brahman qua substance takes on forms and Brahman qua consciousness gives itself content — are primarily qualitative and infinite, and only secondarily quantitative and finite. Essentially, mind is the agent of the supermind's secondary, limiting and dividing action. When mind is used by supermind, its tendency to divide ad infinitum is checked. This is why the self-differentiation of Brahman does not go "all the way down", and why it is impossible to construct reality from the bottom up. When mind is separated in self-awareness from its supramental parent, as it is in us, it not only divides ad infinitum but also takes the resulting multiplicity for the original truth or fact. This is why we keep trying, unsuccessfully, to construct reality from the bottom up.

References

Aurobindo, Sri, 1999, *The Synthesis of Yoga,* Pondicherry: Sri Aurobindo Ashram Trust.

———, 2005, *The Life Divine,* Pondicherry: Sri Aurobindo Ashram Trust.

Feynman, R.P., 1967, *The Character of Physical Law,* Cambridge, MA: MIT Press.

Mohrhoff, U., 2001, "Beyond the Cookie Cutter Paradigm", in *Consciousness and Its Transformation: Papers Presented at the Second International Conference on Integral Psychology,* ed. M. Cornelissen, pp. 333-45, Pondicherry: Sri Aurobindo International Centre of Education.

———, 2002, "Why the Laws of Physics Are Just So", *Foundations of Physics,* 32(8): 1313-24.

———, 2007, "The Quantum World, the Mind, and the Cookie Cutter Paradigm", *AntiMatters,* 1(1): 55-90 (http://anti-matters.org).

———, 2009, "Quantum Mechanics Explained", *International Journal of Quantum Information,* 7(1): 435-58.

Penrose, R., 1986, "Gravity and State Vector Reduction", in *Quantum Concepts in Space and Time,* ed. R. Penrose and C.J. Isham, Oxford: Clarendon.

3

Remarks on the Foundations of The Life Divine

S.E. Bhelke

I

YOGĪ Sri Aurobindo was a great genius of the nineteenth-twentieth century. He did not belong just to India but to the entire world as a *yogī* to make a spiritual upliftment of the whole mankind. He was concerned with man as the most precious creation of the Nature or God where the consciousness has reached to its peak. However, in the wider plan of the universe and universal life, it is just a beginning of life in its proper shape and true content. The real growth has to come yet and it begins at this stage of the most cultured human being with all his achievements and creations in the fields of science, psychology, sociology, political organizations, *yoga* and spirituality. The essence of the existence is spirit and man being a higher stage in existence has his essence of being in spirit. Nevertheless, the spirit, either in nature or in man, is not fully grown and manifest. In its due course it will grow to its fullest extent on its own, since a growth in the form of elevation is inherent to the existence in whatever form the existence appears to be.

Man, as a being living with awareness of his nature and the essence of the Cosmic Existence, has in him the awakening of the inherent drive of the elevation of the status of Consciousness to its limitless infinite form, thinks of and strives for the elevation in a maximum possible speed to achieve the fullest growth in the minimum span of time. Man has a potential to be aware of the growth, to find and follow paths of the growth and become successful in completing the growth. The fully grown and elevated state of consciousness is the final aim for man, since it is the ultimate goal of the Existence to attain the completion of its manifestation in making it remain to be in the perfect and permanent state of harmony, rhythm, balance, peace and happiness. All these are the essential ingredients of the Existence with a built-in propensity to grow through manifestation and reach the perfection. Given this Life it is Divine in its essence and whatever is in essence has to be the nature of it. Thus, this Life has to become the Divine Life. It is, in a way, a journey of Being as the Divine Life to its destination of Becoming the Life Divine as the manifest Being. Becoming is in no way different from Being. They are two perceptions of the same Existence bestowing a vision of the non-difference between them. It is a truth on the trans-physical plane of the Existence and hence without any reference to space, time, action, materiality and so on which are the parameters of the physical plane of the Existence. It is the partial perception of man due to his limitedness that he gets the differences and dualities between being and becoming, manifest and unmanifest, emergence and cessation, creation and dissolution, life and death, progression and regression, rise and recede and so on.

A higher state of consciousness gives a wider and higher view which is not only inclusive of these so-called opposites and differences but is an integrity amongst them as their true nature. The task before us is to realize that the Divine Life is the Life Divine. This realization for mankind is a process of conscious deliberate efforts to transform the Divine Life into the Life Divine through manifestation which is a process of creative evolution. As a seed grows by nature, the Existence evolves itself and this process of evolution is not a mechanical one but it is a creative process.

There is an awareness behind the evolution which provides direction, desire and destination as deliberate and diligent efforts making it Divine. The transformation is into the Divine and hence it is creative. It is a continuity of manifesting into a form and at every point the form further manifests into an evolved form. Each form is fully evolved and it evolves out to its prior form. A transformation is not a horizontally linear progression but it is a vertically spiral progression where there is an upward progression strictly within the track of its own without allowing any deviation or digression in it. It is dynamic due to being self-propelled. Its movements are not discrete or defused. They are focused and concentrated to conjoin within it all the multiple forces operating in it at its smaller parts. Parts are not parts in themselves; they are perceptions of a partial vision. It is one unitary force operating in the Existence as a whole. It is homogeneous. When in its partial perception it appears as differentiated at multiple centres, a comprehensive vision to grasp the Existence as whole is to be attained by rising higher in position.

Such a vision brings to our comprehensive understanding the integrity amongst the apparent multiplicity of parts into whole and forces into energy. Thus it is the whole of the Existence that manifests into a form and each form as a whole evolves into a subsequent form out of its preceding form. This process is infinitely endless. However, we can think of it in two parts belonging to two different levels. In the initial stage the process of evolution is revealing and manifesting each and every element and aspect of its potential. A stage will come, a state of poise, where no element and part of the whole of the Existence remains to be manifest to its fullest extent. The process of manifestation and evolution being endlessly infinite will not come to stagnation at this point but will continue the manifestation of each fully evolved form into a novel fully evolved form. This novelty is the essence of the evolution being creative. It is novel because it is beyond imagination. It is an actualization of that which was not contained into its unmanifest possible potential. Any actualization is necessitated by its preceding and foundational potential. However, a potential comes under the grasp of imagination and hence makes the manifestation lose its novelty. The sense of potentiality on these two levels is different. On the primary level the potential is an unmanifest form which has scope to manifest further. The potential on this level suggests a sense of incompleteness and that incompleteness is completed in the manifestation. However, on the higher level of manifestation the form of the Being which is manifested is fully grown and complete. It manifests not because of its incompleteness in it but it reveals a different form. It is manifested out of its prior form which itself is fully manifest but in its next manifestation it reveals a novel form. The prior form for manifestation has a potential to manifest in the sense that its being there is its being a potential and not any incompleteness in it is its being a potential to manifest. This makes the manifestation creative, endlessly infinite and full of novelty beyond imagination. The sense of "play" is fully expressed on this level of an infinite chain of manifestations.

II

Sri Aurobindo has elaborately and meticulously worked out the process of the creative evolution to transform the Divine Life into the Life Divine as the pre-destined goal of the Divine Existence present everywhere in an unmanifest and latent form. He has an urge to hasten this process of evolution so that much earlier than to its natural course the final goal of completeness could be reached to make the life of human beings the life of true happiness and completeness. Freedom and peace are the main characteristics of this fully evolved complete life. The way to achieve the final stage of the Evolution is the Integral Yoga. However, the practice to follow the path of the integral *yoga* presupposes a clear understanding of the full plan of the evolution. Sri Aurobindo has given the principles of it to understand it comprehensively, mainly in his monumental work *The Life Divine*. It is a vast plan with a complex structure. His vision being vast and deeply penetrat-ing he gives the understanding in a voluminous work. However, the work demands an analysis to simplify for a clear understating of it. Although Sri Aurobindo does not call himself, nor does he like to be called himself a philosopher he calls himself a *yogī* and a visionary (and a *kavi*). His work is a highly philosophical work and it can be better understood as a philosophy following philosophical methods of analysis and synthesis of its underlying structure. He has developed a full-fledged philosophy of life, not just for the life of man but for the Cosmic Life which is a dynamic and evolved form of consciousness exhibiting itself through organisms and non-organic entities of Nature. We call it philosophy because it has a complete logic, epistemology, metaphysics, ethics and aesthetic of its own blending into a complete and consistent system of a rational thought in abstraction as well as its application in practice.

III

There are some sets of basic concepts he uses to develop and elaborate his thought. They have their own logic. In order to understand the structure of his thought, understanding of those sets of basic concepts along with their logic help us to take a comfortable grasp of the kernel of his philosophy. Sets of these concepts are used in different ways with different details as warranted by the context. Nevertheless, they remain consistent in their meanings. He has used the concept of negation as one of the basic concepts to develop his thought. Although the concept of negation is a logical concept and in logic it is used to show various shades and types of oppositions in differences seen in the multitude, Sri Aurobindo has used this concept for an epistemological and metaphysical purpose. As the concept of negation is basic to develop a system of logic, formal or informal, Sri Aurobindo has used this concept to develop a system of his metaphysical thought in a constructive way. An opposition is a threat to an assertion for its being an assertion. An extreme form of an opposition makes the two opposing statements to cancel out each other making them incompatible with each other. An opposition makes an inconsistency in a system. This is so because an assertion and its opposition, i.e. negation belong to the same level and they become incompatible making each other cancel out. If an inconsistency remains or is allowed to be in a system, the system no longer continues to be a logical system, since it loses warantability of logical, i.e. valid conclusion.

Any conclusion follows from a contradiction means that whatever conclusion is shown to be following does not have a logical necessity of being a valid conclusion. This is the reason and significance of negating an inconsistency in a system to keep the system as a logical system. This is the case of a two-dimensional epistemology where all statements are on one and the same plane. But a philosopher has to go beyond the two-dimensional epistemology, because the reality is not two-dimensional. A reality which is multi-dimensional cannot be legitimately and completely captured by a two-dimensional epistemology. The reality has an infinite spread horizontally as well as vertically. Man has to take a grasp of the reality not just on one level or layer of it, but has to take into consideration its multiple layers at a time to make a proper understanding of it in a right direction. Just one layer is a cross-section and it is not representative of the true nature of the reality. The multi-layered structure of the reality is to be grasped through a multi-layered epistemology. In such a multi-layered structure opposition, incompatibility and inconsistency have a wider meaning. The holistic integral metaphysics of Sri Aurobindo gives a different treatment to negation and opposition. His metaphysics is described as a non-dualistic one. The logic of opposition he uses in his metaphysics makes one to transcend uni-layered structure making the oppositions and incompatibilities thought to be otherwise inconsistent as integral parts or aspects of the same unitary reality. This is the logic operative in his thought on the levels of Nature, World, Cosmos, Life, Mind, Consciousness, Existence, Being, Absolute and Divine. This makes his metaphysics unique and novel on the background of various systems of metaphysics developed so far in any of philosophical traditions.

The extended use of the logic of negation and opposition he has made so far is due to another fundamental technique of philosophizing in developing a system of philosophy in the technique of transcendence. In modern times, i.e. past few centuries, the German philosopher Immanuel Kant had introduced this technique in philosophizing and made it a mature and standard procedure to get a profound vision of reality. Sri Aurobindo follows the same procedure to develop his philosophy. However, there is a basic difference between them. Although Kant succeeds in going beyond the existence of the apparent reality to trace the roots of its real existence in its foundations, he ends with an agnosticism by saying that the noumenon is not within the reach of human reason to know it. He is aware of that which makes possible or provides existence to that whatever is there, but fails to develop an epistemology which could make possible to grasp the noumenon. Sri Aurobindo's philosophy is not crippled to take a complete grasp of the reality transcending the empirical world of physical nature. Sri Aurobindo is looking at the Reality as evolving into higher and higher forms. They are vertically ascending planes on which the Reality is manifesting itself. In this ascendance, at every plane there is transcendence. To show that these are subsequently higher states he uses the prefix "supra" to state ascending on higher planes. Although there are multiple countless ascending planes, there is no rapture between any two planes. This process of evolution is not abrupt or broken into parts which are to be joined or collected mechanically and externally. There is a smooth continuity in the process of evolution and yet a correspondence between two contagious levels. In order to capture this logic of evolution he has used the model of a spiral development in which there is continuity across the level-transcendence.

The continuously evolving reality is infinite vast. When it is perceived by man who is limited, whose perception is partial and whose position to perceive is mundane, the reality appears in multiple parts. The difference in the multitude leads to oppositions and inconsistencies which is not an aspect of the reality. Nevertheless, we have to live on and deal with the mundane plane where we have to handle the oppositions in such way that they will neither fragment our life nor annihilate forces of life within it. We have to find out the ways and modes in which the apparent oppositions are essentially integral. In order to understand this aspect of the Reality and live our life accordingly Sri Aurobindo introduces a set of four concepts, viz. harmony, rhythm, centre and balance. There is a harmony amongst the apparent parts of the homogeneous Reality. The dynamism of the Becoming is rhythmical. With this the parts of Being and also of the Becoming remain in balance. This gives centring of the Being — the centre of the Being holds the Becoming in balance and in totality. These four concepts are so interrelated that a mention of one refers to the sense of other three with its own meaning. When the opposites do not cancel out each other, rather harmonize with each other, they transcend into a unity on a higher level. The differences are complementarities to one another. This principle on epistemological level gives a deeper sense of ignorance (*avidyā*) which is not a negation in the sense of absence of true knowledge but is a fragmented knowledge leading to confusion rather than to the realization of the true nature.

The metaphysical application of it in the doctrine of *māyā* which gives the fleeting images of the Reality, which is not its true nature. *Māyā*, according to him, is not something unreal or non-existing as usually claimed to be. In fact, according to him nothing is unreal or non-existing. The logic of transcend-ence, i.e. comprehension from an ascending plane, makes us realize that everything is real and existing including the world which is a reality on the mundane level. Sri Aurobindo radically differs from the position and metaphysics of the Advaita Vedānta mainly on this point where for the Advaita Vedānta, the world is unreal and *Māyā* is illusory. At a later stage the Advaita Vedānta held that *Māyā* is a power of the Absolute Reality called Brahman to cover and conceal its true nature. Sri Aurobindo also treats *Māyā* as a power but with a different role assigned to it. The oppositions, negations, contradictions and ignorance are there when they are observed on the mundane plane of practical life of physicality. With transcendence of plane they get transformed into unity and integrity as we realize the harmony amongst them. The harmony makes the assimilation of the lower to the higher by accommodating it to form a unitary whole and establish a balance in the multitude. The transcendence is with transformation and hence there is an absence of duality. The technique of transcendence is, thus, used by him in multiple ways and in all dimensions. When the transcendence takes place with transformation of the lower to the higher, the evolution takes place where the existence of the lower plane gets transformed through assimilation into the existence of the higher plane. This process does not allow a possibility of duality or difference in the whole, though there appears plurality in it. The plurality remains with harmony and the whole becomes integrated. As the death is not denied but accepted as a transformation of a state maintaining continuity of life, the multitude is not dissolved but retained with harmony to result into integrity. In a way the problem of life felt by man can be formulated as some kind of negation which apparently suggest an absence of something or opposition to something. This negation or absence or opposition is with reference to or in relation to something being there essentially and primarily. On the human level the being is a continuity of life and its absence or negation is seen in death.

On the same individual level the essence of being is poise and happiness and its negation or opposition is imbalance and misery. This duality stands in the form of an opposition. Sri Aurobindo's thought has this ground for beginning the activity of philosophizing. However, he takes this opposing duality, on all possible levels of being and thought, viz. logical, epistemological, psychological, metaphysical, ethical and so on, suggesting its implications in sociological and cultural realms. This, again, is a holistic approach to bring together various approaches of philosophizing and formulating the basic problem in philosophical categories. He suggests that the root cause of the problem lies in our perception or understanding of the situation where we belong to while experiencing the problem. Hence the solution to the problem lies in modifying the perception and understanding the situation by enhancing one's own position to perceive the reality as a whole. This enhancement of position takes us to transcendence and the transcendence takes us to see the rhythm, harmony and balance which is an essence of the reality. The essence of the individual existence, thus, is not misery or sorrow leading to depression and frustration but happiness leading to poise and creativity. It is the fragmentary approach in perception which causes an understanding of opposition in multitude. Transcending the fragmentary approach is perceiving unity and integrity. Thus the logic of transcendence, harmony and integrity is operative in Sri Aurobindo's philosophy on all levels of thought and reality.

The bare basic structure of his ontology has four categories, viz. matter, life, mind and consciousness. These categories are developed in complex structures increasing their number as he goes on developing details and subtleties. Matter is further enlarged into matter, nature and world, life is enlarged into life, mind and consciousness, mind is enlarged into higher mind, illuminated mind, intuitive mind, overmind and supermind, and consciousness is enlarged into spirit, absolute, existence and being. With the subtleties these categories are used mainly epistemologically. However, he transcends this further and presents its categories with specific Vedāntic terms, viz. *Māyā, Ātman, Brahman* and *Saccidānanda*. For him they are on trans-transcendental level. In order to show the difference on vertical level he uses the terms as prefixes, viz. sub, supra, super, supreme and divine. In order to specify the scope of the reality vis-à-vis its level, he uses categories like individual, universal, cosmic and infinite where the infinite is transcendent. The grasp of the metaphysics is an epistemological affair where he uses categories like reason, will, intuition and knowledge. The dynamic aspect is presented through categories like will, force, bliss and delight. These categories reveal the aspect in which the reality is a result or an effect. The same reality is stated as a dynamic continuum through categories of manifesting, ascending, evolving and creating. Thus taking a hold of these basic sets of categories facilitates a deeper grasp of his philosophy.

IV

The grasp of the reality, in the beginning, is through knowledge. Epistemology leads to establish metaphysics. The reality which is a content or subject matter of metaphysics itself is spread on multiple levels. The human capacities to grasp it also has multiple levels. They are the faculties through which the reality is grasped in its various aspects and dimensions. On the empirical level the empirical reality, which is physical and concrete in nature, is grasped through the empirical senses which are called by him as physical senses. They are operative on two levels: physical and supraphysical. There is no leap from empirical knowledge to trans-empirical knowledge but the same faculty has a capacity to perform a function to take a grasp on these two levels. In his philosophy although there is a multitude on the vertical and horizontal level, the multitude does not lead to a rapture or disorganization. Everywhere he maintains a smooth continuity which guards the integrity and homogeneity of a whole. In fact, the human agent, due to his partial nature and capacities, does not get the unitary whole at a glance but gets it in parts without getting through the same faculty the internal relations expressing the unity and homogeneity of the whole. Although it may appear that there are multiple faculties to take a grasp of the reality, the faculty is one but with multiple functions and operations to perform as per the requirement of the nature of the subject matter, the context in which the subject matter is placed or presented and the purpose for which the grasp of the subject matter is meant for.

The reality as an Absolute Being or Existence is transcendental and hence is a-dimensional. But for the human understating of it on a primary level a category of dimension is invented to capture the reality and the dimensions of the transcendental reality are infinite. The physical senses on the physical level get us the three-dimensional empirical nature of the reality which is in a form of a world or nature. Sri Aurobindo uses some of the basic terms either in a small case or in an upper case (i.e. capital letter) as the first letter of the term to indicate the level on which he is referring to the referendum belonging to. He is continuously referring to the mundane and the transcendent levels because his main aim is to understand the reality in its essence as it is and live the life in its full depths to make it complete. The philosophical plane is of the supra or super level and in relation to it the empirical plane is the sub-level. The physical reality, i.e. the empirical world and nature, is the World and Nature on the supra level and the physical senses, which enable us to get the physical world or nature, also have a capacity to bestow us the World or Nature through its supraphysical potential. The physical senses, thus, give us the grasp of the reality on its primary level, which is in a way a data which is to be processed further to get the essence of the reality on the one hand and the completeness as a whole on the other hand. Hence he moves to the other faculties which belong to higher levels. He introduces faculties of philosophical reasoning and impartial reasoning. The physical senses do not perceive the immaterial nor does it capture the organized as gross Matter and hence the supersensible enters into the scene. The entire existence from its lowest form to the highest form is essentially consciousness manifesting or expressing itself on relevant levels of Being. The faculties to grasp the reality are cruder and finer forms of the consciousness corresponding to the levels of the consciousness as Being. Grasping the reality as consciousness through faculties as functioning consciousness in their mutual interaction is free play of consciousness as Being and Becoming. There is an argumentative form to know which is a function of reason. The subtler forms contained in the world of matter cannot be grasped by physical senses. He, therefore, introduces, following the Sāṁkhya metaphysics, the role of subtle senses of subtle bodies (*sūkṣma-indriyas* of *sūkṣma-deha*) to continue his epistemology. The consciousness has material as also spiritual organization. In order to capture that he uses the epistemic functions of consciousness as irrational, rational and thought. For him irrational is that faculty which leads to ignorance. It is *ajñāna* or *avidyā* of Vedānta which is full of contradictions, negations and so on. This is the sphere of *māyā* but not the sphere of non-existence as traditionally said to be. Transcending the realm of negation takes us to the realm of pure Spirit which is free from changes. It is obtained through reason and its furtherance in developing sciences to unravel the secrets of the material world is undertaken by the faculty of thought. This function of reason as faculty of thought is different from enlightenment which is the highest or the purest function of Consciousness to grasp the consciousness.

Thus he comes to the three forms of knowledge, viz. scientific, cosmic and practical, which are, more or less, concerned with the empirical form of reality and life in their dynamic expressions as becoming. Although they belong to a much lower level of mundane plane they are foundational to the ascend of evolution. Praxiological considerations are not free from axiological considerations. The practical knowledge is not limited to skills, techniques and to do things but it covers the cultural and ethical practices which presuppose and develop norms. The scientific knowledge is concerned with the logical and methodological aspect of the reality of which the knowledge is systemized to understand the organization of the reality on the empirical and trans-empirical levels. The cosmic knowledge helps us to understand the transcendental reality in its infinite form. In the realm of discussing knowledge as a result of operations of the faculties he is mentioning various epistemic states which matter for our experience and attitude towards the reality and life. He, mainly, refers to four epistemic states, viz. faith, knowledge, perfect experience and wisdom. The last three stages also correspond to the forms of the reality which are transcendent and spiritual in nature. The last form of knowledge called wisdom is what he takes and develops from the Indian tradition, referred to as *Prajñā*. Wisdom as an epistemic state has a significance both in the Greek and the Indian tradition to take a grasp of the ultimate reality on the one hand and comprehend the cosmic life fully on the other hand to lead to attain the highest goal of life in whatever manner it is formulated. Sri Aurobindo makes the proper use of it to keep it as pivotal to epistemology and metaphysics. At a higher level there is a unity of epistemology and metaphysics, not only in Sri Aurobindo's thought but basically in philosophical systems of Indian tradition. For them philosophy does not remain merely an intellectual pursuit of developing epistemology as a way to approach and grasp the Ultimate Reality or the Absolute but becomes a way of life in which the subject of epistemic enterprise transforms himself into the metaphysical entity as the spiritual being. This being the importance of the epistemic enterprise he points out the force to know, i.e. the emergence of an epistemic operation being twofold, viz. impulsion and reception. A force is an innate and internal power for an action and actualization of the potential. Whatever is there on any level either as being or becoming is within existence itself and it keeps manifesting in a form of evolution for him. Even the negation which is the base and motivation for the philosophical inquiry has two forms, material and spiritual. In its primary form a negation leads to contradiction where opposites cancel out each other. When they are known on a higher level they turn out to be reconciliating factors of a wider whole. This makes us to know the harmony and rhythm as an essential nature of the Reality. Thus we finally come to know the centre as a principle of the unitary whole of the Reality establishing a balance in it. The balance is the final form in which the Becoming is known. This is to be known on the empirical and also the transcendental level. The sense experience gives forms and movements. Forms may be concrete or abstract. The movement gives the glimpse of the motion of matter in Space and also the motion of change in Time. Beyond the sense experience there is a role of self-awareness giving the knowledge of the transcendent. It gives the knowledge of the immovable and immutable nature of the reality which is beyond movement and change, not by denying the movement and change but by assimilating it and going beyond it. Life and death are empirical negations not revealing the nature of the reality but misleading the nature of the reality. Self-awareness gives an integral view by going beyond all life and death. A particular instance of life is followed by death, but all life is not followed by death. Life continues through the ephemeral instance of death as its own transformation. This also helps to get the knowledge beyond all change, formation and action. The difference in a particular and all is not horizontal, it is hierarchical. Hence the self-awareness takes one beyond the truth.

In the hierarchical arrangement of levels and functions of being or consciousness or spirit, Mind plays a crucial role in epistemology as faculty to discharge the results of the epistemic enterprise. Mind for its epistemic role to play is a sense-mind. This sense–mind is all sufficient, pure, sovereign and an extension of faculty. Its first three characterizations assure the validity and soundness of knowledge it bestows. Hence this epistemology is free from the talk and discussion of theories of error and validity (i.e. Khyātivāda and Prāmāṇya-vāda) of knowledge. The sense-mind is pure and sovereign because it is a sufficiently articulate form of consciousness. The faculty above the sense-mind is reason which gives the knowledge of the still higher and abstract forms of the reality in its being and becoming aspects. Higher to this is the faculty of consciousness as subconscient and superconscient. This enables as a deeper penetration into the essence of the reality. It has a refined and evolved form as the Supreme Consciousness which gives the knowledge of the self-existence and he calls it as the faculty of intuitional knowledge. In this case the subject of knowledge becomes the object of knowledge; it does not cease to be the subject. The dichotomy between them remains to make the epistemic self-reflexivity possible. The highest faculty for the epistemological enterprise is supramental which is a state of pure consciousness giving full awareness without any interactive structure of it. Nevertheless, the consciousness in its full awareness is not static, it is illuminating and reflecting. Thus the realm of epistemic enterprise is a self-propelling play of the dynamism of consciousness. It is a play of the sense-mind generating the images of the Reality as Forms and Movements. It is a play of the Consciousness which takes to the Truth beyond. The play of intuition not only gives the consciousness of the immovable and the immutable but also whatever is behind and beyond of the focus of the play. The higher aspect of awareness of the self-existence in various forms like *"aham brahmāsmi"*, *"tat tvam asi"*, *"sarvam khalv idam brahma"* and *"ātmā ca brahma"* are the expressions of the highest forms of the realization of the Ultimate Reality in union with the experiencing and knowing agent as an ontic entity in the Existence. This play in the epistemic realm is a primary level of *Līlā* which involves interactions, intercourse and illumination without any constraints and external force. This is the essence of the functions and operations of consciousness on various levels to grasp the reality through epistemic enterprise. The play of the reason orders perceptions, actions and thoughts on the praxiological level of dynamic functions of the consciousness. This notion of play (*Līlā*) reveals the becoming of the existence when it comes to develop on the transcendent level metaphysics of evolution. However, at this stage the perception of metaphysics is made on a primary level through the epistemological aspect.

While developing the thought of faculties to get knowledge of the reality Sri Aurobindo seems to be following the basic model of Sāṁkhya system of philosophy and supplementing it with the contributions of the Western philosophical tradition and categories. The physical senses give an empirical knowledge of the material world and along with the sense-mind they operate to give the knowledge of the non-physical world. The sense-mind, for him, includes *Manas* and *Buddhi*. However, the more subtleties are captured by the pure reason which, according to him, is a deputy to intuition. Knowledge of the spirit in its primary form is not possible through the sense-mind. It is the pure reason which enables this type of knowledge where the dependence on the means of knowledge is more than the consciousness.

He also speaks of perception of senses which is of the physical world and of reason which is of the reality beyond the physical world. *Manas* gives an awareness of an object which belongs to the external world and also of a subject who is the knower itself. An awareness operates not through the means of senses or mind or even reason. There is directness in the operation of the awareness. Knowledge, basically, is indirect being known through sense-organs. Knowledge which is also direct is known either by identity or through self-awareness. Knowledge by identity is knowledge of the knowing self and knowledge through self-awareness gives the knowledge of *ātman* and it further leads to the knowledge of Brahman. This is how in his scheme, knowledge is both physical and metaphysical, i.e. knowledge of the empirical world and knowledge of the transcendental reality. In the realm of epistemology there are some other functions which take place to organize knowledge for a specific purpose. There is conception, ratiocination and imaginative variation to construct complex structures giving more conclusions as an addition to the available knowledge. The level of the reality as an object of knowledge determines the type and function of the epistemic faculty and its operations. In this scheme the highest faculty is Intuition. Beyond this Intuition there is Supreme Experience and it is followed by the Supreme Intuition. The Intuition and Supreme Intuition go parallel to what Advaita Vedāntins call as *aparokṣānubhūti* which appears as something mystical in the logico-rational structure of epistemology. However, in Sri Aurobindo's system, with his explanations, it does not appear to be mystical in nature but logically and rationally a justifiable faculty to grasp the Absolute which is infinite and trans-transcendental. He has used the concept from the Indian philosophical tradition, viz. *prajñā* as apprehending consciousness. To explain its role he makes a fundamental division of *puruṣa* and *prakṛti* which he explains as Conscious-Soul and Force-Soul or Nature-Soul. Although these terms come from the Sāṁkhya system of philosophy he gives a different meaning to *prakṛti* as being traditionally understood.

For the faculty analysis Mind is the central category of his metaphysics. However, Mind is basically metaphysical in nature with its finer and higher forms. One of the much higher forms of Mind is Supermind to which he assigns some roles to play in the realm of epistemology. In Supermind the action of mind is consciously subordinate since it is transcendent. In it there is a return of self-concentrating conscious-being. The individuality of the self is retained but heightened. Its outward expressing direction reverted to inside. The identity is obtained not in the extrovert functions of the consciousness but through the self-reflective operations of it. The Supermind makes the return of self-concentrating conscious-being. The Consciousness is illuminating, expressive, expanding and pervasive. Its locus is its centre, i.e. the self itself. Just to be aware of the self is not sufficient to make further higher operations possible. It has to focus in a retrospective way to generate its energy to express itself in the inner dimension of its being. This is achieved by concentrating on the self itself. The being is conscious, its consciousness is operative in both ways, i.e. expressing and expanding outward and penetrating deep inside itself. This gives self-concentration and it is the self-concentrating conscious being which is the higher state of mind that makes its epistemic and praxiotic functions possible. It is due to this that the identity emerges and the self-identity makes possible further developments seen in the process of evolution. Although the evolution is basically and largely understood as a metaphysical process, it also has an epistemological dimension along with the praxiotic dimension. For epistemic functions to be performed and for praxiotic operations to take place the identity of the self as an agent needs to be formed. Such an identity, rather a self-identity of the conscious-being emerges when there is a return of it in its self-concentrating function. This epistemic and also the praxiotic formulation of the Supermind helps the dissolution of the aggregate into the infinite nothingness. The higher evolved form is without particularities of being and its functions. This state is attained, to begin with, in the epistemic realm and further spread in the realm of aesthete and pure being. Although there is dissolution of it into the infinite nothingness the epistemic and praxiotic functions do not cease to be, since they are integral to the very essence of the Consciousness. They universalize themselves as becoming the universal feature of the Consciousness in its being illuminating. We get epistemic and praxiotic functions as recognizable when the universal Consciousness reflects in a limited form narrowed by our partial glimpses of it. Hence the state of the Supermind is a state balancing and projecting the epistemic, praxiotic, aesthetic and ontic dimensions of the Consciousness.

The various functions of Consciousness are held and directed by an agent which is pointed and individuated locus in the Consciousness. This is identified as a Self. The agent to know, to act, to enjoy and to be (in itself) is this Self. He is the bearer and the source of operations in these realms. He is the connecting bridge, in the thought of Sri Aurobindo, between the being and the operations of the being. This self gives the foundations of the ontology in his metaphysics. As an agent this self has a constitution to make possible the various functions through assuming concerned role. Mind and Reason are the two main and basic structural components of the Self. They make epistemic, praxiotic and aesthetic operations actual. They are on the empirical level. But as there is an ascent of the higher levels the individual operations of the Self tend to become universal, cosmic and infinite. They are functions of the individual self but a higher self to get the grasp and interact with the transcendent forms of the being. The Reason develops into the subconscient All to take to the superconscient All. The superconscient all gives Life where actions take place. The subconscient All gives Light which leads to the Supreme Consciousness on the one hand and the Conscious Identity on the other hand. This manifests into the All and gives Intuitional Knowledge. Due to the Intuitional Knowledge the self-existence gets captured in the epistemic context. The higher form of the Intuitional Knowledge is the Supreme Consciousness which gives Self-awareness in which the own self and also the other self are grasped. This is how the luminous self-identity is established. This is a state both in epistemic realm and in the ontic realm. It develops into the self-luminous intuition leading to the Supramental. This is the highest possible state of knowledge giving the grasp of infinite absolute. Knowledge is imprisoned in the act. However, mind and reason enable knowledge to liberate from its imprisonment. This further enables know-ledge to resume its essential primacy. The liberated knowledge retaining its primacy makes the upsurge into the Supramental to attain the highest possible epistemic state. This state is not just an epistemic state but also reveals the features of the ontic state of consciousness. Thus the epistemology not only gives the grasp of the object but also transforms the epistemic state into the onticity. This is a unique transcending function attained through the transformation of the luminous intuition into the luminous being or consciousness.

V

The formation of the consciousness in the state of Mind makes epistemic, praxiotic and aesthetic functions possible, its structure as an ontic being explains the continuity of the metaphysics of consciousness. At the level of mind it is a sentient being and the primary identity of sentient being is in its epistemic functions. In the case of a human being the identity and epistemic functions are more articulate and more evolved. The metaphysics of Sri Aurobindo is carved out on the model of a human being. The sub and supra levels, the ascent and the descent, the mundane and the transcendent — all are with reference to a man at the centre. There could be an epistemo-logy and praxiology with reference to non-human sentient beings. But we are not capable to conceive its nature, structure and details. The behaviour of human beings in the sentient world is unique in its operations and achievements. This is so because of the elevated and articulate nature of consciousness of human beings. This articulation is the nature of Mind. It is sense-mind to discharge its basic functions. It is self-sufficient, pure, sovereign and an extension of the faculty. It is not a psychological entity of passions and emotions as understood in the Western tradition, but it is an articulate storehouse of consciousness to make possible the activities and extension of the inner world against the external physical world. It does not depend on anything else than itself for its being, operations, control and directions. Hence Sri Aurobindo describes this Mind through the metaphor of a mirror and says that it is a reflective mirror. Its operations belong to and are restricted to the physical world and hence it is a faculty of relative thought. It gives images of pre-existent Truth and serves as a faculty of forecasting new modification. This means that it is not limited to the space and time where it belongs to but extends beyond it to take into its stride a wider span of life and goes deeper to penetrate into the foundation of everything which makes the thing exist. The truth in metaphysics is existence and Mind gives images of that Truth. It is a chained and hampered sovereign of our life. In essence it is consciousness. It contains parts of whole as separate integers. However, it is the root of the great ignorance, i.e. *avidyā*. Its grasping and handling parts of a whole as separate entities do not lead to the Truth, but only to the images as glimpses of the Truth. It is an illusion of body being a physical instrumental and so, being dynamic, it gives an illusion of Life — Life as a higher form of consciousness. Nevertheless, it is the highest of the three lower principles of existence. It is, in another context, a creative cosmic energy which makes secondary creations of new combined forms. It functions also on the subconscious level to work at Force and Matter. It is responsible for its own emergence, since it is sovereign and all sufficient. It is equally responsible for life, nerve's consciousness of plant and ever developing mentality of evolved animal and man. In fact, with mind the evolved sentient life in organisms gets marked to make it unique. Thus it is a final individualizing operation of Supermind and it is a consciousness force to make all epistemic, praxiotic and aesthetic movements possible in a direction and with a meaning or purpose to them.

VI

Mind having this specific place in the scheme of his philosophy has some functions affecting epistemy, praxis, aesthetic and ontology. In fact, these functions have direct bearing upon the metaphysics of consciousness. This mind measures things and accordingly limits them into parts. The Absolute being infinite is immeasurable. But the Mind cuts out forms of things from the indivisible whole. Precisely this is the function of *māyā* in Advaita Vedānta. When Mind is used vis-à-vis the reality to appear in the ordinary discourse, then the empirical world is taken as the apparent world presented through *māyā* for Vedāntins. Sri Aurobindo takes this part in his metaphysics. The measuring and limiting of the parts of the indivisible whole presuppose an epistemological preparation and Mind fulfils those requirements by undertaking the operations of conception, perception, sensation and creative thought. The last function is unusual to the ordinary epistemology. But in order to exclude the thesis of falsity of the empirical world, which is a thesis of the traditional Vedānta, Sri Aurobindo focuses on this function of Mind to continue the metaphysical truth of all levels. Whatever parts of a whole are taken out Mind treats them as small wholes of a greater Whole. Mind's actions and enjoyments are on these small wholes. This means that Mind does not seem to have a capacity to act on a greater Whole. Hence it divides, subtracts and multiplies them, it does not go beyond it. It handles images, forms and worlds, and not, obviously, the essences. This is a Vedāntic doctrine of name and form (*nāma* and *rūpa*). It has a capacity to perceive particulars but not the universal. It views every phenomenon as a separate part of a whole. It is an action of the Infinite; nevertheless, this action is consciously subordinate to Supermind. Thus Mind makes divisions which are not in the reality. Framing and presenting the reality in this form, according to Sri Aurobindo, is a perversion. This is an original perversion and Mind is responsible for it. This shows the limitations of Mind. It does not perceive universals. It possesses simply a formless vast and not the real spaceless infinite. The Real is beyond its reach. It is determined by the body and hence causes a fall from self-knowledge.

Sri Aurobindo gives a hierarchical spread of Mind as seen in the process of evolution. He begins to give the formation of consciousness as Mind and explains its nature in various dimensions as elaborated above. It has refined and higher forms. It is to be noted here that in the process of evolution he speaks the state next to Mind is consciousness as its evolved state. However, in another context Mind has refined and higher forms which are more subtle, overcoming many of its limitations and attaining the state of consciousness leading to Absolute, i.e. *sat–cit–ānanda*. These forms are made clear in the analysis by taking a cross-section between Mind and Consciousness. In the process of evolution the third stage after Matter and Life is Mind. In its higher sphere it is Higher Mind. Next to it comes the Illuminated Mind. This has a refined form of Intuitive Mind which helps to get the self-identity. This level is followed by Overmind which basically works as a mediator between the Supermind and Ignorance. It takes to the essential Truth but falls short of establishing the integrity. It works separately on each aspect of the Existence as an independent entity. It expresses in multiple sources of action and does not reach to their unity as a whole. It is a principle of cosmic Truth, but it retains differences in manifestations as independent one. It gives the original cosmic *māyā* which is a power making possible the Ignorance.

Sri Aurobindo views Overmind as a Power or Force which is metaphysical in nature. Its functions and operations are metaphysical, more than epistemological or praxiological. There is a thin line between the Overmind and the Supermind which is the Truth-Consciousness. In fact, the Supermind is beyond the level of Mind, though it may exhibit similarities with Mind. It is metaphysical and it is the highest culmination in the process of evolution. There is *sat–cit–ānanda* next and beyond to it. Thus he shows that the faculty performing epistemic functions develops itself into a metaphysical entity which is transcendent. As being or existence it is transcendental and in its epistemic role it transcends its epistemic level to evolve into the metaphysical essence of consciousness. There seems a subtle difference between the epistemic role and the praxiotic role played by Mind. Mind, in its higher evolved forms, is essentially performing epistemic functions and providing force for praxiotic functions. In a way, the third type of functions, viz. aesthetic, is not so elaborately mentioned by Sri Aurobindo. Nevertheless, when he speaks briefly about *rasa,* which belongs to the aesthetic domain of faculties, he brings the three most crucial concepts together, i.e. an essence of a thing, a taste of a thing and the delight one gets. Thus in this domain also the faculty giving awareness of a certain aspect is both, an existence qua existence and the highest state of being on the experiential level as delight. The experiential states being private and personal, or not fully sharable and objectively expressible. The aesthetic domain being completely an experiential one, the state it refers to as the highest one, is delight and in another aspect delight is a higher metaphysical category in his philosophy.

Ordinarily what we experience and the level on which we live our life is our bodily experience. The body is active and interactive not merely on its own but because of something which belongs to it and is supposed to be within it. To this kind of entity Aristotle, the ancient Greek philosopher, referred to by the expression psyche. To begin with, it is rather a vague expression to specify precisely an entity, though it is successful to focus our attention to the realm which needs to be investigated for further studies to understand the reality in-depth as far as the existence of a person is concerned. Sri Aurobindo makes use of this logic and says that something beyond the body but belonging to the body is a psychic principle. By this expression he refers to the soul. That which is beyond body but belonging to or residing in body, according to Upaniṣads, is a *puruṣa* and this entity of *puruṣa* is captured by Sri Aurobindo through the expression, psychic principle. He holds a doctrine of double soul in which he says that there are two minds and two lives. One is the surface mind and the other subliminal mind. The real focus is the subliminal mind. Mind is a form of consciousness and the soul is pure consciousness. All other are states of consciousness in a hierarchical structure. The consciousness on a deeper level is the subliminal mind which makes possible universal knowledge of the cosmic mind. On a material and practical level the surface mind is operational which is seen in surface desires. This is a soul entity and it gives vital cravings, i.e. urges for the organic and biological life. It also makes possible emotions, mental seeking for power, knowledge and happiness. Its functions are not limited to the carnal level, rather Sri Aurobindo does not admit such a carnal level which is otherwise detested from the spiritual point of view. All these functions are required to enrich the primary level of life. He adds to it one more function of aesthetic faculty. Although all these functions of surface mind belong to the basic, i.e. physical level, they are the potential sources of energy to enrich and enhance the basic level of life to the higher level. Its function is on the social level when there is mental seeking for power and then it rises to free itself from the bodily level when it takes care of knowledge, aesthetic pleasure and happiness. It is supported by the subliminal psychic entity which, according to him, is the pure power of light, love, joy and refined sense of being. The feeling of love is a heightened form of emotion which encircles in it the entire humanity into a tender but stronger and wider feeling of love. There is strength, durability and universality in any of the pure forms or states of consciousness. He is concerned not merely with the life and existence of an individual person but his thought is wide enough to take within its scope the society as an entire humanity. The thought and hence the philosophy of Sri Aurobindo is cosmic or universal, though it begins with an individual and a particular. This mind, in either of its forms, makes life possible.

Corresponding to double soul there is also life explained on two levels or in two forms, viz. outer and of the vital being. The life of the physical body is the outer one. This is made possible by the force of life which is deeper at its core and is called as the subliminal force of life and to this form he calls as the true vital being. It needs to be noted here that by the term "vital" he refers to the principle of *prāṇa* as spoken in Upaniṣads and this point he has made explicitly at any other places. The *prāṇa* is a purer, subtle and essential force which makes the existence of a living organism possible and in the case of human beings this *prāṇa,* i.e. the vital life-force energy is in the purest form matching with the cosmic life-force energy of vital existence. The only difference in both of them is not of levels but of forms, one is in a particularized form belonging to an individual being and the other is cosmic or universal which has no limit whatsoever. Thus he calls the subliminal life as the universal force of the cosmic life. There is a subliminal physicality which is a universal force for formation of the cosmic Matter. The final form of the subliminal life is the subliminal soul which, according to him, is nothing else but the universal delight. We have noted and we need to repeat it in this context that the delight is the final, formless and infinite state of expression of the pure existence. But the practical life is lived more on the physical level where the agent performs different roles on different lairs. In the Indian tradition philosophers have used the model of a sheath (*koṣa*) as cover around the delightful soul. Sri Aurobindo uses these as roles of the *puruṣa*. The physical agent is the *annamaya-puruṣa*, the vital energy agent is the *prāṇamaya-puruṣa* and the contemplative agent is the *manomaya-puruṣa*. All our feelings, emotions, passions, desires, deviations and aspirations belong to the *prāṇamaya-puruṣa* which makes the practical life to live fully the way in which it is and it is to be lived. Beyond this is the form of consciousness called Supermind to which he uses also an another expression, viz. the Truth-Consciousness. A finer and the cosmic form of this is the Absolute which is the purest, the highest and the most evolved form of the existence which has within itself the Truth and the Delight or happiness as its inherent aspects.

VII

Sri Aurobindo talks about the consciousness not merely in its being aspect but also in its becoming aspect. There is a dynamism, a process and creativity of the existence which is revealed in its becoming aspect. This way of thinking and developing metaphysics on these lines is a peculiar Indian way of philosophizing. The dynamism becomes possible due to the operation or expression of energy in the Being. The Indian tradition has used the principle of *śakti* to explain this phenomenon of dynamism, manifestation and transformation. Sri Aurobindo has adopted this doctrine in his metaphysics. In order to emphasize the strange part of the energy, which is really responsible to make possible transformations, he uses the term force instead of energy to represent the category of *śakti* in his philosophy. The evolving and modifying element of the individual and the cosmic Existence is so far stated in the form of consciousness through its various states. Nevertheless, this is an anthropocentric presentation of the metaphysics. He has developed the cosmocentric metaphysics also, though it is not exclusive of the becoming aspect of the reality which is dynamic and modifying in nature. This metaphysics gives us an understating of his thought of the Ultimate Reality and how it keeps on evolving within itself to transcend its levels.

The Existence as given to us is in the form of Nature. This is the wider and cosmocentric perspective which does not get limited to particular physical objects but takes the view of all objects in totality as they are there. This is not merely the physical existence. He says that this Nature is a secret God. He presents the thought in an anthropomorphic way to make it easily intelligible to common people. He is not addressing to a philosophical community and hence, as far as possible, he uses the style to approach an intelligentsia on the common level. The human mind has personified the spirituality in an image of a God which is higher in the level of existence and a source of being for the human World. Whatever is given to the human experience has a form and shape of human categories through which it is received. The Nature in generality is the existence, to begin with, for his purpose. It is an inseparable combination of life and physical substance but in a cognizable form which can be manipulated on the epistemic and the praxiotic levels. The concreteness of this level of existence is in the Matter which is the next form or level of the Existence. This Matter is not bereft of consciousness, spirit is involved in it. However, this is the non-specified form of existence which can be grasped by an intellect rather than senses. This matter manifests itself into its next form which is called Life. He is talking of Life and life. It is not just a biological living of an organism but it is a cosmic phenomenon which is dynamic and ever progressing with reference to the living of animate beings in totality and the living of the cosmos as a whole. The Life is an expression of "Will to be". This "Will to be" is the key and base of the Divine Life. From the anthropomorphic point of view the final goal of evolution is the Life Divine. It is a transformation that passes through a creative process from Divine Life to the Life Divine. Divinity of Life is its transcendent manifestation. The Divinity is in the seed form in Life as its essential nature. The end of the creative process is to transform the Life itself into Divinity which is the culmination of Absolute in its final and infinite form. Life is a formation of consciousness on a particular level which initially develops into Mind and then into the Higher Mind.

VIII

The consciousness is a cosmic entity. It is relative when in relation to its particular forms and specific functions, but in itself it is absolute and hence transcendental. It is an essence of existence. In one direction of its transformation, which is an evolution also, it forms into Mind. It is the Consciousness on a much lower level which is spoken of here and hence Mind is an evolved form of it. It further evolves into the Ego. This is a state of formation of a personhood but not on a mundane level. Thus its further evolute is a form of Being which is transcendent. From this Being there evolves Time which further evolves into Space and then the Cosmos which is the all-pervading nature of consciousness. At this stage the Ego evolves into self-enlargement which is the highest state of humanity. This goes in an abstract dimension but in the direction of man and human life. In an another context he shows the existence of Matter transforming into Spirit. In fact, these are roughly the two points between which his metaphysics runs. Usually they are opposed to each other but in Sri Aurobindo's philosophy both are positive forms of the same essence called consciousness. The line connecting them provides a basic frame of his philosophy which is applicable in every context in which he has employed the logic of evolution. This Matter, in one dimension of dynamicity, evolves into Force. In the context of a human person this Force is the life-force energy (*prāṇa*) which makes life as a dynamic and growing process. This Force results into Life and the cosmic abstract form of it is Will. It is that state of Force which enables all activities of life. But it is not limited to an individual being's will, it develops into Collective Will which is, in fact, the will not restricted to an individual being, but expands over the entire humanity to make the Will of the humanity. It gives rise to the social structures which generate authority and sovereignty. This is its form of Superconscious Might which rules the human life as a whole. Sri Aurobindo identifies it as the God in man. This is the divinity and transcendence in man which is operative through man in his individual and cosmic life. In all these various forms of existence the strong principle in nature is that of Unity. Negations may be apparent but the underlying harmony amongst the negating points drive towards balance and establish unity amongst all. This explains the homogeneity of the whole which is one without anything other than one. In this way the monism or non-duality (*advaita*) is understood of the Existence. The Unity is not only in the vertical dimension but it is also on the hierarchical dimension. The Absolute in his metaphysics is multi-dimensional. However, to begin with, the base of his metaphysics is Matter which is obtained through physical senses and physical senses are evolutes of the Matter. The Existence in the world of Matter is suprasensible as also the Physical Realities are suprasensible.

IX

While elaborating on existence Sri Aurobindo points out three levels of existence. In the beginning the existence is seen as phenomenal, i.e. as it appears to human senses. This is obtained by observing consciousness. There is an active objectivity in the phenomenal existence. On the next level it is material, i.e. physical existence which is experienced through sense-organs and is concrete in nature. In fact, it is an existence on the mundane level. The next to it is an eternal self-existence. It is transcendent. The matter is potent with spirit, though it is not manifest in it. He calls it as spiritual monism which is connected to *māyā*. *Māyā* is neither non-existent nor imaginary in his system of thought. It is phenomenal and transitory. It is an unreal object world. When he talks about the phenomenal existence he makes a point about phenomenal Life which is the life of an individual ego. It is fictitious. The human existence as a part of this phenomenal life, also, is fictitious and purpose-less. Tending towards the Absolute, which is full of Delight, is the highest culmination of evolution and it is the purpose inherent to human existence. However, in the phenomenal life it is missing. It is called Non-being which is a relationless Absolute. In order to clarify and elaborate this aspect of existence, he uses the Vedāntic category of *māyā*. In Vedānta, especially in Advaita Vedānta, *māyā* is used to indicate the ephemeral non-existence. However, in the system of Sri Aurobindo, nothing is non-existent and he gives a positive understanding of *māyā* and also of the World, which, too, is non-existent in Advaita Vedānta. For some other varieties and later developments, *māyā* is a power which confuses ordinary understanding by creating an illusion that imaginary objects get treated as concrete existents when they are neither even tangible nor graspable through reason as essences of objective entities. It conceals or perverts cognitive capacity to confuse it.

Sri Aurobindo accepts *māyā* as the power not as concealing or perverting but as misrepresenting the limitless with limits, infinite with finite and permanent with impermanent. He says that *māyā* is the power of the infinite consciousness. It is a comprehending and containing consciousness. It makes to understand an object to be known in totality. It makes an object to engross into consciousness. The basic technique of knowing an object is measuring and limiting an object. An object is limited by putting a frame around it to separate it from the limitless existence. In a way, for practical purpose this is necessary in the case of human beings who are limited beings with a carved out consciousness into a personhood. The limited capacities of a knowing subject count and compare the object in terms of its limited nature. This is measuring and the human process of knowing follows this procedure. The existence is infinite but it is known in parts. The categories of understanding capture, within their limits, parts of the limitless infinite existence. This *māyā* forms and formulates an object. In order to do this, it puts outlines and moulds to embrace it. Sri Aurobindo calls this as psychologizing. The Existence is approached and embraced by a subject and from a subjective point of view, it does not have universality. In this process *māyā* makes the Unknowable knowable, i.e. that which is beyond the reach of limited human capacities is brought within the reach by imposing moulds of limits on it and thus the limitless is brought under the function of measuring it. The technique of measuring, limiting and knowing is done by using Name and Shape. The Advaita Vedānta has introduced these techniques of *nāma* and *rūpa* to bind the Ultimate Reality within them and then identify it with them. This makes the appearance unreal and non-existent. However, Sri Aurobindo gives a turn to this technique and holds that Name and Form are the moulds which limit parts of the limitless Existence and make them to appear as the existence on a lower plane. *Māyā* does not make a claim of non-existence but brings the transcendent on a lower level. The task in epistemology is to transcend the epistemic function to grasp the transcendent existence in its pure nature.

X

The Being is stated by Sri Aurobindo in three forms which are three levels of existence. In the primary state it is physical. The next to it is vital and above it, it is mental. In fact, these are not separate and independent lairs from each other. They are identified by focusing prominent functions they exhibit in concerned contexts. The vital belongs mainly to the animate World. It has a base in physical materiality and it tends to evolve into a higher level of mental. This is a perspective about the objective world. The same logic is employed on an individual person. A human person is cognized in a body which is physical and made out of five gross elements. Nevertheless, it is a living body. It is living because consciousness is seated into it. This is called by him as an Instinctive soul which is a conscious being and identified otherwise as a physical *puruṣa*. This living body functions through the physical *puruṣa*. It has a force which makes functions possible and that is a vital force (*prāṇa*). The vital force makes this *puruṣa* an impulsive source which is the *puruṣa* as the vital conscious being, i.e. *prāṇa-puruṣa*. This has a base and energy of Consciousness which is on the level of Mind and thus it is recognized as Mental energy making it a mental *puruṣa* or *manomaya-*

puruṣa. This is known as an intellectual and emotional soul, i.e. *vijñānamaya-puruṣa*. The highest culminating form of it is the Soul (*Ātman*) which is the inner Consciousness. The Vedāntic tradition has used these as covers or sheaths of the soul. A sheath is separate and does not have the existence of the type of existence the soul has. However, in the system of Sri Aurobindo these are the structures of *puruṣa* as persons performing roles required in life on various levels. This is a metaphysical understating of a person. It has also another aspect which, too, is revealing the nature of existence of an individual being as a person, but from a different perspective, i.e. as a social being. This understanding is from an ego sense, i.e. the formation of an "I" which makes him an agent to decide, deliberate and do. Basically he is a social being and as an agent he is never lonely, without any reference of other members of the society. He is always unified with others and hence motives and consequences of actions performed by him have a context of the social milieu. Although, as an agent to initiate and perform an action, his actions are never actions only by him but others related around him have a contribution to make him an agent through pouring their intentions and aspirations into his deliberations and decisions. This makes him a moral being. Morality itself is an expression of spirituality. It assures and enhances the betterment of life and this is achieved through a moral sense. An ego is undesirable especially when it generates antagonism and obstacles to others. However, when an ego becomes a moral agent, it establishes values to direct and channelize the social life to elevate it on a higher level. A person on the higher level is a mental being in which the functions of consciousness become more vivid. This makes him to reflect on himself and thus it becomes a subjective self. Beyond this there is only one state and it is a bridge to the metaphysics of the being as a person or individual. Sri Aurobindo calls it as the divine being. It should be noted that in every realm like faculties, epistemic, praxis, aesthetic, ontic, social, psychic and cosmic, he brings the endpoint in divinity. As seen from the anthropic point of view the life is divine and from the cosmic point of view the existence is divine. The culmination of the being as a person is concluded by him as a divine being.

The various roles an agent plays are due to a particular formation of consciousness within him. For Sri Aurobindo Mind is that articulation of consciousness which makes various roles to discharge through them the varied functions as a part of an expression of consciousness. The articulation of Mind results into the Cosmic mind, the universal expansion of the self. This is the Supermind, an extension of consciousness. It is an enlargement from an individual to the cosmic. At this stage the self withdraws its initiative and involvement and it becomes Witness (*sākṣī*). This is a transcendent position of a knower, doer and enjoyer. The self performs these roles and rises above them just as an uninvolved rational spectator who remains detached from these roles, in spite of performing them with fulfilment.

A person as a being on the Mind-plane is a person with pure thought and intelligence. In this category come philosophers, thinkers, scientists, intellectual creators, men of idea, men of word, idealists and dreamers. This is the plane where consciousness tends to be creative in performing its specific roles. These persons change and enrich the human life by making advancement and enrichment of culture to make the life happier and fulfilling. The idealists have a vision to project into future. This makes them dreamers. This is the highest position of an active person living on the Mind-plane. Sri Aurobindo calls such a man a Mental man. In him the spirit is expressed in an evolved form. So he is identified also as a Spiritual man who is the supreme supernormal. It is an evolved state of normalcy without any addition, subtraction or modification to it. Such a spiritual man is a mental creator, i.e. a creator on a transcendent plane. The examples of such a spiritual man are seen amongst thinkers, sages, prophets who are directly descending from the order of divinity carrying with them the light of the Divine in the form of their message to uplift the ordinary human life. They are the agents helping to realize divinity in mundane life. They are self-controlled and self-disciplined persons. They live by their own rules and do not come under anybody's rules. Their status is that of a supreme being and hence they do not come under any rule, but the regulation comes in them from within. Thus they are harmonized mental beings. The final or the essential feature of any rule or discipline is harmony which is inherited by them in their nature. They are identified in different cultural contexts differently as spiritual sages (*yogīs*) or Gnostics of Sufis or mystics. They pose themselves as God-lovers, but they themselves are incarnations of Godly essences. On the human plane and in the context of life this is the highest role played by a person remaining with and working for the mundane.

Such a position becomes possible because of the descendence of the Supreme Consciousness in a channel which is meant for performing functions of it through a person as mentioned just now. The Supreme Consciousness formulates itself into the Supermind. This is a process of particularization of the Supreme Consciousness to perform specific functions in life, especially in social life. The Supermind gets formulated into the Supramental Consciousness which is a still transcendent level of the Supreme Consciousness. It is from this the Active Will is produced. The Active Will is responsible to make contributions enhancing the mundane level life. This Active Will generates the Active Knowledge. This Active Knowledge is a direct path for man to the Absolute. Thus the Mental Consciousness puts us in front of the Truth-Consciousness. The Truth-Consciousness gives an order in the infinite multiplicity of manifestation of the Absolute. It establishes harmony in them which provides a definite direction to the epistemic functions of Mind to grasp the Absolute in totality. Mental consciousness is more particularized as discharging, basically, epistemic functions. The Truth-Consciousness, although plays a certain epistemic role, basically tends towards fulfilling ontic requirements of the metaphysics.

XI

The first foundation for all these higher forms and their functions is, in fact, the Matter. This is the base of existence as discussed here. When this Matter ascends it manifests as Nature, the form of existence we live in and interact with as a normal course of life. In this Nature there is an unconscious or may be half-conscious integration. This evolves into the completely conscious form. This is the occult subliminal which is now the new spiritual foundation for further elevation and developments. This leads to the Integral Consciousness which is a very significant state. Because in this formation the harmonization of Life takes place. The Absolute is integrated, ordered and accommodative of all possibilities irrespective of their apparent inconsistencies amongst them. The unity and oneness this whole gets is due to the assimilating harmony amongst the infinite multiplicity of possibilities. In a dynamic aspect of reality harmony plays the crucial role to maintain its onticity.

There is a connection between the anthropocentric and cosmocentric understandings of the ultimate reality. In the wider aspect of existence man has to become and live as a universal being. It is not only universalization of the human being but a transformation of the anthropocentric into the cosmocentric. For this the mental consciousness has to widen to the superconsceint unity. The fulfilment on the mental level gives happiness, on the supramental level it gives bliss. In its cosmocentric counterpart the fulfilment of the Being gives delight. The mental consciousness is a way to the universal delight. The final stage of consciousness is *Saccidānanda* consciousness which is universal and transcendent. A human being, at a stage, reaches this state. This is an elevation of the anthropocentric to the cosmocentric. The path to reach or attain the state is a loss of ego which comes from surrender. This is the merger of the anthropic being into the cosmic Absolute. In the case of a human being this has a practice (*sādhanā*) which passes through the surrender. This happens because the spirit in Nature creates higher type of being. This is the unfolding of the existence towards the divine life. In reaching or realizing the divine there is both — the evolution in the form of manifest-ation and creation in the form of expression. This is how the spirit keeps itself continuously unfolding. In this process one gets all psychic or mystic experiences described in religion, occultism, *yoga* or supranormal psychological experiences. This makes the self the occult self which is the unfolding spirit.

All Existence, for Sri Aurobindo, is, thus, Being. In one form it is the Consciousness. In a form to promote the dynamicity it is Force or Will. This is in both the aspects, viz. anthropocentric and cosmocentric. The cause of cosmic existence is Delight which, too, is a form of Existence. In its subjective aspect it is Bliss which is active and creative. In one form it is God and in its objective final form it is Divine Consciousness. He relates it to the Advaitic parallel of it, *ātman* and Brahman. The self has three states, viz. mental ego, false self and veiled self. This thought of Existence can be presented in a diagram. It is a diagram of a triangle. In one triangle life and body make a base while the mind is at the apex. In another triangle representing the existence, Existence and Consciousness make a base and the Bliss or Delight is at the apex. The same triangle is represented in the Vedāntic model. The *sat* and *cit* form a base and *ānanda* is the apex of it. This is how he conceives the triad of *sat–cit–ānanda* which is the final form of the Existence as the Absolute. In its another aspect this Existence is depicted in a triangle where the base is made by one Existence and Consciousness and the apex is Delight. These triangles present his metaphysics to show the integrity of Existence on different levels and in different manifestations. This enables him to make a metaphysical statement about Delight which comes in every realm of his system of thought as the ultimate culminating point, not just as experimental but also as existential. The Divine is All Existence, One Existence; it is the Conscious Being and also the Truth-Consciousness. This is the final revelation of the last potential of an existence and hence all Existence in its every aspect aspires to realize itself as the Divine. The given Divinity is the essence of Existence and it is to manifest as the highest evolved form of the Absolute.

The presentation of the Existence in a diagram of a triangle joins triple worlds together in an integrated way to reveal the dynamic aspect of the Absolute. In the first triangle of Mind–Life–Body the base is Mind and Body where the dynamic aspect is presented through Life. For human beings what really matters is that which goes in life as continuum of process. The realization, happiness, bliss, delight, creativity, evolution — everything is centred around the man and it is placed in his living the Life. It is the Consciousness which is expressed in the form of Life. To make it as the crucial aspect for man to achieve and fulfil it needs to have that capacity which can make the fulfilment possible. It is in the form of intelligence that the Life gets a direction, purpose, deliberation and fulfilment.

The intelligence is an articulation of the Consciousness. It forms the core of Life. It is a manifestation of Mind in a specialization of Force. It serves as a Force — the energy which takes care of the dynamicity and the fulfilment. It has a form of an appearance as Being and the basis for it is Matter. The grossness of a category makes a base to its higher form. All are ascending forms in continuity without any break in them. The Matter holds life as a form of one Cosmic Energy. Life is to be seen in the form of an energy. It is a play of the Force which is the cosmocentric metaphysical category. The Force is never stable, it is volatile and fluctuating but in an ordered or a disciplined manner. It is a free play but not a chaotic one. There is no constraint either from within or from outside to its dynamism. The dynamism is pleasurable heading towards happiness in the form of delight. There is no specific purpose to achieve something in particular, but just dynamism of expression and manifestation resulting into Delight. This play of Force builds up and energizes forms which are an aspect of creation.

The process of life is an endless process. Usually we think of the antagonism between life and death where death is understood as a cessation of life. Sri Aurobindo, in his constructive approach and keeping himself consistent with the Indian philosophical tradition, holds that life and death are not opposed to each other, death does not end life. Nothing perishes in the continuity of life. There are constant renewals of everything that lives and the renewals are out of the force from the within on their own. What are the apparent changes in the continuity of life are these renewals without any destruction. In a play life hides from itself and that is called death. In death the positive being tempts to seek for its immortality. Death serves as means to reveal the unbroken continuity of life. A negation gives a limitation and indicates a defect. There is neither a limitation to life nor any defect into it. On the mundane level always there is seen a struggle for life. This struggle is a form of survival. It tends to realize its perfection which is within it. The perfection is an everlasting survival and it is a continuous permanence. The process of life is an interchange of forms. It is an intermixture of expression coming variedly. This is a fusion of being with being and not being with non-being, since there is nothing like non-being. The variation of forms is related not with oppositions but with fusion. Thus it continues and continues permanently. Life is a self-expression. It is also self-preservation by nature. It progresses in continuity, because it is self-assertion. The assertion here is neither to overpower the other nor to suppress the other but to express itself with the other. There is a kind of aggressiveness in life, but it does not harm or win over the other. It is an expression of itself with its force to manifest in a direction to proceed ahead. Thus life is, basically, a play of force which is seen in the animal kingdom, vegetative realm and also in the material world. The force is force, it is neither restricted to the animate form nor limited to an inanimate form of the Existence or Being. This force has three aspects: viz. it builds, i.e. creates and constructs novel form; it takes care of sustaining them by maintenance; and in order to change and rejuvenate it destroys earlier forms to make space for the newer forms. This is the model of *utpatti-sthiti-laya* which is a celebrated doctrine of the Indian philosophy for ages. Since Life is the play of Force it is a form of Energy and in its objective form of World it is Force. This explains the Life-Force, i.e. *prāṇa*, Mind-Energy, Life-Energy and the material Energy. In a way, these types of energy are varieties in the expression of Life itself. Because the universal Life is an all-pervading existence and this existence, at times, assumes the form of Matter.

XII

Life as the dynamic play of the universal Force is a combination of the mental consciousness with the nervous vitality. Although the nervous plane is physical, it is not gross as the rough material of the body is gross. It is an elevated state of physical energy which takes to the level of the mental consciousness. The level of vitality as *prāṇa* is used, by Sri Aurobindo, in many ways. Vitality is that form of energy which simultaneously works on the material level as well as on the spiritual level. It gives the Existence an anthropic dimension to manifest itself, which is the crucial aspect of Life as an evolved category of Consciousness. The continuum of life is an interchange of stimulation and response. An act is a response to some previous situation and a response becomes a stimulus for the next response. Neither is there any beginning nor any end to this dialectic of stimulus and response. Being a response an action gets a meaning since it is in the context of and for the purpose of the stimulus. A response is a completion of a stimulus and a stimulus is an expectation for becoming in a particular form. Both stimulus and response are forms of consciousness and they constantly take into themselves. It provides Force to breath and energy for movements. It absorbs the conscious energy and gives it back when and how required. The process of life on the ordinary level is a dialectic of attraction and repulsion. A kind of tension is created for a process to go on. This tension generates force. On a mundane level a meaning lies in a fulfilment of an expectations. There is a purpose appearing in the form of an expectation and a response is a fulfilment of a purpose to complete an act which is initiated out of a tension. This is achieved by a force which, on the one hand, evolves out of Matter and culminates in Mind, on the other hand. Thus Life is an active span between Matter and Mind carried out by the Force. Although there are many levels in the World, both in animate as well as in inanimate, the play of Life is the same everywhere from an atom to a man. As all these levels are essentially forms of consciousness and functions of consciousness they are regular and homogeneous everywhere. Thus it is a universal operation of conscious Force. This Force and Life subconsciously act on and in Matter. The cycle of creation, maintenance or sustenance and destruction continues in re-creation. These are the constant transformations of forms and such a transformation is Life. In this way the play of Life becomes a creative force of existence. It is a middle state between Matter and Mind and it is distinct from them. Life is also viewed as the pulsating nerve-energy which is taken as *prāṇa*. It is a final operation of the Consciousness-Force. This itself is an early form of the energy of Divine.

Sri Aurobindo's philosophy is based on Satkāryavāda. In the anthropic formulations he puts the final culminating form of the fully evolved being, i.e. the Absolute as the Divine. The divinity is present in a seed-form and it becomes manifest through the process of evolution in the final form. There is divinity in the Life and in the Play of Life. On the basis of this he advances the thought of Life Divine. The play of Life is the energy of Divine. The divinity in a seed-form evolves due to the energy which is divine and thus the goal of the Life Divine gets achieved. This is the form of the energy of consciousness. It is appropriate to the action of Mind and Matter. It is seated in Matter and it is an energy aspect of Mind. It continues due to the Consciousness-Force it has at its back. With this Force there are stages of operations. At the first place there is vibration. It resides in an inactive form in the Matter. It is mechanical and in a subconscious form. On the higher stage which is the submental stage, it is capable of giving a response. In the first form the operation is just within itself without a reference to something else. In the next form it is with reference to the other, tending by consciously towards the other. In the last stage operations develop consciously. With these operations life appears on the material level as a submerged consciousness. On the vital plane, however, it appears as an emerging consciousness. It is half-apparent as power of life. It is also expressed through growth, activity and decay.

Sri Aurobindo takes a psychological aspect to explain his metaphysics of becoming. The Life is a continuity of emergence, transformation, cessation and re-emergence of forms. On the human level the Consciousness-Force in human relations takes the form of the feeling of love. This love is not a carnal animosity for him nor it is a sensuous consuming for sensuous pleasure. He calls it a law of hunger, certainly not the carnal hunger meant for temporary tinglings of the physical sense-organs. It is a hunger of and for receiving. It is receiving oneself by oneself but through surrendering oneself to the other. There is an impulse to realize and fulfil oneself in others and by others. On the social plane for the life of individual the priori and significance are to the other and not to oneself. One gets fulfilment not in the completion of one's desires, impulses, needs, etc. but in the completion of the desires, impulses, needs, etc. of others by him. He is an agent to perform acts. Those acts are performed primarily for himself but for others. The field of fulfilment for one is the life of others and not of his. At the same time his life is a field of fulfilment of others. Others have to surrender themselves for his fulfilment and he has to surrender himself for the fulfilment of others. This is a mutual interaction and the meaning of love is complete only in this mutuality. Love enriches life but, again, it gets enriched when one enriches other's life. In enriching the other one gets enriched. In love one has a feeling of possession. But in Sri Aurobindo's philosophy the possession is neither selfish nor self-centred. One possesses when one is possessed. In this respect, the mutuality of human relations reveals his social thought in which society itself is an indivisible homogeneous whole. Society is not made out of individuals taking an initiative and completing the action. But actions in society or in social life are initiated and performed by individual agents on behalf of the society and for the sake of the one who is the other to the agent. This essence of social life lies in relationship which is realized in the form of love.

The Life as vibration has some forms on the practical level. The Consciousness proceeds through the process of evolution. There is an imperfect evolution due to which vibrations take forms like pain, pleasure and indifference. These three states are the usual experiences of the practical life on the mundane level. These vibrations lack harmony and rhythm of life which is present in the balanced state of the Consciousness. Life functions in the space between Matter and Mind where the Matter evolves to attain the form of Mind. This evolution has to be free from defects.

Pain and pleasure are felt in a particular contact of consciousness through body with an object or situation. They are forms of experience and such forms of experience develop attitudes like aversion or attachment. Such attitudes do not lead to happiness, fulfilment, satisfaction, bliss or delight. In between these two attitudes there is a state of indifference which is not a state of detachment but a state which creates stagnation in the dynamism of a process. These states are habits of our nature where the nature is not normal and stable. Pain of body and mind is a transitional end in Nature's upward evolution. Pain is an impulse of self-defence against "others". It is an unnatural reverse in the proceedings of the life. Pain and pleasure are currents of delight of existence in an abnormal way. When the current of delight is imperfect it is recognized as pleasure and when it is perverse it is recognized as pain. The reason for this is the self-division of the being. This self-division of the being takes place due to the measuring and limiting functions of *māyā*. This leads to sufferings in the lives of men. This suffering can be reduced and ended. For diminishing the sufferings the Mind in man has to become capable of being free, unegoistic and in harmony with all other beings. This is possible when the play of the universal forces takes place rhythmically. The suffering can get eliminated when the human mind cultivates the state of *titikṣā* which is tolerance to extreme states that disturb the poise of mind and patience to hold against adverse conditions. *Titikṣā* is not to fight against sufferings and eradicate impatience but to tune the human mind in such a way that sufferings, impatience, intolerance, etc. will not arise. It gives poise to personality in such a way that the human mind does not tend to extremities like excitement or depression, but rises above these states to keep the consciousness functioning rhythmically and in harmony with the Cosmic Consciousness which is integrated and delightful. In the process of life a man has to face various situations, endure with adversities and conquest the threats to the will to live. He gets strength to pass through these states without getting affected by them when he cultivates *titikṣā* as an integral feature of his nature. This is the way to the self-disciplining of the Soul. Once *titikṣā* becomes a nature, the life of the Soul follows a regulated way. It develops neutrality to the imperfect touches of pleasure and neutrality to the imperfect touches of pain. The Soul remains unaffected by pleasure and pain and makes it way towards the spiritual evolution leading to Delight. On the cosmic level the Universal Soul has all contacts of things having essential delight. To this state Sri Aurobindo calls *rasa*.

The term *rasa* is more known as used in the theory of art and aesthetics. However, its origin and base are metaphysical. Upaniṣads use the expression *rasa* to refer to the ultimate reality as *ātman* or Brahman. In a theory of art *rasa* is a higher-level experience caused by relishing an object. In metaphysics, the real itself is full of the pleasure of relishing, it does not depend on anything external to it, it is an integral part of itself. *Rasa* as a metaphysical entity is the real and at the same time it itself is happiness. This is the reason the Soul is capable to see harmony and beauty in the world. The essence of the dynamic aspect of the reality, i.e. of the becoming and the essence of the relations amongst multitude is harmony. This harmony is at the base of beauty which gives happiness. The beauty, he speaks here, is a higher experiential state of consciousness. In the perfection and completeness of the reality, the experience one gets is an experience of beauty. This experience leads to bliss when it is heightened due to the level and the density of the object of an experience. The principle of harmony is seen in the dynamic aspect and in the aspect of the being as being there is a principle of unity. There is a totality. The ingredients of the totality, in spite of their multitude, retain the consistency and coherence in them and it leads to unity. The principle of unity leads to Supermind in which we get conscious unity of diversities. At this level will and knowledge come down and operate on the same level. They become equal and perfectly harmonious. At this state the Consciousness and Force get into a divine equation. Thus from the lowest level of evolution to the highest culminating point there is harmony and unity amongst the multitude which establishes the metaphysical monism of his philosophy.

This metaphysical base shows the integrity and continuity of different status of Life. On the primary level life is expressed in the form of a robust drive or urge which is crude and hence dumb and inconsistent. It is a form of an involved will in material existence. Nevertheless, it is not particularized but is possessed by universal movement. A less crude and higher state of life is seen in a desire which is self-oriented. There is an eagerness to possess in this state but in a limited capacity. The refined state of life is that of love which consists in possessing and being possessed and receiving by giving itself. The developed state of life is the pure and full emergence of the original will. This state gives a high and deep satisfaction of conscious love. It is an interchange of love by the unification of the possessor with the possessed. The dichotomy results into union or unification of Being. These states of life keep ascending because the ascent of life is the ascent of the divine Delight. Sri Aurobindo also personifies the Absolute and presents it as God. This God has a conscious-force and Life is an energy of god's conscious-force. On this level the life is the Life of a gnostic being who is the divine being. In this life the living agent has a complete consciousness of the self of others. In this consciousness the principle of harmony reflects, because it is a natural rule of the Spirit. On such a higher level and in a context of society simultaneously many agents are active in their interactive and mutual actions. This has an intricate complexity, and harmonization in such a complex situation is a challenge. However, an intuition and self-knowledge of awakened spirit has a capacity to harmonize the complexity. It is a complexity for an ordinary consciousness but not to an evolved one where the consciousness is not limited to an individual bearer of it but takes into its stride the entire society and evolves as a consciousness of the society. The bearer of the consciousness remains an individual agent but functions of such a consciousness extend over the entire society of which the bearer agent is a member. In such a social context the bonds of relationship are established as the Law of Love and Sympathy. This is the natural rhythm of consciousness. The individual is the initiating agent of all activities and also of knowledge. He becomes conscious of the Reality and hence he is the key to the evolutionary movements. The Truth of life consists in the life of unity, mutuality and harmony. This Truth is born of deeper and wider truth of our being. Our practical life is based on values which are followed in performing actions. These values are of the normal ignorant Nature within us. Gnostic Supernature transcends these values to elevate the states of Life. Our standards, norms and values are created by ignorance, i.e. it is not aware of the Life fully as in its hierarchical spread. Hence, these values fall short of determining the life of the Supernature. The laws and structures of the content of the lower level cannot capture that which forms the content of the higher level. The epistemic state of a lower level is an ignorance being limited and incomplete. There are oppositions, inconsistencies and contradictions on the lower level. When Life ascends on the higher level of Gnostic Consciousness all oppositions get fused in this consciousness with a result of their cancellation. The life for Gnostic Consciousness, i.e. for the achieved spiritual consciousness is bound to be the manifestation of the realized truth of spirit.

Gnostic life has a twofold rule — one is of the self-expression of the Spirit and the other is the Will of the Divine Being. The expression is an operation of the Will and the Will is the functional aspect of the Being when it becomes Divine. The manifestation of Will and

Self-expression are simple and they maintain the natural balance. The powers of expression of the Spirit are enlisted as beauty, plentitude, sweetness, laughter, sunshine and gladness of life. All these are the positive and constructive aspects of the Spirit and indicate why and how the bliss will follow as a necessary consequence of spiritual experience. These powers refer to the realm of aesthetics and suggest that the aesthetic properties are spiritual in nature. The beginning of the journey towards *rasa* is in beauty which is a step in the Spiritual Life. The pleasure results in relishing beauty which is an early form of Delight and it is ever new. It continues to be relishable and enjoyable due to its novelty. The forms of beauty of spirit are innumerable. The godhead of Spirit is ever young and the taste of delight, i.e. *rasa* of infinite is eternal and inexhaustible. It is the Delight of being. By nature it is infinite, since the being is infinite and it is an essence of the being and so it is inalienable from the being. This Delight itself is a form or manifestation of existence and a secret of creation. Although creation is a result of a free play, it has a certain direction and the direction follows a purpose. Delight is the purpose of creation. But it does not operate overtly, it is secretive to creation. It is, therefore, understood as a cause of remaining existence. It is both a root and an end of birth. The creation finally ceases into Delight. It is an eternal and immutable being and variable of becoming as a root of the whole matter. The principle of Delight, i.e. divine Being is fourfold, viz. Existence, Conscious-Force, Bliss and Supermind. It manifests on the level of the Supermind and operates through the Conscious-Force to culminate into Bliss. In all these forms it is the Existence. The Existence is omnipresent in the entire material cosmos. It is veiled behind things, i.e. things are its expressions but such expressions which do not allow it to reveal itself in its bare form. So it is called as substance, i.e. that which is Being and holds all appearances or modifications of it, on it.

As a Conscious-Force the Delight is omnipresent in the entire material cosmos. It is veiled and operates secretly and in this form it is called as Life. The Bliss also is omnipresent in the cosmos and veiled. The Supermind, too, omnipresent but veiled in the material cosmos. That it is veiled does not mean that it is unmanifest but it means that it is fully operative but it's being and operations are behind a curtain, i.e. do not make themselves aware of their being and operations. The Delight gives the unity of Existence, Being, Conscious-Force, Life, Supermind and Bliss. Although Bliss and Delight are the expressions which presuppose a bodily organization for sense-organs to attain a stage of experience, Sri Aurobindo's thought does not make it a necessary requirement to have a personification of the bearer of an experience to make a statement about Bliss or Delight. He, on a transcendent level, ascribes Delight to the Being to reveal an aspect of the Being. When the Being is seen as having Delight the Delight itself becomes a Supracosmic Reality. It is self-existent and it is a secret underlying the whole manifestation, as pointed out previously. It is infinite and inalienable from the Being. The culminating form of the Existence is stated by him in the Vedāntic categories of *sat–cit–ānanda*. It is a trio of the essence of the Existence understood from three basic aspects or points of view. In his philosophy the World, though an appearance of the Existence, is as real as the Existence itself. Nevertheless, there is a practical difference between them. World is a masked form of *sat–cit–ānanda* which is a delight of the transcendent, immanent and universal. In the trio of *sat–cit–ānanda* — *sat* is *cit* and *ānanda, cit* is *sat* and *ānanda, ānanda* is *sat* and *cit*. From this point of view Life is the conscious-force of God. In every state of Existence, whether particular or universal-cosmic, there is a fundamental instinct to seek the delight and in Becoming there is a motive to find, possess and fulfil the delight not outside but within itself as its inherent trait. The Life is, thus, full of delight in a seed form. As the Life continues, it continues with transformations and in each emerging form of transformations there exhibits delight, both from the anthropocentric point of view and from the cosmocentric point of view.

XIII

The existence of the Being is determined by itself and the dynamism of the Becoming is not controlled by anything outside to it. Whatever is, is real and existent on its own without anything else other than it. The only variation is due to the levels. Each level is transcended by a following level and thus the Existence gets more and more evolved in its continuum of manifestations which are a form of self-expression. Unless they are seen from the anthropocentric point of view their metaphysics is not teleological. However, if the philosophical system is centred around a man and organized using categories of human life, a talk in terms of purpose, end, goal, etc. becomes a structural aspect of language in which such a metaphysics is presented and understood. In this way we can justify the mode of explanation of the metaphysics of the philosophy of Sri Aurobindo. As he says, there is a final goal of an emergence of the infinite consciousness in the individual. The path to reach this goal is of the self-knowledge and self-recovery. Sri Aurobindo said in the context of the human life that to fulfil God in life is man's manhood. God is a personified version of the universal Reality with human traits. One has to realize, i.e. bring into existence God in one's own life and then in the cosmic life. This is self-realization and it proceeds following the rule of progressive comprehension. That which is on the lower level, right from emotions to Existence is not to be abandoned. It is to be transfigured on the higher level. This is done by assimilating the content of the lower level to the higher level. This is how there is an integration where the duality or multitude of levels and contents of levels do not remain. The content of the lower level gets assimilated and then transformed into the higher level. For this process there is a descendence of the higher level to the lower level. The higher level takes the responsibility to elevate the lower level by assimilating into itself. The responsibility is carried on by taking an initiative. The content of the lower level belongs to the lower level because its capacity is limited to the level to which it belongs to. Hence, the higher level has to exercise to pull the lower level by pushing it upwards from the lower level. The dynamics of pull and push is a key factor in the process of evolution. Evolution is not mechanical, it is conscious, it is *līlā*, it has a direction, goal, purpose and fulfilment. That is why he calls it as creative evolution. The element of intention and purpose is on the level of Mind. The Mind descends down on the level of, or rather into, matter and vital (*prāṇa*) to transform it to belong to the higher level. In Matter there is hidden and unmanifest life, and Life is hidden and unmanifest consciousness. Thus there is a sequence of Matter, Mind, Vital, Life and Consciousness.

There are mainly three forms of consciousness. The basic form of consciousness is individual. It is a centre of the universal consciousness and it is operative in an individual human being. The next to it is the universal form of consciousness. It is a form and definition of the formless and indefinable. The Absolute is infinite. It has no form and it cannot be identified with any marks of particularities. However, going beyond the individuality the consciousness at this stage makes it general to understand its universality. The form of consciousness beyond this is supracosmic and transcendent. In this form the unknowable descends into universe and individual. It is the pure consciousness which descends for manifestation in particularized forms as the free sportive play of the Force. The Force is the self-expression of Existence. It is a dynamic aspect of the reality which makes dynamism an all processes possible, though all of them are *sui-generis*. It follows the law of an expression of an innate knowledge to show that the state is not chaotic but an organized and rhythmic one. This has stages followed sequentially. At the first stage there is an involution and self-absorption of conscious being. The conscious being itself absorbs and comes back to the previous state. The force is imprisoned in a state. In the next stage this self-imprisoned force emerges into a formal being as a manifestation of it. At this state the being is a thinking being and releases itself into the free realization of itself as One and Infinite. This self-realization is not constrained but comes spontaneously. Here we have to note the order in which the Consciousness or Being evolves itself. He begins with Matter for the ascent of the Divine Existence. The Existence is there and it is divine. The expression of the divinity passes through the stages of manifestations. The Matter ascents into Life making it Divine. The Life manifests itself into Psyche, the locus of the particularized existence. This ascends into Mind where various aspects and functions of the Consciousness appear to be operative in a direction. There is a transcendence of this state ascending into Supermind. This further ascends into the state of Bliss where it enjoys its freedom and beings unconditionally.

This proceeds further into Consciousness-Force which is the dynamic aspect of the being expressing itself as the becoming. And the last stage of the ascend is the Existence which is Divine as its essence. The divinity is not a characteristic but it is the original nature in its fully manifest form. This is how the ascend proceeds in a hierarchical way of transcendence.

Sri Aurobindo has also introduced the category of World. It is more or less, a conception of the World (*jagat*) as formulated by Śaṅkarācārya. It is the existence which appears as the practical context of physical being and all interactions amongst human agents, constructs of human contemplations and the ephemeral structures of Name and Form (*nāma* and *rūpa*) through which the process of living for man and cosmos continues. He says the World is *māyā* which is a creation of the self-conscious being. Certainly it is not the essential truth of that. It is a phenomenal truth of Its free multiplicity. This World is, basically, the concern and context of human affairs. It has layers mentioning the normative considerations of actions, behaviour and conduct. The first or the basic layer is infra-ethical and the next to it is ethical. Actions performed by human agents and their conduct as members of the society are evaluated in terms of goodness, and morally good actions are acceptable in a healthy and happy society. Nevertheless, there is a layer which takes the plane of the World beyond its ethical status making it Supra-ethical. This layer shows the propensity of the World to ascend on the spiritual level. The spirituality has, mainly, three prongs in the human life, viz. ethics, aesthetics and pure knowledge. The spirituality is inherent in the human life and world in a hidden form where it is eager to unveil the cover concealing it. This is the sportive play of evolution.

XIV

The major thrust of Sri Aurobindo's thought is the process of evolution. Whatever is and especially whatever is in a world of sentient experience is in a state of the dynamic continuum of Becoming on the hierarchical axis of the Being. The Becoming is a process of manifestations which is an unending chain of transformations in an ascending order. Not only the man or mankind but the Existence itself is aiming at the highest end which can be achieved through a sequence of transcendence at every level. Thus his metaphysics is the metaphysics of evolution. Whatever is to be understood is to be comprehended keeping the evolution as its central focal point. The beginning of the evolution is in Inconscience. This is the lowest level given to Existence where consciousness is not traced because no operations of consciousness are seen. It is neither a state of absence of consciousness nor a state opposed to consciousness. The process of evolution continues on a deeper level. The middle state of the evolution is evolution in ignorance. In the previous, i.e. the beginning state, it is not deliberate, since reason is not functional. In the middle state there is no awareness of the process of evolution. In the last, i.e. the end state there is a liberation of spirit into true consciousness. In this state there is a self-awareness and hence the evolution is in the knowledge. The evolution is not merely an expression of that which is latent but it is a manifestation of assuming novel forms at every point. A form which is manifested need not repeat its manifestation in similar or parallel conditions. Its appearance is beyond imagination of a normal thinking mind. A manifestation comes up with new powers of existence. The Existence is infinite. The manifesting forms are also infinite and the powers of Existence which make manifestations are also infinite. The recurrence of manifestations and the evolution of new forms is neither repetitive nor mechanical. Hence the Evolution is called as the Creative Evolution where an occurrence of a manifestation is a creation. The process of evolution is a process of continuously creating new Worlds. On the base level it appears as a material inconscience but in its higher forms the material transforms into spiritual and becomes Spiritual Consciousness. It is, in a way, a progress of consciousness from a lower grade to a higher grade. The progress is not on the material straight line but it is on the spiral line. The spiral progression keeps continuity without a rapture in an ascend and makes the process three-dimensional without difference of layers. The layers are changed but without any effort to change or lifting up. In a spiral progression the points of the lower or earlier level correspond to the same place but on a next or higher level. In its circular movement it exhausts the entire region and without any employment of an extra energy it keeps ascending. The Existence or the Consciousness has a direction within itself as its essential ingredient which automatically keeps the progres-sion hierarchical, i.e. upwards. The end or the culminating point of Existence in the dynamism of the Creative Evolution is the Absolute which is an origin, support and secret Reality of all things. It is a source of its being and becoming, it provides foundation to hold the existence and without making itself vivid it is the Reality in itself. The Absolute is in two aspects, Being and Becoming. The aspect of Being is the static way of the existence. The aspect of Becoming matters for cognition, sensation, praxis and aesthetic. It is an effectual reality. It is a dynamic power and also the result of the dynamism. The dynamism is a creative energy actualizing the evolution. It is a persistent mutable form and also a process. He calls this Absolute *sat–cit–ānanda*, the Vedāntic concept covering all aspects of the Ultimate Reality. This is the Divine Existence for him, a form of Consciousness.

The Evolution is first understood on the material level. It comes under the scope of ordinary perception and experience. The beginning of the Evolution is experienced in the material universe. Mind and along with it Life evolves in Matter. The material substance transforms its substance into living substance which is a conscious substance. It has a movement of conscious-ness, feeling and life. This is the state where the life in a human form appears functioning in its full aspects. The dynamism of the Becoming takes place due to Energy. The primary form of this energy is Material Energy. It leaves its materiality and becomes Energy, the pure form of energy which is required for movements, dynamism and process. It evolves into the Consciousness-Force which is Supramental, i.e. above the level of Mind. It further evolves into the Mind-Consciousness, the state above the Force and nearer to Spirit. This, then, transcends into the Life-Consciousness, a more spiritual in nature. However, these stages are contextualized, either into a structure of Mind or into a structure of Life. It evolves into a state of consciousness which is context-free and pure. Still this state has an ahead of it, viz. the Supreme essence which is the Power of Spirit. This Power has twofold functions, one is the Creative Energy of Mind and the other is the Creative Life-Force. Due to this the Evolution does not remain a mechanical or monotonous evolution but becomes a creative evolution. This dimension of evolution is a progressive self-manifestation of the Spirit.

Sri Aurobindo has explained the process of the evolution even as beginning from an atom, the tiniest form of the material existence as Matter. Though he speaks of spirituality, consciousness, transcendence and so on, he is thoroughly scientific in his outlook and he never overlooks the scientific development and the scientific approach. His spirituality is not in opposition with science but it respects and accommodates the scientific way and the scientific approach as a stage in evolution. The atom, for him, is a miniature of the cosmic reality. So he states that the atom has life, mind and Supermind besides it having the material existence. The Mind at this level is the Physical Mind which is brain-mind, i.e. the contemplative power of consciousness functioning through the brain which is the physical entity. This further evolves into the Life-Mind which is the function of Consciousness in the Life as a whole. This evolves into the intelligence of Life-Mind which is dynamic, vital, nervous and more open. This evolves into the Life-Soul to which he calls as *puruṣa*, the person as an articulate entity of Consciousness functioning as an agent to perform various kinds of activities like knowing, doing, enjoying and so on. This personhood has intelligence and it evolves first into Life-mentality which is a vital mind in a kinetic version and then into the Mind-plane which functions to produce thought and makes the intelligence operative to play its cardinal role. He has used the Vedāntic parallel to present his process of Evolution in terms of the Vedāntic categories. The base of the personhood is the Physical man who is *annamaya-puruṣa*. The evolved form of it is the Vital man, i.e. *prānamaya-puruṣa* who expresses feelings (*bhāvanā*), emotions (*vāsanā*), dispositions (*vikāra*) and desires (*icchā*). The elevated form of this man is the Mental and intellectual man, i.e. *manomaya-puruṣa*.

In the case of *puruṣa* the significant centre is Mind. In the Evolution of *puruṣa* we have to follow closely the Evolution of Mind. Mind has more an epistemic role and for epistemic functions a human personhood is necessary. With the Evolution of Mind as seated in man, the person evolves to higher and higher state and at a point he gets depersonalized and takes a cosmic form. The Mind evolves as the Higher Mind and then proceeds to become the Illuminated Mind. This has wider and deeper epistemic potential. It evolves into the Intuitive Mind where the epistemic states are attained without any means between the object and the subject. It becomes the Overmind where the powers and functions are heightened. But the real transcendence takes place in Supermind. This is, in fact, a form of de-particularized Consciousness. It takes that form from evolving out of the line of the Mind. Next to the Supermind comes the state of the highest or Ultimate Reality as *sat–cit–ānanda*. This *sat–cit–ānanda* is the Truth-Consciousness. It is omnipresent. It harmonizes everything in one rhythm and one unitary whole. It is dynamic, creative, self-expressed, infinite and transcendent. It is also a delight and this *sat–cit–ānanda* manifests everywhere where there is a manifestation. This is the state where there is an awareness of self-completion, eternity, a-temporality, beyond verbalization and bliss. It limits itself and transforms into Matter for forming the World as a practical interplay amongst particularized constituents, human and non-human. In the Upaniṣadic context *sat–cit–ānanda* is the nature of the Ultimate Reality called Brahman, revealing the essence of Brahman. The world is produced out of Brahman by limiting itself and transforming into Matter. It is immutable, unchanging and permanent. It manifests itself through extreme motion. The Being and Becoming are fully intermixed in it. When it transforms itself into Matter, it is an intense heightening of the Consciousness-Force. The smallest particle of Matter is an atom which passes through the states of Life, Mind, Supermind, Spirit and finally the unmanifest transcendent.

When the Evolution is spiritual there is a self-expression and self-manifestation of the transcendent into a tangible, experimental form. It is a result of the superconscient creative energy. It has an internal force to emerge and so it is called a Nisus. It is an upward journey, i.e. an ascent. However, it begins with a descent and them it rises above as an ascent where the pull from upwards and push from downwards take place simultaneously. This is how, it becomes a manifestation of unmanifest. In this process an awareness and an expression are involved. In the process of evolution there is an integration at various levels. The ascent is an intense elevation of transcending levels. This is the heightening in the ascent in which the consciousness of the higher level comes down to the lower level and then assimilates the consciousness of the lower level to transform it into the higher level. In this mechanism there is also of widening the scope of consciousness leading to concentration making it firm, stable and solid. In this process there is a manifestation which is a determinative form. This happens because of the Consciousness-Force which functions as a creative agent. The Consciousness-Force is the very nature of Being. The Consciousness as a Being is manifested as a creative knowledge which is an aspect of the Will. This Will inspires the evolution which is a creative process. Within Consciousness there is an element of divinity which aspires to manifest itself. The expansion of the divinity gives satisfaction to man which is the fulfilment of his being as a form of Consciousness. In this process man produces out of himself a greater being. In one dimension such a production leads to create a divine humanity and in a different dimension it makes a Superman to come to an existence. The potentiality in the human existence is *sat–cit–ānanda*. This makes him to realize himself in a certain harmony and unification of individual life and universal life. Basically it depends on the positions of relations between the Consciousness and Force. It is a poise in the being of *sat–cit–ānanda*. It is also a poise of being in the material universe which is the great denial of *sat–cit–ānanda* by himself.

Materiality and spirituality are two different positions; they might suggest an opposition on a lower level. However, the essence of both is the same and that establishes a poise in their relation. There is a struggle against a denial but it is made ineffective due to the poise of the being in Mind and Life. There is this poise of being on the still higher level, i.e. Supermind. This is the fulfilment of the Existence. Man realizes his true life in this poise of being. The creative force of consciousness of the Being within us is Nature. This is concealed by *māyā* in the inverse creative movement. This *māyā* is an illusion or power of concealing of the highest being either God or Brahman. Finally, there is a unification of Spirit and Matter which is a result of reconciliation between them. This is a form of harmony and on this higher level it is a Divine Harmony. This harmony is between Mind and Life and also between God and Life. There is a reconciliation in the Cosmic Consciousness as well as in the Transcendental Consciousness. Hence the Universal Force and Universal Consciousness are one as also the Divine Knowledge and the Divine Will are one. These unities are results of the principle of harmony which is a basic and central principle of the philosophy of Sri Aurobindo. The harmony is the whole rhythmic idea of the universe. The Law of the universe originates from it and maintained by it. The harmony is inherent in the Existence which comes up as an expression of self-nature. Thus the harmony suggests that the entire development which is to take place is pre-determined in its self-Knowledge.

What matters from the anthropocentric point of view is the Life which is the reality of being and becoming for man as the human life or the cosmic life. This is functional through Mind which is a form of the Consciousness. This picks up the spiritual dimension in its evolution where the spiritual life grows into divine living. To realize the inherent divinity in an expressed form we have to create ourselves and our world. The striving for perfection is within us as our nature. That is how in the growth in the divine life our first occupation is the spirit and the second growth comes from the within. It is an expression of the Force of Nature to be and to become. Our true being and the divine being is to reveal on its own to give it a form of becoming and keep it active. Our growing and living within are a search of the divine being. An individual person has to discover the spirit within him which is a discovery within himself is to be expressed in his being and living. The discovery within himself is self-awareness and it is the spiritual knowledge. The Will-force of being is expressed in a conscious action. The expression of the Self has to be full. In full expression the being is full and this is the full delight of the being. The meaning of Divine Living has several aspects. It is to become complete in being. It is to become complete in consciousness. It is to become complete in force of being. It is to become complete in delight of being. All these aspects are to be integrated and the Divine Living is living in this integrated completeness. The manifestation of Divinity in the every aspect of

Life is the Life Divine. This makes man to be and to live transcendentally. The Life Divine is the transcendental form of the divine life. In this transcendence one transcends the consciousness of body, transcends mind and transcends life.

XV

This entire process of evolution, expression, manifestation, creation, transformation and transcendence is out of the inner will of the Being to have sheer pleasure without any specific goal or purpose. It is the nature of the Being to be Becoming. This is concised in the concept of *līlā* (free sportive play) which is essentially a concept of the Vedāntic philosophy. *Līlā* is a rhythm of the creative consciousness. It is a play of self-concealing to self-revealing as a process of joy. There is an extreme attractiveness in this play which, too, gives a pure joy. In this play there is a victory of knowledge bestowing pleasure and victory of power and creation bestowing delight. An attraction gives a joy of discovery. There is a surprise of new creation which is an adventure of the soul. *Līlā* gives the delight of existence. In fact, the Cosmic Consciousness or the Transcendent Existence creates into it itself and enjoys this creation. The Becoming is a creation of the Being, i.e. *līlā* and the Becoming is enjoyed by the Being which also is *līlā*. This is an Upaniṣadic thought expressed through the concepts like *ātmarati* or *ātmamithuna* or *ātmakrīḍā* which results into *ātmatuṣṭi*. The transcendental reality has within itself the Delight which gets expressed through the rhythmic and harmonious dynamism of the Existence. The *līlā* is the transcendent form of the Life Divine. The Self, the spirit, the Reality discloses itself in its evolution and returns into the Absolute through a spiritual completeness of itself in life.

XVI

Sri Aurobindo had a good exposure of Eastern and Western traditions of thought and culture. He has studied them seriously as an academic enterprise and also as a spiritual pursuit. His thoughts were highly articulate. A study into his writings, especially the text *The Life Divine* makes us aware of various sources he has adopted for formulating, adopting and developing his thought as a universal philosophy. He has used concepts, doctrines and methods of philosophizing mainly from Immanuel Kant, Henri Bergson, Benedict Spinoza and Morgan Llyod from the Western tradition and Śaṅkara, Upaniṣads, Īśvarakṛṣṇa and Vedas from the Indian tradition. What appears to be the contribution of his thought in moulding the Advaita Vedāntic metaphysics greatly owes its sources and bearing upon the Āgamic traditions of Tantrism with a particular focus on Kashmir Śaivism. He has been very brief and scanty in making references to sources from traditions earlier to him. But the terms, concepts, procedures and structures he has used are obvious and vivid references to the material he has used. Sri Aurobindo has a holistic approach to his thought and philosophy as a way of life to be contemplated and pursued in practice to life and fulfil it. His philosophy is a homogeneous whole with an inherent design to it. Every part of his thought in the form of a concept or doctrine or theory is precisely and perfectly placed in that whole. As the whole has its own design an every part of it, too, has its own design determined by the design of the whole. His bearing upon sources is in the form of borrowing concepts, doctrines, methods and procedure, etc. from the early traditions. As if he has borrowed stones from those traditions to construct his unique and palatial structure in the form of concepts, doctrines, etc. from schools, sects, philosophers, etc. He has carved out those stones to give them the design and meaning of his system of thought to fit into the grand holistic system of his metaphysics in his own way and for the purpose of his system. With this way of utilizing the sources already available, he stands as a novel and an independent thinker of the world of thinkers uptil now. In using the borrowed material he has not tied himself to the contention of those schools or philosophers but provided the material with his own meaning and purpose to fit into his context. In giving this treatment he has neither tormented those systems nor distorted those concepts and doctrines. In fact, it is our acquaintance with those concepts which arrests our understanding to flow with the thought of Sri Aurobindo and creates confusions in our minds. He uses the term *puruṣa* at different places. In some places it refers to the meaning of the term coming from Upaniṣads while in some other places it refers to the meaning of the term coming from the Sāṁkhya system of Īśvarakṛṣṇa. He is clear in his use but we have to get the clarity in our understanding by following the context in which he uses it and the purpose for which he uses it.

The thinking and philosophy of Sri Aurobindo are his own contribution. He was a well-read great scholar. He was deep in Indian philosophical thinking. He was highly influenced by the Vedāntic philosophy and he has used the basic important concepts of Indian philosophy. It is useful for our purpose to trace the roots of his philosophical thinking in the Indian and Western traditions. He was influenced by and using concepts and categories of the philosophies of Aristotle, Immanuel Kant, Morgan Llyod, Henri Bergson, Śaṅkarācārya, Upaniṣads and so on. The Vedāntic concepts of *ātman*, Brahman, *māyā, sat–cit–ānanda, parātpara, ananta, śāśvata, nitya, puruṣa,* etc. are very prominent in his writings. But more importantly, the basic and unique categories of Kashmir Śaivism appear to be shaping and structuring his philosophical thought. He says that consciousness and being qua existence are not different but are one and the same. This is the position of Kashmir Śaivism. He uses the further developments of the Kashmir Śaivism. It holds that all being is supreme consciousness, all consciousness is self-existence and eternal, the world is real and it exists only in consciousness, the conscious energy is one with Being that creates, conscious being is the truth of supermind, conscious being lives independently, world lives by that, we can enter into the cosmic consciousness and also enter into the world-transcending consciousness, become superior to all cosmic existence, etc. are the doctrines which come from the Kashmir Śaivism. The concepts like *cit-śakti,* i.e. *prakāśa, unmeṣa, āviṣkaraṇa, viśvamaya* and *viśvottīrṇa,* creation, evolution, *prāṇa, spanda, utpatti, āvirbhāva* and *tirodhāna, bheda-abheda, jīva, caitanya, parāsaṁvit, śuddhasaṁvit, sāmarasya, manas, buddhi, jñāna, icchā, spanda, krīḍā, sṛṣṭi, saṁhāra, ānanda,* etc. are the concepts unique to Kashmir Śaivism and they are used by Sri Aurobindo adopting their uniqueness and nuances. His thinking is more Kashmir Śaivaite than Vedāntic. Nevertheless it makes his own contribution of an all exhaustive philosophy rejecting contradictions and advocating creation as the metaphysics.

4

God's Last World
Sri Aurobindo's Argument for Divine Life

Stephen Phillips

IN Western philosophy, the theistic problem of evil is well known and well-rehearsed. Beginning with an idea of God as perfect and thus both omnipotent and omnibenevolent, philosophers reason that this world should be, in the famous phrase of Leibniz, "the best of all possible worlds". However, this does not look very much like the best of all possible worlds. It takes only the tiniest bit of imagination to compare our world to one that is better, a world with just the tiniest decrease in pain or suffering. Since the decrease we are imagining — one less headache, for example, or one less birth defect — is possible, why didn't God arrange things so that that world — and not this one — is the one that came about? As Epicurus (342–270 BCE) a younger contemporary of Aristotle's reasoned, God is either incapable of preventing evil or unwilling. If incapable, out the window goes God's reputed omnipotence (God is a weakling). And if God is unwilling, out the window goes omnibenevolence (God is a bully). If God is neither incapable nor unwilling, why evil?

The theistic problem of evil, as the difficulty is dubbed (sometimes called instead the problem of theodicy, "justification of God's goodness in the face of evil"), appeared early in Indian thought. It is no accident that the "three evils" famously identified by the Buddha, namely, disease, old age, and death, are natural evils; no one escapes these and it is these natural evils that cause the greatest difficulty for theism. Moral evil — the evil that is voluntarily perpetrated, that did not have to be had people behaved differently, having made different choices — is not much of a problem for theism. For in both the Western and classical Indian conceptions, God is not responsible for karma, the just consequences of free choices of the likes of us. But natural evil cannot be explained so easily as the consequences of our free will, since disease, old age and death are natural phenomena which our choices have not plausibly brought about.

Let us get ready to look at how Sri Aurobindo sees natural evil by reviewing classical Vedāntic theory. *Brahma-Sūtra* has a long section explaining how God is not the author of evil, and Śaṅkara, the oldest commentator, makes plain a mainstream position.[1] Although Śaṅkara is an Advaitin, he takes seriously the theistic teachings of the Upaniṣads and *Gītā* as meditational aids. Scripture says that Brahman is the source of the world, and so since Brahman is unsullied value and bliss, whence evil? How could evil have its source in what is inherently its opposite? Here it is of course important that it is the Upaniṣadic concept of Brahman that is being defended and not the Western concept of God. Nevertheless, Brahman is said not only to be the source of the world but also its "Lord" (*Īśvara*) and "Inner Controller" (*antaryāmin*). So, indeed, conceived as *Īśvara*, Brahman looks pretty similar to God as conceived in the Western theological mainstream. Furthermore — and this is an important point — evil is perhaps even more of a problem for a concept of Brahman as opposed to the Western concept of God since Brahman's nature is foreign to evil and the world is not only shaped by the Lord but in its stuff it is, or comes out of, Brahman, the One.

But let us go slowly looking at Śaṅkara. His explanation of the *Brahma-Sūtra* passage is complex, and only the second part of his theory is taken over by the more genuine Vedantic theists such as Rāmānuja. That part, however, remains the central-most plank on God and evil within the long history of theistic Vedānta. The first part relies on the distinction between Brahman as "without" and "with" qualities (or attributes), *nirguṇa* contrasting with *saguṇa*-

---

[1] Śaṅkara's "Commentory" or Bhāṣya (*c.* 750) on the *Brahma-Sūtra* (*c.* 200 BCE). 2.1.34, tr. G. Thibaut, *The Vedānta Sūtras of Bādarāyaṇa* (1890, 1962), part one, pp. 357-59.

Brahman. According to Śaṅkara, Brahman without qualities is supremely real. Brahman with qualities is talked about in scripture as an aid to meditation. Scripture is like a patient teacher (*guru*) and it is difficult to appreciate that Brahman as supremely real has no qualities. Scripture talks about God, i.e. Brahman with qualities, as a preparatory to the austere truth — which is that nothing but Brahman without qualities is really real. God, too, is part of a cosmic illusion due to Nescience or spiritual ignorance, *avidyā.*

Brahman with qualities is God, the Lord and Creator, *Īśvara.* How then could the Lord, who is perfect — much as in the Western conception — allow evil in the world? Śaṅkara asks this question and moves to the second part of his theodicy, the part that is shared. Here karma as affecting rebirth is the absolutely hinge notion and the theodicy seems a *saṁskāra* extension of the free-will theodicy of the West. For, not only are we responsible for our karma in making our future births; the Lord is just in arranging the universe so that it embodies principles of karma justice. Rebirth is fair. Mental dispositions, *saṁskāra,* underpinning our habits and character, maintain, at least in part, our personal identity over lifetimes, and we are responsible for our own *saṁskāra* in that we etch them by our choices or reinforce them by endorsing and acting out of even so-called natural desires. So rebirth is fair in two ways: (1) we make ourselves by our choices (virtue is its own reward), and (2) there is karmic payback in future pain and suffering or pleasure and happiness.

But why should there be any creation at all. And why should God permit bad karma, permit us to do evil things for which we must pay in seemingly natural suffering? Why does God permit *avidyā,* the spiritual ignorance that is at the root of evil here? In response, Śaṅkara turns back to the first part of his defence; the world is *māyā* and *inexplicable* in relation to *nirguṇa-Brahman.* We will come back and consider whether this response is successful in a moment. But first let us note again that this is where the theistic Vedāntin parts company with the Advaitin. The world is not inexplicable in relation to God; it is His or Her expression, the body of God, reflecting somehow God's intrinsic nature. The work of the first part of Śaṅkara's two-part defence is done, in the theistic views, mainly by a sense of gratefulness, it seems to me. Let me elaborate.

God creates many worlds much better than this. But in those worlds I do not exist. Our world is definitely not the best of all possible worlds, but it is a world where I exist. So I am grateful that God in Her infinity suffers it. Indeed, this could be God's "last world", as I shall explain, a world which is only barely possible as bordering on incompatibility with Brahman's nature as Saccidānanda (in Aurobindo's conception), which will be our focus presently.

What I am proposing might be called the Parallel-Worlds Defence of God's Goodness. Leibniz reasoned that God should create the best of all possible worlds. The problem is that this world does not seem to be that world, because of evil. But suppose that God does create the best of all possible worlds. What about the second-best world, the runner-up in world competition? Should not God give the creatures in the second-best world their day in the sum? Why should some marginal flaw, in comparison with the champion world, prevent God from letting the runner-up world be? God, it seems, would create the second best universe as a parallel universe, with its own space and time, etc. alongside the world with the first prize. Similarly, with the third-place universe, the fourth, the fifth, and so on down to a universe where the balance of good and evil is so tenuous that God says, "Okay, this one and no more". That last universe is ours. Thus so long as we judge that there is not absolutely so much evil in this world that God would refuse to give us our day in the sun, then the evil here is compatible with the idea of God as Good. This defence has the further virtue that it matches our gratitude for being at all. That is, so long as we are, all told, glad that we exist, we would feel thankful toward a Creator, despite evil.

Again, this is not Śaṅkara's view. Specifically, he voices the theory — which is quite widespread, appearing in Buddhism as well as Śaṅkara's Vedānta and which seems to me to be simply an elaboration of the inexplicability doctrine, *anirvacanīyatva* — that there is no first creation, that the transmigratory round or universe is beginningless (*anādisaṁsāra*). Śaṅkara in responding to the objection that at the beginning of the universe there was no good or bad karma denies explicitly that nescience (*avidyā*), spiritual ignorance, has a beginning.[2] This is to shift back to the first part of his defence, relying on the distinction between Brahman as with and without qualities, *saguṇa* and *nirguṇa*, which is unavailable to the genuine theist.

With Śaṅkara the deep question is: Why is there nescience (*avidyā*), spiritual ignorance? If Brahman is the supreme reality, our own true self, why is it we are unenlightened? Advaita has no answer to this, it seems to me.

Vedāntic theism struggles with a similar problem: Why, given the possibility of living enlightenment such as Kṛṣṇa's, are we not all enlightened? The answer, again, is karma. We somehow deserve not to be enlightened. But why does God let us get into such straits? This is the further question for which the theist owes us an answer, it seems to me (as it does to Aurobindo, as we shall note). The best answer seems to be that otherwise we would not be who we are and there would not be the opportunities we have for development. This is the problem space in which Aurobindo works and frames his explanation of evil. First, let us sum up the classical response.

Habits, which we have ourselves made and for which we are responsible, the fundamental dispositions of the soul, carry over into and determine the course of a soul's next incarnation. In this way rebirth is fair. Along a second dimension of the karma concept, karmic payback, the Lord guides the workings of *adṛṣṭa;* "unseen force" is not blind, according to the theists.

So, in this way beyond virtue and vice being their own reward (a truth of the karma-doctrine independent of rebirth) there is to be justice, just payback for bad acts — i.e. beyond the badness of bad habits — and pleasure and happiness for good karma. And why not? There are pretty horrible sinners out there especially in comparison with the saintliness of some of our ancestors. Compared with the saints and *avatāra*s we are all sinners to some degree — at least I may speak for myself. So God's universe could well be just, it seems to me, at least "just" in the sense required to defend the thesis that God is good and worthy of worship. Thus some of what

---

[2] Śaṅkara, *Brahma-Sūtra-Bhāṣya* 2.1.35-36 (Thibaut, op. cit., pp. 359-61).

we see as natural evil would be payback for which, then, the Lord should not be blamed.[3] And of course some evil, such as pain, has a biological or other instrumental function without which our world would not be possible. And so an Eastern version of free-will theodicy, coupled with instrumentality considerations, could be quite compelling, it seems to me. Aurobindo inherits karma and rebirth doctrines which seem in themselves quite promising, I should say.

Let us now turn to *The Life Divine* (*LD*) of Sri Aurobindo and take up the specifics of his *darśana* with respect to evil. He starts, like the Vedāntic theist, with a concept of Brahman, the One, who creates by loosing forth the world out of herself. Everything is in some sense Brahman. Now that Brahman is essentially *ānanda*, "bliss" — the fuller characterization of Brahman's *sva-rūpa* is *Saccidānanda* for Aurobindo but this of course includes "bliss" — means above all that the immanent Brahman is so intrinsically *valuable* as to be forcing "divine life".

Aurobindo does not explicitly address the nature of value. He does not explain the character of the value that he believes is implicit in Brahman and *ānanda*. It is clear, nevertheless, that he believes that a kind of *ānanda* scores high as a hedonic value, since he often repeats traditional claims that a yogī's experience of Brahman is ecstatic.[4] But *ānanda* is in his view more. As I read Aurobindo, it is a basis and touchstone for moral and aesthetic value, though, do not mean to suggest that he is an ethical or aesthetic hedonist. He explicitly contrasts divine *ānanda* with just about all that we humans ordinarily regard as evil, in particular pain and suffering.[5] Indeed, it is crucial to his central argument in support of his prediction of

[3] Rebirth theodicy is in this way similar to the theory of Augustine (e.g., *Of True Religion*) that natural evil is payback for sin. The Indian theory has the advantage, however, of the punishment better fitting the crime than in the Western version because there are lines of individual continuity as opposed to our paying for the sin of remote ancestors. However, there must be, then, continuity in the consciousness making choices and after-death awareness of the connection between payback and choice. Otherwise, there could be no moral lessons and the retributive nature of karma would make no sense.

[4] *LD*, pp. 990-91 as well as numerous passages in his voluminous writings as a teacher of yoga.

[5] Ibid., pp. 404-06; see also p. 98.

divine life that the prominent forms of what we know as evil, both moral and aesthetic, be intrinsically repugnant to Brahman's essential nature, although, as will be explained, they have an instrumental value to the development of divine life. Divine *ānanda* is presumed to be incompatible with any *purposeless* enjoyment on Brahman's part of pain, suffering and other evils.

Although Aurobindo has no explicit theory of value, he does embrace a means/ends value distinction. He endorses the view that the positive intrinstic value of an end may compensate and justify the negative intrinsic value of its necessary means. Further, he holds that pain, suffering and evil in general have such "instrumental" value, compensating for their negative intrinsic value. They are not to be present in divine life, though he believes that there could not be the development of divine life without them:

> . . . if that [Divine] Reality is what we have supposed it to be, there must be some necessity for the appearance of these contrary phenomena [of evil], some significance, some function that they had to serve in the economy of the universe.[6]

According to Aurobindo, Brahman as *ānanda* blocks the real possibility of any universe where there would be any evil that was not an indispensable condition for the realization of some great good.

The future good has to be great indeed: not only is future "divine life" conceived as so wonderful that it would rather directly express the essential *ānanda* of Brahman, it is conceived as more wonderful than what Brahman's "bliss" would have been without this self-manifestation. Otherwise, Aurobindo reasons, earthly pain, suffering and evil in general could be unredeemed, i.e. incompatible with Saccidānanda, since, as he says, Brahman as *ānanda* would not undergo a *meaningless* depletion:

> . . . nor can they [pain, suffering and evil in general be a mere mistake of the Divine Consciousness without any meaning in the divine wisdom, without any purpose of the divine joy . . . to justify their existence. Justification there must be . . . .[7]

---

[6] *LD*, p. 597; see also pp. 623-24.

[7] *LD*, p. 407; see also the surrounding text, pp. 405-11, as well as p. 682.

Thus it is that *ānanda* is to involve not only "delight" understood hedonically but also the value of a significant process of achievement. Mere delight of play is not Brahman's motive for creation.[8] Brahman wants to accomplish something. There are to be "new riches"[9] from the cosmic adventure as well as a return to an awareness of an intrinsic bliss. That Brahman is essentially *ānanda* means that where there is or has been evil there Brahman is itself moving to greater value, in Aurobindo's view.

This interpretation of Brahman's motivation may appear controversial: no earlier commentator, to my knowledge, has expressed it. Also, the references to *The Life Divine* which I have given thus far may not, I admit, seem clear in their expression of this conception — which I feel is none the less present. So let me fill out in further detail the reasons why I read Aurobindo as proposing Brahman's motive in manifestation to be not only a "bliss" understood hedonically but also the accomplishment of a "significant" achievement. Then we shall examine Aurobindo's central argument in support of his prediction of "divine life", which I take to hinge on construing Brahman's *ānanda* of manifestation as involving a "significant" process of creation.

Nowhere in *The Life Divine* does Aurobindo say in just so many words that Brahman's reason for manifestation is the value and significance of the development of divine life. But that this is his view is suggested by his reflection on other views of Brahman's motivation in creation, as well as by the central position enjoyed by the theory of divine life in his entire project.

There are three distinct views of Brahman's motivation for creation that are considered in *The Life Divine*. One is the view that *mukti* (liberation) might be Brahman's goal in cosmic becoming and reason for manifestation, just as in many Hindu circles it is viewed as the supreme value in a person's life, *parama-puruṣārtha*. While regarding *mukti* as the kind of experience which he calls both "mental silence" and *nirvāṇa* and thus seeing it as having a great but limited value, Aurobindo reasons that *mukti*, on his or indeed on a traditional

---

8 See in particular *LD*, pp. 104-11, 303, 386 and 835.

9 *LD*, p. 150; see also pp. 1069-70.

conception that he identifies, could not be Brahman's motive for manifestation. Brahman could not be motivated to self-manifest just for *mukti* as conceived in the traditional Hindu idea identified — the return of (human) consciousness to Brahman awareness — for why should Brahman undertake a cosmic process only to return to its native state? And *mukti* as interpreted by Aurobindo would also leave world processes as meaningless. Why should the achievement of a *nirvāṇa* type of experience be Brahman's sole intention for individuals? *Mukti* on either construe could not be a sufficient motivation for Brahman to subject itself to any finite experience much less to the pain, suffering and evil which are part of our world. Aurobindo rejects the idea for these reasons.[10]

A second position he scrutinizes is the Vedāntic one that the world is God's *līlā* (play or amusement). He never really rejects this view or its complement that Brahman's or God's "delight" (*ānanda*) in manifestation is motivational. The question is then the nature of *ānanda*. In fact, Aurobindo's most explicit answer to the motivational question appears to be an endorsement of the *līlā* view.

> If . . . [Brahman] being free to move or remain eternally still, to throw itself into forms or retain the potentiality of form in itself, it indulges its power of movement and formation, it can be only for one reason, for delight.[11]

But if by "delight" he means *ānanda,* which is intrinsic to Brahman, it could be no reason for Brahman to undertake manifestation since Brahman is supposed to have an infinite delight without manifesting in any finite fashion. How could this *ānanda* which Brahman is said to enjoy enough an inessential self-manifestation be then the same *ānanda* which Brahman is presumed to have intrinsically? That is, how could it be so if there is also to be a distinction between the essential self-presentation of Brahman to itself on the one hand and finite manifestation which is held to be contingent upon Brahman's free "choice" on the other? Thus presumably Aurobindo means that Brahman realizes a different sort of delight in manifesting in finite

[10] *LD,* pp. 39-41, 446-61, 667-69 and elsewhere.

[11] *LD,* p. 91.

forms. This is, I maintain, the delight of a "significant process of achievement".

Note that in an extended passage Aurobindo finds, contrary to the traditional notion, the view of Divine amusement and equal delight in everything "little more than the facile dogma which tells us that all that is right, because all is perfectly decreed by the divine Wisdom",[12] and poses it to his view of evolutionary progress. It appears that his considered opinion is that the traditional *līlā* view is incomplete.[13]

In contrast to his attempt to preserve at least something of additional ideas of *mukti* and *līlā,* Aurobindo rejects outright a third view that is held by Advaitins, namely, that the question "Why this world?" cannot be answered, *anirvacanīyatvāt* (because it is impossible to say). The practical realm's reality to itself cannot be explained in relation to the absolute one because from that perspective it is an illusion only, Advaitins hold. Thus it would be impossible to say why or whence it originates. Although apparently "illusion" is an attempt at some sort of explanation of a presumed relation between the Absolute and the practical world, the point would be that it is necessarily an incomplete explanation.

Aurobindo expresses two principal objections to this view. First, he argues that Advaitins by proclaiming "world as illusion" to be *anirvacanīya* make their own position that Brahman-experience is the *summum bonum* unintelligible.[14] And here he has a good point. How could Advaitins coherently view Brahman-experience as the humanly greatest good without admitting some fuller relation than strict illusoriness between Brahman and our human world, specifically in regard to human values? Aurobindo in spite of his

---

12 *LD*, p. 394; see also the surrounding pages.

13 The quotation above from *LD*, p. 91 was published in 1914 in the *Arya*. It was not revised in the rewriting of 1938-40 although the chapters added at that time show further reflection on the motivational issue. See in particular *LD*, pp. 408-09, 754, 835 and 1069-70.

14 Aurobindo wrongly attributes this view, which is indeed dominant in Advaita, to Śaṅkara, who uses the term *anirvacanīya* in a different sense (see Hacker, op. cit., pp. 84-87). Where Aurobindo says "Śaṅkara" in this regard, we shall say "Advaita" or "Advaitins".

own occasional use of the terms "ineffable", "unknowable", etc. mounts a cogent attack on Advaita for postulating a self-defeating cognitive gap between the human and Brahman.[15]

Second, Aurobindo appears to find it a duty for a philosopher to try to affirm a cosmic meaning and value for life, while finding the doctrine of *anirvacanīyatva* an unjustified neglect of that duty. He presents many variations on this theme. He believes that we cannot be satisfied intellectually with a view that finds our lives and universe to be without a true significance and value.[16]

According to my reading, that some value or allure from Brahman's perspective accrues to the manifestation of divine life follows simply from assuming that the motivational question *can* be answered. Aurobindo definitely assumes that it can be. He presumes that unmanifest Saccidānanda is the natural state and that manifestation has a sufficient reason that we human beings can understand — on analogy to our own reasons for undertakings.

Aurobindo's central argument for divine life is that Brahman as *ānanda* would be incompatible with evil — with pain, suffering, incapacity, death and the rest of our miseries — were these not instrumental to the development of divine life, that our present world could not exist if these phenomena were not contributing to Brahman's goal. Divine life is to provide the world its significance, both from Brahman's and from human perspectives, by justifying all evil in a historically achieved state of earthly beatitude.

Aurobindo's central argument in support of his prediction of divine life is that two facts or premises, (1) Brahman's being *Saccidānanda*, particularly *ānanda*, and (2) the reality of evil, together indicate that divine life will emerge.

Now a perception of a tension between these two facts is not all that Aurobindo brings forward in support of his claim that divine life is inevitable. Biological evolution and the course of civilization to date are cited as further evidence in support of the proposal. Evolutionary theory provides a parameter for Aurobindo's

---

15 *LD*, pp. 469-76.

16 See especially *LD*, pp. 674-82.

theorizing;[17] it may also be counted as a premise in the argumentation for divine life. And here our yogin-philosopher seems on dangerous grounds, and it is unclear that he means by the word "evolution" the same as do biologists. Something similar may be said in criticism of Aurobindo's understanding of the course of civilization. He discerns progress along several dimensions, biological, intellectual, moral and spiritual, and claims that the "fact" of progress to the present suggests that there will be further progress and that a "diviner" future will come to be. Thus several ideas converge in the prediction of divine life. However, yogic indications of Brahman as Saccidānanda viewed by the side of evil is where Aurobindo finds the only certain sign of divine life's eventuality.[18] In other words, that Brahman is Saccidānanda is a "yogic claim" based on yogic perception, *yaugika-pratyakṣa.* Without yogic perception indicating Brahman as Saccidānanda, evolution, as he says, might seem "a queer freak in a bit of inanimate Matter".[19] So too human civilization. And without evil, this might be what he calls a "typal" world whose denizens are content in a fixed world order, one of other worlds that God creates before She creates this, as I say, Her "Last World". Here again Aurobindo:

> There is a possibility of self-expression . . . in perfect types fixed and complete in their own nature: that is the principle of becoming in the higher worlds; they are typal and not evolutionary in their life principle; they exist each in its own perfection, but within the limits of a stationary world-formula.[20]

Aurobindo views evil as tied to human dissatisfaction and aspiration (as the disease with its symptoms).[21] They are, he says, the clear indication that, assuming the reality of Brahman, ours is not a world having reached the stability and perfection of its type and that there

---

17 *LD*, pp. 835-36.

18 Ibid., pp. 306 and 1042.

19 Ibid., p. 851.

20 Ibid., p. 681; see also pp. 591 and 784ff.

21 Note that the first chapter of *The Life Divine* is entitled "The Human Aspiration" and that the idea of human aspiration/dissatisfaction has a pronounced importance throughout the book: pp. 1-5, 117, 243-47, 395ff and 842-43, among other places.

inevitably will be an evolution to divine life. Evil in Aurobindo's conception is rooted in our material evolutionary inheritance. The inconscience of matter itself may be said to be for him the fundamental evil, for it stands in sharpest opposition to Brahman's essential nature and gives rise to all the specific evils of life. Above in encapsulating Aurobindo's argument for divine live, I did not mention matter, since the perception of a tension that leads to the prediction centres on (the emergent material phenomena of) human evils, not on matter in general. But to understand Aurobindo's sense of how precisely evil is necessary to the evolution of divine life, one has to take up his views of matter and biological evolution. This we cannot do, however, here, since there are too many details. My point is that the tension which Aurobindo perceives between Brahman and evil is intended to motivate his assertion of the instrumentality of evil. It is also intended to motivate his view of the root of evil which he identifies as the insentience and other apparently adverse characteristics of matter and of life forms emergent in matter.[22]

Aurobindo provides a lot of details concerning the instrumentality of evil (and of matter) for divine life. However the basic point is just this: the creation of distinct individuals who would be in part responsible for their own growth and development as complex personalities would not be possible without matter and the evil that its insentience entails. Working from this fundamental intuition, Aurobindo tries to make plausible his story of the ways in which such untoward phenomena as aggression, incapacity and death might be serving indispensably the great good of divine life.[23] This story could prove to be Aurobindo's chief philosophical accomplishment.[24]

---

[22] See in particular *LD*, pp. 593-95 and 757. The most important chapters in *The Life Divine* for this reasoning are bk I, chaps. 9 and 10 on divine "bliss" and chaps. 19-23 on life, bk II, chap. 4 on the divine and the undivine, chaps. 11-14 on the transitional necessity of evil, and then almost the whole of bk II, Pt 2, excluding the long passages that are devoted to description of certain sorts of mystic experience. Among the clearer, summary statements of the argument for divine life are passages on pp. 233, 288, 591-92, 623-25, 834-35, and in the book's last paragraph, pp. 1069-70. See also pp. 417ff.

[23] See in particular *LD*, bk I, chaps. 19-25 and bk II, chaps. 11-14.

[24] Aurobindo's view of the instrumentality of evil is in many respects close to various Romantic or "soul-making theodicies".

Ends can justify means, although, as John Dewey points out, means can also justify ends, i.e. when the ends most desirable would require much less favourable means.[25] Still, in certain circumstances ends can justify means, and so I feel that the plausibility of the details in Aurobindo's story of evil's instrumentality for divine life is important of gauging Aurobindo's overall philosophic accomplishment.

Finally, let me mention another aspect of Aurobindo's response, where he is in line with the *bhakti* aspect of Vedāntic theism, where he himself is *bhakta* as opposed to a philosopher defending the concept of Brahman. In the view of the *bhakti-yoga* practitioner, suffering is an opportunity to pay off bad karma. We should be grateful and not generate further bad karma by whining and complaining. Far from disproving the existence of God, pain and suffering are manifestations of God's love and concern for our welfare. Better to pay off bad karma now than to let it fester, than to let it blindside us later or in another life. Who cares about it really anyway, since essentially life *is* delight, is *ānanda*? Our business is its relishing.

References

Aurobindo, Sri, 1972, *The Life Divine*, Pondicherry: Sri Aurobindo Ashram.

Dewey, John, 1948, *Reconstruction in Philosophy*.

Śaṅkara's "Commentary" or Bhāṣya on the Bramha-Sūtra, tr. G. Thibaut, *The Vedānta Sūtras of Bādarāyaṇa*.

[25] Dewey 1948: 170-72.

5

Does the Delightful Absolute Provide for Evils?

Indrani Sanyal

EVILS, sorrow, sufferings obviously snoop into human affairs. Man's tussle with obstreperous ways of evils and his consistent strive to pull through the harmful and despicable invasion of evils during the course of his existence characterize his activities as humanly. Meddlesome bearings of evils are difficult to confront and still more difficult is to make the notion of evil intelligible. Evils, sorrow and sufferings are necessary accompaniments of beings. Evils of various shades, shapes and strength do intrude into each and every human's existence. Any attempt to provide a definition of evil is no doubt a Herculean task. It is an arduous task to categorize or to classify evils or to theorize about their nature. Whether evils are absolute or relative, whether these are objective or subjective — are no doubt important issues which need deliberations. Evils do occur — whether physical or moral — but their occurrences are questionable. Again discussion about evils cannot altogether avoid, any consideration about the nature of the perpetrators of evils and the sufferers of evils. The *Mahābhārata* and the *Rāmāyaṇa* are abound with the stories and anectdotes of evils. Pages of any daily newspapers are flooded by gloomy incidents of evils. Most of the TV news channels are busy in catering to the ominous events of evils with minute details. The omnipresence of evil and suffering in our world seems to pose a serious challenge to the belief in the existence of a perfect God. In the world it is not uncommon to see the untold suffering of the virtuous person, whereas the wicked have good time in spite of his unrighteous deeds. Thousands and thousands of good-hearted people, innocent people, scrupulous people fall prey to the wildness of nature, suffer from diseases, death and old age, experience the roguery of heinous crime. In this essay, I avoid all nitty-gritty issues relating to the definition of evil and its scope. Everyman's perceived sense of evils is the starting point of this discussion. Instead of citation and enumeration of varied instances of evils, I refer to the following excerpts from the writing of Sri Aurobindo as providing a rough but comprehensive list of items to be brought under evils; Sri Aurobindo writes:

> . . . grief, pain, suffering, error, falsehood, ignorance, weakness, wickedness, incapacity, non-doing of what should be done, and wrongdoing, deviation of will and denial of will, egoism, limitation, division from other beings with whom we should be one, all that makes up the effective figure of what we call evil.[1]

Evils as befallen on somebody mostly challenge the perceived sense of justice. In the Vana-Parva of the *Mahābhārata*, Draupadī questions the very idea of God as a just and good ruler of the universe on the ground that Yudhiṣṭhira, who was well known as the embodiment of virtue was being subjected to untold sufferings, whereas, Duryodhana, the well-known arch-fiend was enjoying immense prosperity. To quote Draupadī:

> *na mātr̥pitr̥vad rājan dhātā bhūteṣu vartate* ।
> *roṣādiva pravr̥tto'yaṁ yatho'yaṁ itara janaḥ* ।।[2]

In the Western philosophy, the problem of evil has been dealt with as the problem of reconciling the belief in God with the existence of evil. The orthodox theistic claim that there exists a perfectly good God comes into conflict with blatant facts about evil and sufferings. Discussions about the paradoxical and unsettled characteristics of evil and their elaborate explanations are made in Indian philosophy and Western philosophy but not always from the same viewpoint. All the schools of Indian philosophy excepting Cārvākas speak of worldly existence to be sorrowful because of sufferings.

In the present discussion, keeping the vastness of the problem

---

[1] "The Divine and the Undivine", *The Life Divine*, p. 423.

[2] O king, god does not bear his creatures in the same way as borne by parents. He seems to be provoked by wrath like an ordinary person." — *Mahābhārata*

in mind, I would like mainly to elaborate the viewpoint of Sri Aurobindo on evil which I consider in several respects as providing the most elegant explanation of evils and sufferings. Our discussion will consider closely the viewpoint of *The Life Divine,* one of the main contentions of which is to offer not philosophical balm for wounds but to "lit the flame of aspiration"[3] for transcending evils and suffering. Sri Aurobindo's candid admission that suffering is a great stumbling block to our understanding of the universe led him to search for avenues for transforming undivinely imperfection into divinely perfection. He acknowledges:

> . . . the presence of evil, the insistence on suffering, the large, the enormous part offered to pain, grief, and affliction in the economy of Nature are the cruel phenomena which baffle our reason and overcome the instinctive faith of mankind in such an origin and government or in all-seeing, all-determining and omnipresent Divine immanence.[4]

Evils exist as stern reality; evils are not treated by Sri Aurobindo as illusions. We shall see in course of our discussion how Sri Aurobindo's arguments aided by his persuasive skill established that the spectacle of evils is not so miserable. This world being temporary and unhappy, *anityaṁ asukhaṁ lokamimaṁ,*[5] Sri Aurobindo emphasizes upon enthusiasm of human beings towards self-development and self-transformation. Sri Aurobindo's explanation of evil is to be comprehended against the vast canvas of his integral monism. Sri Aurobindo though an avowed interpreter of the Upaniṣads, a staunch Vedāntist, sharply distinguishes his viewpoint from that of Śaṅkarācārya[6] and his followers. In his framework evils are real for evils have their origin out of the interaction of different forms of consciousness. But he does not treat evil as any universal principle subsuming under its fold all aspects and levels of consciousness. What is interesting to find that Sri Aurobindo is not at all baffled

---

3 "The Divine and the Undivine", *The Life Divine*, p. 414.

4 Ibid., p. 423.

5 *Gītā* IX.33.

6 In *Śāṅkara-Bhāṣya* on the *Vaiṣamyanirghṛnyādhikaraṇaṁ sūtras* 34-36 his response to the problem of evil is provided.

by the presence of evil in our surrounding. Sri Aurobindo finds out some significance for the appearance of these evils, sufferings or what may be called "contrary phenomena". For Sri Aurobindo, evil or falsehood is not an accidental phenomenon. Since Brahman is all-knowledge, such phenomenon as evil or falsehood cannot be taken to be something whose occurrence is accidental. His belief in an Omnipresent Divine Reality prevents him from rejecting the existence of whatever that falls short of that standard. He argues, on the other hand, that workings of the Omnipresent Divine Reality do adumbrate the necessity of falsehood and error, necessity of wrong and evil and their functioning.

Explanations Rejected by Sri Aurobindo

Sri Aurobindo does not share the view of those who would like to explain evils by attributing these to an involuntary forgetfulness or confusion of the Consciousness-Force of Brahman, the All-Wise. The suggestion that evil could have been the handiwork or manoeuvre of some miscreant to defame the All-Wise is discarded by him. Sri Aurobindo does not try to evade the explanation of evil or falsehood by labelling these as mysteries of the Being, of the original and eternal. Neither does he succumb to the temptation to say that evil and falsehood are so mysterious of all mysteries that even All-Wise is at its wit's end to provide explanation for all these. His straightway rejection of all these viable options does not imply that Sri Aurobindo had no definite clue as to the nature of evils. According to him the All-Wise Brahman is the source of all evils and falsehood and it is significantly responsible for evils and falsehood. He emphatically asserts that evils have significance in the working of our self-experience and world-experience.

Evils Are Possible Only in Cosmic Manifestation

Sri Aurobindo characterizes evils with various qualifications and at times it may seem that all these adjectives do not match with one another. To grasp Sri Aurobindo's idea of evils we need to give up our many unfounded prejudices about tallying one qualification with the other. If something is fundamental then it is authentic, if it is authentic then it is real, hence if it is fundamental then it is real.

Does this style of arguing endorse something to be real in spite of being non-fundamental in the sense of Aurobindo? Is it acceptable to say something to be real but unauthentic? The constructive suggestions from *The Life Divine* provide answers to these baffling questions. The first pronouncement about evils is that these are relative in status but he reinforces that the relative status of evils and falsehood does not necessarily imply their unreality. This is where Sri Aurobindo differs from other philosophers who forsake evil to the domain of unreality. In this connection, we are reminded of Śaṅkarācārya's resolution of the charge of being partial with regard to God by relegating evils to the domain of unreal. While explaining the nature of evil in relation to the Absolute, Sri Aurobindo is straight-forward in rejecting the possibility of taking the Supreme Reality as the locus of evil. He does not hold that evil and falsehood have any direct root in the Supreme Reality itself. Sri Aurobindo made it categorically explicit that falsehood and evil are not to be supposed to have any kind of fundamentality, or power of infinity or eternal being. Evils neither have any authenticity of the original inherence. He views self-existence as essentially and eternally inhering in the self-existent and that is the condition of absoluteness. Sri Aurobindo speaks of one Absolute, i.e. Brahman and for him this absoluteness of Brahman is a well-defined concept. However, in his view, as pointed out by Sri Aurobindo:

> This self-existence reveals itself again in three terms of its essential nature, Self, Conscious Being or Spirit, and God or the Divine being.[7]

The Indian concept of Brahman, the Reality as *Ātman, Puruṣa, Īśvara* more satisfactorily explain Sri Aurobindo's viewpoint.

We are all sensitive about evils, evils are something that happen, evils are thus episodic. Hence the question as to what occasions evil is an important question. Now, let us turn to Sri Aurobindo's answer:

> But it must first be noted that it is only in cosmic manifestation that they become possible; they cannot pre-exist in the timeless

[7] "Brahman, Purusha Ishwara", *The Life Divine*, p. 340.

> being, for they are incompatible with the unity and bliss that are its substance.[8]

The question, as to why there should be the kind of manifestation in the cosmos that originates evil, is disquieting. Sri Aurobindo admits ignorance (*avidyā*) as the cause of evil and falsehood. This notion of *avidyā* is not a unique idea that has been introduced by Sri Aurobindo but in the whole domain of Indian philosophy this is one of the very meaningful concepts. In the Aurobindo's writings, especially in *The Life Divine* we find his vivid account of *avidyā*. However, in this discussion no attempt will be made to compare Sri Aurobindo's idea of *avidyā* with that of other Indian philosophy or a detailed elaboration of Sri Aurobindo's idea of ignorance. However, in order to grasp the nature of evil and its origin, Sri Aurobindo's explanation of *avidyā* needs to be touched upon. He does not desist from considering the problem of evil on the basis of the integral Oneness as the truth of existence. According to Sri Aurobindo ignorance is also knowledge, in its nature it is a self-limiting knowledge oblivious of the integral self-awareness. The process of consciousness has brought ignorance into existence. At this juncture, an answer to the question as to how does this happen, seems to be imperative. In other words, how could this manifold ignorance or this narrowly self-limiting and separative knowledge arise and come into action or maintain itself in action in an absolute being who must be absolute consciousness and therefore cannot be subject to ignorance? The profundity of the question rests on the anxiety to match multitudinous and separative something with the eternal absolute. In fact, this is the perennial question which bothers the metaphysicians from the time immemorial. The other intriguing question is as to why, even if it arises, does it need to arise? Sri Aurobindo's response to these questions is, particularly, to be elucidated in this article.

To understand the nature, the origin and the influence of evils and suffering on the universe and the individual, we need to comprehend Sri Aurobindo's explanation of the same. Within Aurobindonian scheme, transcendent, universal and individual are

[8] "The Origin of Falsehood and Evil", *The Life Divine*, p. 625.

the three aspects of the one existence, and "each of these always contains secretly or overtly the two others". An enquiry into the problem of evil needs to be taken up from these three angles, which are not supposed to be absolutely separate from one another:

1. In the first place, Sri Aurobindo provides an explanation of evil in its relation to the Absolute, the Supreme Reality.
2. He provides an elaborate account of the origin of ignorance and falsehood by tracing its relation to the cosmic workings of the Saccidānanda.
3. He tries to fathom the nature of evil by its action and its hold on the individual being.

Evils in Relation to the Absolute Reality

What is Reality according to Sri Aurobindo? Sri Aurobindo begins with the idea of an omnipresent Reality, a reality which is independent and exists in its own right. Is it possible to say that reality is *asat* or *śūnya* in Sri Aurobindo's philosophy? Sri Aurobindo criticized Nihilism or Śūnyavāda in the ordinarily understood sense. On some occasions, he attempted to show why it would be too hasty a conclusion to argue that the Buddhist conception of reality is antagonistic to the Vedas. Referring to the poems of *Taittirīya Upaniṣad,* wherein it has been stated that the Being was born of non-Being, Sri Aurobindo interprets the expression *asat* (non-Being) as not mere *śūnya* (null) but as that which exceeds even the purest conception and the highest experience of existence in the cosmos. Reality defies all attempts to limit it by either negative or positive descriptions. Sri Aurobindo interprets the expression *asat* as implying the indescribability of reality. *Asat* is not the whole conception of reality nor does its experience represents the limit of our knowledge about it. So what is *asat* or non-existence in the vision of Buddha is also an aspect of reality according to Sri Aurobindo. In the view of Sri Aurobindo *sat* is also an aspect of reality. He would say that *sat* and *asat* are just categories for apprehending consciousness. Thus in the view of Sri Aurobindo, Existence is Consciousness and he derived this view from the Upaniṣads. He also adds that Consciousness is Consciousness-Force, *cit* is *cit śakti.* Consciousness is the ultimate light in the illumination of which everything is manifest but which needs no light other than itself for the manifestation of its own existence. According to Sri Aurobindo self-awareness of Brahman is the background and possibility of the self-knowledge of Brahman. One line of interpretation of the Upaniṣads denies that Brahman knows itself. It is Pure Consciousness but not conscious or self-awareness. Sri Aurobindo affirms that Brahman is Pure Consciousness and accepts that knowledge of Brahman is a movement within its own being. The self-awareness of Brahman is also world-awareness and that is what Sri Aurobindo calls the Supermind.

Brahman is conceived and experienced in three aspects: *Ātman* (Self), *Puruṣa* (Soul or Conscious Being) and *Īśvara* (Divine). The first aspect of Brahman is *Ātman*, the pure Self which represents the basic aspect and is considered to be static and provides support to the creative adventure. In its second aspect, the self as a witness of the process of dynamic manifestation which it initiates in its own being by its conscious power is a conscious Soul, *Puruṣa*, the self of the cosmos. The third is the aspect of Brahman wherein it is as *Īśvara*, the Lord and Master of the cosmic manifestation. None of these aspects is to be considered as more authentic than or superior to others. Our emphasizing of only the aspect of Self to the exclusion of other aspects amounts to concentrating only on the static silence of the Infinite. Again overemphasis on the aspect of *Īśvara* would imply making the dynamicity more important at the cost of its eternal status and infinite silence. Our concentration on *Puruṣa-prakṛti* alone would highlight the dichotomy of Soul and Nature, Spirit and Matter and its unity aspect will be overlooked.

> We must not commit the mistake of emphasizing one side of the Truth and concluding from it or acting upon it to the exclusion of all other sides and aspects of the Infinite.[9]

The integral supramental knowledge reveals these three as the same Reality simultaneously without losing the distinction among them. *Ātman* has an impersonal and static aspect. It is not by itself active in the manifestation of the universe. It provides the foundation of the cosmic creative act, but not itself active. *Puruṣa* is in comparison

9 "Brahman, Purusha, Ishwara", *The Life Divine*, p. 348.

to *Ātman*, more active and closer to the act of manifestation. It gives sanction to the manifestation and enjoys the creation. It is not the aspect of reality which dynamically controls the creation. *Īśvara* is the masterful governor. Divine being or *Īśvara* is the Supreme Person. It is not an impersonal reality nor is it static and aloof from the act of manifestation and the manifested universe. Divine Being is free from his creative act and is not bound by it. None of these aspects of Brahman is either superior or inferior to the other. They are on the same level and equally real and represent three sides of the omnipresent reality when it is approached from the standpoint of cosmos.

Coming to the question of evils and sufferings, thus we find that Sri Aurobindo denies evils and falsehood as belonging to the "fundamental or primary aspects of the Being".[10] He was quite categorical in his denial about the existence of any absolute of evil or absolute of falsehood. Evils and falsehood are not native to the Absolute.

Evils in Relation to the Cosmic Manifestation

Evils and falsehood arise at the level of cosmic manifestation. According to Sri Aurobindo, Brahman is an inherent self-consciousness inseparable from its being, throws itself out as a force of movement of consciousness which is creative of forces, forms and worlds. According to Sri Aurobindo, as we have already discussed Consciousness is also Consciousness-Force. In relation to the three aspects of Brahman, Self, Soul and the Divine Being, Consciousness-Force also assumes three aspects. According to Sri Aurobindo, they are *Māyā*, *Prakṛti* and Śakti. It is the *Cit-Śakti* (Consciousness-Force), conceptually creative of the universe. It does not execute what it conceives. The dynamic execution is the work of *Prakṛti*. Śakti is the synthesis of these two aspects of Consciousness-Force, i.e. *Māyā* and *Prakṛti*, and is both conceptually creative and dynamically executive. *Īśvara* is the synthesis of the other two aspects of Brahman, Self and Soul. For Sri Aurobindo, the notion of manifestation is important and this should not be

---

10 *The Life Divine*, p. 622.

confused with the notion of creation, which has a different connotation. He says:

> In fact, the Infinite does not create, it manifests what is in itself, in its own essence of reality: it is itself that essence of all reality and all realities are powers of that one Reality.[11]

If one still insists on the notion of creation in accounting for the diverse multiplicity around us Sri Aurobindo would suggest drawing a line of demarcation between two sorts of creation. Sri Aurobindo's position is not difficult to understand from the perspective of Indian philosophical tradition which speaks of two sorts of doctrine regarding the nature of causal relation, known as Satkāryavāda and Asatkāryavāda. Unlike the proponents of Asatkāryavāda, who maintain that effect has no existence (*asat*) in the cause but brought into being anew, Sri Aurobindo as a proponent of Satkāryavāda argues that effect or origination is the actualization of pre-existing potentialities.

He clarifies further:

> The Absolute neither creates, nor is created — in the current sense of making or being made; we can speak of creation in the sense of Being becoming in form and movement what it already is in substance and status.[12]

The world is a manifestation of Brahman, but it is from another point of view a self-concealing of *Sat–Cit–Ānanda*. The self-concealing does not in any way affect the existence of Brahman, it remains what it is for ever and yet the act of self-limitations is the beginning of the process of manifestation of the universe. The transcendent limits itself as Cosmic Being, the Self and Soul of the universe. And the Cosmic Being self limits itself as the individual self. These three, the transcendent, the cosmic and the individual are the three aspects of *Sat–Cit–Ānanda*.

The following passage from the "Brahman, Purusha, Ishwara" explains the reason for exploring the problem of evil from these three angles:

---

[11] *The Life Divine*, p. 350.

[12] Ibid., p. 350.

> Brahman is the absolute, the transcendent, and incommunicable, the Supracosmic Existence that sustains the cosmos, the Cosmic Self that upholds all beings, but It is too the self of each individual: the soul or psychic entity is an eternal portion of the *Īśvara*; It is his supreme Nature or Consciousness-Force that has become the living being in a world of living beings.[13]

It is in the supermind and by the action of the supermind that *Sat–Cit–Ānanda* becomes the subject knowing itself as the object. This ideal of twofold bifurcation-cum-unification presupposes an integral consciousness.

In the *Gītā*, according to Sri Aurobindo's interpretation, the Supreme Divine has three aspects, *Kṣara Puruṣa*, *Akṣara Puruṣa* and Puruṣottama. The first is the Reality in the flux of the world and all creatures, the second is immutable and away from all movements of *prakṛti*, and the third reconciles in its being the mutable and immutable *puruṣa*s, their apparent contradiction is resolved in this supreme aspect of the super personal Person who is both unmoving and moving and yet transcends these formulations of his self-existence. The *Bhāgavata Purāṇa*, Trika philosophy, accept both the dynamic and the static aspects of Reality.

The progressive process of self-variation of the one Self is called descent of consciousness by Sri Aurobindo. Ignorance, according to Sri Aurobindo, is not an original power of creating unrealities and illusions, but it is a development by limitation from Knowledge. From the point of view of the descent of consciousness, it is knowledge hiding itself partially. It is to be differentiated from that of the ascent of consciousness which is developing knowledge. Ignorance arises from the third poise of the Supermind, its projecting and apprehending activity in which it looks at an aspect of itself as if it were an object other than itself. Ignorance arises from this apprehending status and the function of the Supermind. Ignorance is not entirely devoid of consciousness. It is in Sri Aurobindo's language, half-light and half-shadow. Sri Aurobindo thinks that in the Indian ascetic ideal, the great Vedāntic formula "one without a second" has not been understood properly in relation to the other

---

13 *The Life Divine*, p. 341.

formula equally imperative, "All this is Brahman". To enjoy Himself in material existence, divinized so as to reveal and not to veil Him, the Divine created the world which is a manifestation of this creative delight through Consciousness-Force in His Divine Being. The instrument of this self-manifestation is the Supermind, the link between the unitary divine existence and the world of multiplicity.

In his opinion, evil and falsehood are products of Ignorance and being products of Ignorance, these cannot exist where Ignorance does not reside. Naturally again question will arise as to why should Brahman at all throw out force of consciousness to create in itself these worlds of forms?

Sri Aurobindo is quite categorical in maintaining that Ignorance has been brought into existence by the process of consciousness. He cites from *Muṇḍaka Upaniṣad* and *Taittirīya Upaniṣad* at the beginning of his chapter on "The Origin of Ignorance",[14] in support of his claim about the origin of Ignorance.

Muṇḍaka Upaniṣad I.1.8 states:

> *tapasā cīyate brahma tato 'nnamabhijāyate* ।
> *annāt prāṇo manaḥ satyaṁ lokāḥ...* ॥

> By energism of consciousness Brahman is massed; from that Matter is born and from Matter Life and Mind and the worlds.[15]

He also quotes a passage from *Taittirīya Upaniṣad*, II.6 stating:

> He desired, "May I be Many", he concentrated in *tapas*, by *tapas* he created the world; creating, he entered into it; entering, he became the existent and the beyond-existence, he became the expressed and the unexpressed, he became knowledge and ignorance, he became the truth and the falsehood: he became the truth, even all this whatsoever that is. "That Truth" they call him.[16]

---

14 *The Life Divine*, bk II, Pt 1, chap. XII.

15 "The Origin of the Ignorance", *The Life Divine*, p. 588.

16 Ibid., p. 588. Also *Taittirīya Upaniṣad*, II.6.

so 'kāmayata, bahu syāṁ prajāyeyeti । *sa tapo 'tapyata* । *sa tapastaptvā* । *idaṁ* । *sarvamasṛjata* । *yadidaṁ kiñca* ।*tat sṛṣṭvā tadevānuprāviśat* । *tadanupraviśya* । *saccatyaccābhavat* । *niruktaṁ cāniruktaṁ ca* । *nilayanaṁ ca anilayanaṁ ca* । *vijñānaṁ ca avijñānaṁ ca* । *satyaṁ ca anṛtaṁ ca satyama bhavat* । *yadidaṁ kiñ ca* । *tat satyamityācakṣate* ।

Sri Aurobindo establishes thus, evil and falsehood as the by-products of the world movement; to quote from Sri Aurobindo:

> the sombre flowers of falsehood and suffering and evil have their root in the black soil of the Inconscient.[17]
>
> Falsehood and Evil are, unlike Truth and Good, very clearly results of the Ignorance, and cannot exist where there is no Ignorance.[18]

Evils in Relation to the Individual

Evils, to be reckoned as evils, resulting out of interaction of consciousness, are episodic in nature. This intermittent or occasional aspect of evils, contra absoluteness of the Supreme Reality has already been discussed. Since the cosmic manifestation of the universe is in Time, and whatever occurs in Time is a historical phenomenon, we may admit that evils are in a sense historical phenomena. It is needless to admit that by maintaining Brahman is the Timeless and Time, Sri Aurobindo has given rise to lots of confusion. In this article, there is not much scope for discussing about Sri Aurobindo's notion of Time. However, he has said distinctly that *Īśvara*, the omniscient and omnipotent All-ruler by his Śakti, by his conscious Power, manifests himself in Time and governs the universe. To Sri Aurobindo's viewpoint evils are just certain happenings, certain forms of cosmic manifestation of consciousness. Evils-like phenomena to be perceived as ghastly, obnoxious and threatening presuppose mental-consciousness. Sri Aurobindo admits that evils, suffering and falsehood are facts of the world-consciousness and strongly resisted the move to dump evils and similar phenomena as fictions and unrealities. The individual valuation of the movements of consciousness "one of the greatest powers of the human mentality".[19] Hence the role of human individual, especially that of human mentality, is significant and positive in our understanding of evils.

Sri Aurobindo has allocated a definite provision for individual also in his metaphysics of *The Life Divine*. The question may be asked, as to who is an individual?

---

17 'The Origin of Falsehood and Evil', *The Life Divine*, p. 622.

18 *The Life Divine*, p. 602.

19 Ibid., p. 420.

> Thus when we speak of an individual we mean ordinarily an individualization of mental, vital and physical being separate from all other beings, incapable of unity with them by its very individuality.
>
> If we go beyond three terms of mind, life and body, and speak of the soul or individual self, we still think of an individualized being, separate from all others, incapable of unity and inclusive mutuality, capable at most of a spiritual contact and soul-sympathy.[20]
>
> By individual we mean normally something that separates itself from everything else and stands apart, though in reality there is no such thing anywhere in existence: it is a figment of our mental conceptions useful and necessary to express a partial and practical truth.[21]

If we carefully go through these passages we may have some idea about the nature of individual in Sri Aurobindo's metaphysics. The individual in his world-view has to be understood as the product of the creative, in the sense of self-manifesting, action of Infinite Consciousness-Force.

> There is a phase or movement of the self-manifestation, a descent into an apparent material inconscience, an awakening of the individual out of the Inconscience. . . .[22]

In the first place, the individual is an individualized being. Again Sri Aurobindo considers individual as "a practical constitution of our consciousness devised to centralize activities of Nature in us".[23] He maintains that individualization of our being exists because of our "world-being" and further, "by virtue of a consciousness which uses the world-being for experience of its possibilities of individuality".[24] Thus he introduces a world-being and individuating consciousness which is the cause of all our self-experience and world-experience. For him cosmic differentiations and the multiple

---

[20] "The Eternal and the Individual", *The Life Divine*, p. 390.

[21] Ibid.

[22] Ibid., p. 382.

[23] Ibid., p. 384.

[24] Ibid., p. 385.

individualities are the power of the Infinite being which is being constantly displayed by the Infinite being out of Delight. Here we need to be very cautious in distinguishing Sri Aurobindo's position from that of Śaṅkarācārya. For Sri Aurobindo our individualization in the world is a becoming of that Self, and the world is also a becoming of that Self. Thus, in this philosophy, cosmos and individual are manifestations of a transcendent Self.

It should not be supposed that individual has been accorded an inferior status. Since individual has the power of self-transcendence and the power of self-transformation by self-knowledge, God cannot be held to be disastrous or ruthless. Sri Aurobindo offers an opportunity to individuals to understand their significance in the whole of cosmic process of manifestation. The following forthright remark is noteworthy:

> In that power lies the justification of individual existence.[25]

According to Sri Aurobindo, the eternal Brahman, the Īśvara, by his *yoga-māyā*, by the power of his Consciousness-Force self-manifests. The Omnipresent Consciousness is beyond the cosmic manifestation, it is within the cosmic manifestation and it is also immanent in each individual. Broadly, this three-tier existence of Consciousness is Sri Aurobindo's metaphysics.

> We see then that there are three terms of the one existence, transcendent, universal and individual, and that each of these always contains secretly or overtly the two others.[26]

Why Should Brahman Throw Out Force of Consciousness into Forms?

In this case, the most baffling questions are the "why" question and also the "how" question. Sri Aurobindo also had these very questions in his mind in his endeavour to explain the nature of ignorance and its consequent suffering. The vexed question, why Brahman should throw out force of consciousness into forms, is none the less challenging. He has placed ignorance:

---

25 "The Eternal and the Individual", *The Life Divine*, p. 404.

26 Ibid., p. 403.

> as a part of the movement of the One Absolute Being, a development of its consciousness knowingly adopted, to which it is not forcibly subjected but which it uses for its cosmic purpose.[27]
>
> If then, being free to move or remain eternally still, to throw itself into forms or retain the potentiality of form in itself, it indulges its power of movement and formation, it can be only for one reason, for delight.[28]

The question as to why does this manifestation take place? Sri Aurobindo answers:

> . . . the only reasonable explanation of such a paradoxical manifestation or creation is that it is a cosmic game, a *līlā*, a play, an amusement of the Divine Being.[29]

We may conjecture variously about such a paradoxical manifestation. It may be supposed to be a pretension of the Divine being to make itself appear as an undivine: the Divine being, presumably comparable with a stage performer or a film star who is enacting someone else's role for the sole pleasure of a false show. It may be suggested that the Divine has created the undivine, created ignorance, created suffering and other evils to be ecstatic about its own abundance of creativity. Does it not sound to be ridiculous and vain? Some have portrayed the Divine Being in the image of a powerful but selfish and wicked human being. To retain God's glory and power some inferior creatures have been created by God so that those creatures praise and glorify Him. When Sri Aurobindo is presenting his view of Divine *līlā*, it would be erroneous to suppose that any such rash, "crudely stated"[30] viewpoint would receive any sympathy from Aurobindo.

Some may propose an interpretation of *līlā* which is less obnoxious. Whatever explanation is offered it may sound awkward. Sri Aurobindo has made two points clear which are very much required in order to make sense of this Divine play or *līlā*. His first

---

27 "The Eternal and the Individual", *The Life Divine*, p. 589.

28 "Delight of Existence: The Problem", *The Life Divine*, p. 100.

29 "The Divine and the Undivine", *The Life Divine*, p. 426.

30 Ibid., p. 426.

observation is that it has to be understood that imperfection is a necessary requisite for making sense of manifestation and second observation is that the evolutionary manifestation requires an intermediate stage of manifestation for human consciousness, "a stage as the mental consciousness of man, part knowledge, part ignorance, a middle power of being still leaning on the Inconscient but slowly rising to the all-conscious Divine Nature",[31] a stage that marks a decisive point of transition.

According to Sri Aurobindo, *Māyā* of Brahman is at once the magic and the logic of an infinitely variable oneness.

> As with being of Brahman, so with its consciousness, *māyā*: it is not bound to a finite restriction of itself or to one state or law of its action: it can be many things simultaneously, have many coordinated movements which to the finite reason may seem contradictory; it is one but innumerably manifold, infinitely plastic, inexhaustibly adaptable.[32]

Sri Aurobindo's *Māyā* is the Supreme, Universal Consciousness-Force of the Eternal and Infinite Brahman. As it is by its very nature unbound and illimitable, it can put forth many states of consciousness at a time, many dispositions of its force without ceasing to be the same Consciousness-Force forever:

> *Māyā* is at once transcendental, universal and individual; it is the Supreme Supra-cosmic being that is aware of itself as All-Being, as the Cosmic Self, as the Consciousness-Force of Cosmic nature, and at the same time experiences itself as the individual being and consciousness in all existences.[33]

Hence from this metaphysical perspective the Absolute One can see itself, experience itself triply, whether from above in the transcendent Existence, from between in the Cosmic Self or from below in the individual conscious being.

According to Sri Aurobindo, a being's ignorance of himself and of the Self of all is the outcome of an original cosmic Ignorance. This

---

[31] "The Eternal and the Individual", *The Life Divine*, p. 427.

[32] "Brahman, Purusha, Ishwara", *The Life Divine*, p. 358.

[33] Ibid., p. 358.

cosmic Ignorance gives rise to self-limitation, divisions in living beings, division in consciousness, division in will and force, division and limitation in knowledge, egoism, misuse of knowledge and will, disharmony, weakness and suffering. Thus we find among many factors that owe their origin to cosmic Ignorance, suffering an exemplar of evil has its origin. Sri Aurobindo insists upon the feature of exclusiveness as the essence of ignorance, in his language "exclusiveness is the very soul of ignorance".[34] In his metaphysical system if anything is to be held responsible for suffering and evil, it is the "strange" power of Consciousness. For him for that reason it appeared to be more important to find out details about the principle of operation of Consciousness, its power and process of operation. He enquires, "How is it that the Ignorance exists?" The other pertinent question is that, "How has any principle or power in the Infinite Self-awareness been able to put self-knowledge behind it and exclude all but its own characteristic-limited action?"[35] He puts the question a little bit differently,[36] when he asks, "How could this manifold ignorance or this narrowly self-limiting and separative knowledge arise and come into action or maintain itself in action in an Absolute Being who must be Absolute Consciousness and, therefore, cannot be subject to ignorance?"

Brahman's Delight

According to Aurobindo, thus we find that Brahman, as an inherent self-consciousness inseparable from its being, throws itself out as a force of movement of consciousness which is creative of forces, forms and worlds. Neither compelled by its own nature, its potentiality is creative. Why should Brahman throw out force of consciousness into forms? It can be only for one reason, for Delight.

> To loose forth and enjoy this infinite movement and variation of its self-delight is the object of its extensive or creative play of Force.[37]

Now the question may be raised as to how are we to account for

---

34 "The Knowledge and the Ignorance", *The Life Divine*, p. 506.

35 Ibid., p. 506.

36 "The Origin of Ignorance", *The Life Divine*, p. 588.

37 "Delight of Existence: The Problem", *The Life Divine*, p. 101.

the universal presence of grief, suffering and pain? It is well known that the very starting point of all schools of Indian philosophy, except the Cārvākas, the life is fraught with suffering. No one can escape from suffering so far his existence is bound with this world. But the universal existence of suffering does not justify its existence. To grasp the exact implication of this issue, we may further elaborate the question into the following sub-questions:

> 1A. "All being Saccidānanda, how can pain, suffering at all exist?"[38]
>
> 1B. "How came the sole and Infinite Existence–Consciousness–Bliss to admit into itself that which is not bliss, that which seems to be its positive negation?"[39]
>
> 1C. "All-Delight being necessarily all-good and all-love, how can evil and suffering exist in Saccidānanda?"[40]

Thus, the problem of evil may assume an ethical tone. Sri Aurobindo, however, has difficulty in accepting the meaning of the term "All Delight" be understood in terms of the ideas of love and good. He accuses human mentality for introducing this sort of dualistic and divisional conception of things. He opines that in the Vedāntic concept of Saccidānanda which is one, the dualistic and divisional concept of good and love is not to be found. He ridicules the attempt of human thought to force an ethical meaning into the whole of Nature. According to him, it is not correct for human beings to judge all things from the standpoint to which he has evolved in course of the process of evolution. He thinks that ethical viewpoint prevents human beings from arriving at real knowledge and complete sight. Sri Aurobindo pronounces clearly that "Material Nature is not ethical".[41] In his view animal or vital nature is also non-ethical, although as it progresses it manifests the crude material out of which the higher animal evolves the ethical impulse. According to Aurobindo, blame and condemnation or rather self-blame or self-

---

[38] *The Life Divine*, p. 103.

[39] Ibid., p. 104.

[40] Ibid.

[41] Ibid., p. 105.

condemnation are the beginning of true ethics. When we blame others without applying the same law to ourselves, we are not speaking with a true ethical judgement.[42]

In Sri Aurobindo's philosophy all is a divine manifestation, hence what is marked as undivine must be essentially divine. Sri Aurobindo writes:

> A primal reality — the Self, the Divine, Brahman — which is forever pure, perfect, blissful, infinite: its infinity is not affected by the limitations of relative things, its purity is not stained by our sin and evil; its bliss is not touched by our pain and suffering; its perfection is not impaired by our defects of consciousness, knowledge, will, unity.[43]

According to Śaṅkara, there is oneself which in *māyā* appears falsely as many individual selves. In Śaṅkara's view the individuality ceases to be real in the state of liberation For Sri Aurobindo, there is one Self who manifests Himself as many individual selves. In this view individuality is real and abiding though fundamentally the many selves are none but the Supreme Self. They are the many self-varied centres of the Supreme Self of its self-knowledge and self-enjoyment.

Thus we find that the background of Sri Aurobindo's metaphysics is Vedic and Upaniṣadic or Vedāntic. Though the basic categories of the integral Advaita of Sri Aurobindo are found in the Vedas, Upaniṣads and *Gītā*, his world-view is more comprehensive and positive in its practical implications than is found in these ancient texts of spiritual philosophy and *yoga*. The main spirit of Sri Aurobindo's Pūrṇādvaita view and the Vedānta view merge in their belief in an uncreated, immaterial principle of being which is free from the material force, vital force and mental force.

Evils Are Purposive

Sri Aurobindo is convinced that what are presented to mental consciousness as adverse and evil have individual utility and cosmic utility. This perspective of Sri Aurobindo may seem to be downright bizarre. Common sense may revolt against this viewpoint as totally

42 *The Life Divine*, p. 105.

43 Ibid., p. 409.

unfounded. How can we discover utility amidst outpouring dismay of suffering, grief and other shapes of evils? The very notion of utility is ambiguous and evokes many questions. How do we measure utility? Should we interpret utility in the pragmatic sense, as practicality? In the domain of economics, business and other related studies interested in the language of profit and loss, for whom utility is interpreted in terms of profitability. Utility is such a misnomer, which may give a false impression about what Sri Aurobindo meant by it. Let us proceed with Sri Aurobindo's remark:

> For without experience of pain we would not get all the infinite value of the divine delight of which pain is in travail, all ignorance is a penumbra which environs an orb of knowledge, every error is significant of the possibility and the effort of a discovery of truth.[44]

Sri Aurobindo further points out:

> But at the same time our present feeling of this evil and imperfection, the revolt of our consciousness against them is also a necessary valuation; for if we have first to face and endure them, the ultimate command on us to reject, to overcome, to transform the life and the nature.[45]

Now evil, sufferings are creations of Mind Consciousness but according to Sri Aurobindo it is not right to maintain that these are unreal circumstances, non-existent in God. Hence it may be suggested by some that it is better to be indifferent to these dualities and to get out of the manifestation into God's being. In Aurobindo's philosophy evils are creations of Mind Consciousness but Mind is only secondarily responsible. Aurobindo harps on saying that these are all creations of Divine Consciousness. These functions of Divine Consciousness are not eternal, not in the fundamental truth of being. This does not imply that Divine manifestation is to be viewed as a mistake of the Divine Consciousness. Sri Aurobindo uses the concept of *līlā* to designate this self-creation of the Absolute Brahman. His view may be summed up in his own words as follows:

> A Reality of Oneness manifesting itself in reality of numberless

[44] *The Life Divine,* p. 424.

[45] Ibid.

forms and powers of its being is what we confront everywhere.

Sri Aurobindo is confident in maintaining that "there must be some necessity" or utility of wrong and evils in the working of the Omnipresent Divine Reality. Are not these remarks simply gibberish? Sri Aurobindo cites quotations from scriptural sources at the beginning of a chapter entitled "The Origin of Falsehood and Evil" to explain the existence beyond evil and for that matter of good. The following is the quotation from the *Gītā* II.50 maintaining:

> *buddhiyukto jahātīha ubhe sukṛtaduṣkṛte* ।
>
> One whose intelligence has attained to Unity, casts away from him both sin and virtue.[46]

The other quotation is from the *Taittirīya Upaniṣad* II.9:

> He who has found the bliss of the Eternal is afflicted no more by the thought, "Why have I not done the good? Why have I done the evil?" One who knows the Self extricates himself from both these things.

The question comes up: what happens to all sorts of evils? Sri Aurobindo refers to the *Gītā* V.15:

> The Lord accepts the sin and the virtue of none; because knowledge is veiled by Ignorance, mortal men are deluded.[47]

It is difficult to resist quoting the following passage from Sri Aurobindo's "The Eternal and the Individual":

> For certain practical ends we have to say that a thing is good or bad, beautiful or ugly, just or unjust and act upon that statement. . . . A great war, destruction or violent all-upheaving revolution, for example, may present itself to us as an evil, a virulent or catastrophic disorder, and it is so in certain respects, results, ways of looking at it; but from others, it may be a great good, since it rapidly clears the field for a new good or a more satisfying order.[48]

Instead of predicting doom for mankind, Sri Aurobindo reveals

---

46 "The Origin of Falsehood and Evil", *The Life Divine*, p. 620.

47 *nādatte kasyacit pāpaiṁ na caiva sukṛtaiṁ vibhuḥ* ।
ajñnenāvṛtaiṁ Jñāiṁ tena nuhyanti jantavaḥ ॥

48 *The Life Divine*, p. 400.

that man can overcome evil. Philosophical explanation of evils is to make man aware that however devastating and traumatic evils may be, man bears within him the courage and capacity to go beyond these evils.

References

Aurobindo, Sri, 2001, *The Life Divine*, Pondicherry: Sri Aurobindo Ashram.

Viswarupananda, Swami (ed.), 1996, *Vedāntadarśanam*, vol. 2, Kolkata: Udbodhan Karyalaya.

6

"Sāvitrī" as a Religio-Literary Composition

Raghunath Ghosh

It is a remarkable fact that Sri Aurobindo, the philosopher and *yogī* is also a poet. In consonance with his philosophy of integralism, as a part, he has wielded an intense art form, developed an integral style and word power to match his experience and vision. This statement is true of his poetry in general and *Sāvitrī* in particular. Like his philosophy, the material of his poetry is provided by a developing pattern of spiritual experiences and realizations. Hence the poetry of Sri Aurobindo is to be understood in terms of motion of poetic integralism, i.e. the universe of poetry lying beyond ordinary creative intelligence. Sri Aurobindo's poetry is generally called "overhead poetry" or the poetry of the overmind. The overmind, in terms of Sri Aurobindo's philosophy, is nearest to the identity of being and becoming, the supermind, the sovereign truth — consciousness. From this plane of expression and vision, word and rhythm become at once intense and immense to the utmost. The overhead utterance is marked by a value and form which all the realities of the subordinate planes fuse in something diversely ultimate, and variously transfigured by an inmost oneness with the cosmic harmony and with the supercosmic mystery. Language in such an atmosphere becomes *mantra*. Sri Aurobindo's poetry has shown how and when *mantra* is possible. A gate of dreams ajar on mystery's verge.

Most of the studies of Sri Aurobindo's poetry have been undertaken with reference to the poetry of Europe. This is but natural, since he wrote in a European language. But it is also a fact that a great bulk of his literary criticism is devoted to studies of Sanskrit literature. Sri Aurobindo has written extensively on Vyāsa,

Vālmīki and Kālidāsa. He rendered into English Kālidāsa's *Vikramorvaśīya* and *Kumārasambhava.* It is true that Sri Aurobindo's perspective of literary criticism has always been that of world literature, yet he always stressed the fact that the poetry of *mantra* has been found in the Vedas, Upaniṣads and *Bhagavad-Gītā,* besides elsewhere. He also wrote *Vāsavadattā,* modelled on the drama by Bhāsa. The chapter on Sanskrit literature of Sri Aurobindo's *Foundations of Indian Culture* is an instance of writing the history of the literature in a creative manner. It is surprising that no discussion is undertaken by way of evaluating Sri Aurobindo's poetry in the light of religious and aesthetic standpoints. And it is precisely to this task that I propose to address myself.

II

The Sanskrit rhetoricians have laid importance on the use of *alaṁkāra* in a Kāvya. According to Daṇḍin, the attributes or merits or excellences that go wholly to adorn or embellish Kāvyas are called *alaṁkāra* (figure of speech).[1] Vāmana also admits the use of *alaṁkāra* as the cause of poetic beauty. The word *kāvya,* as Vāmana observed, applies strictly to word and sense embellished with *guṇas* (excellence) and *alaṁkāra* (poetic figures).[2] Sri Aurobindo also used series of similies and other *alaṁkāras* in his *Sāvitrī,* perhaps keeping their theories in view. When Aśvapathy, Sāvitrī's father, realized the higher harmonies of Consciousness, the unity of truth and idea has been described by a beautiful simile:

> There is a gulf between thought and fact; ever they replied like bird to calling bird.[3]

We come across many such passages where he used different figures of speech.

> *As a star unaccompanied moves through heaven*
> *Unastonished by the immensities of space,*

---

1 *kāvyaśobhākarān dharmānalamkārān pracakṣate* I — *Kāvyādarśa,* chap. 2

2 *kāvyam grāhyamalaṁkārāt* I — *Kāvyālaṁkarasūtravṛtti,* 1.1.1; *kāvyaśabdo 'yam guṇālaṁkārasamskṛtayoḥ śabdārthayorvartate* — Commentary *Kāvyālaṁkārasūtravṛtti,* ed. A. Basu, 3rd edn., Calcutta, 1971

3 Aurobindo 1995: 317.

Travelling infinity by its own light,
The great are strongest when they stand alone.[4]

As an evidence of the use of Rūpaka *alaṁkāra* in which Sri Aurobindo shows his par excellence, the following passage may be quoted:

Offered to the daughter of infinity
His passion-flower of love and doom she gave.[5]

Let us consider the reasons of Sri Aurobindo's writing *Sāvitrī* in a poetic language but not in a language of prose. The poetic feelings of Sri Aurobindo refused to be rendered in a language of prose. The reason for this is found in *Dhvanyāloka* where Ānandavardhana says:

> Poetic language ... is different from the language of prose; it arouses in the reader echoes and feelings in word, aesthetic experience foreign to prose whose value is purely informative and didactic. The words in a prose text have, according to Indian linguistics, two or, in the view of some writers, three powers, of which the chief one is the power of denotation (*abhidhā*), the faculty, that is, of denoting a given object. Clearly, the power to arouse aesthetic experience cannot be reduced to this.[6]

From this statement it is known that the power of denotation (*abhidhā*) which is prominent in prose cannot give rise to the aesthetic excellence, and hence poetic language in which the suggestive meaning is prominent is necessary. Denotation is based upon words alone. The suggestiveness depends on both words and senses.[7] Sri Aurobindo also emphasizes on the suggested meaning of *Sāvitrī*. Through this poetry Sri Aurobindo tries to suggest that just as *Sāvitrī* does one can also be the abode of knowledge, religion, love, emotion, power and yogic experience, and can transform oneself into Divinity. And after bringing down the supramental consciousness in oneself

---

4 Aurobindo 1995: 522-23.

5 Ibid.: 9.

6 *An Introduction to Indian Poetics*, Macmillan, p. 78.

7 *evam tāvadvācakatvā-danyadeva vyañjakatvam; itaśca vācakatva – vyañjakatvasyanyatvam yadvācakatvam śabdaikāśrayamitat-tuśabdāśrayanarthāśrayam ca śabdārthayordvayorapi vyañjakatvasya pratipāditatvāt* । — *Dhavanyāloka*, chap. III, p. 202 (K. Krishnamoortti), Delhi: Motilal Banarsidass, 1982

one can conquer death, the king of decay, and can prepare in this world firm footing of an immortal world, full of bliss where there is no suffering, no injustice, after constructing a bridge over the inaccessible ocean situated in the midst of heaven and earth. This is the message of *Sāvitrī.* The epic opens with the description of the first flush of self-consciousness from the sleeps of unconscious, which is symbolized as Dawn (*Uṣā*). The Divine Consciousness (*Bhāgavatī Cetanā*) comes to this kingdom of ignorance in order to make Her manifested and give Her Divine glimpses. But after noticing that this world, full of ignorance, is not prepared for Her absolute manifestation, She returns to Her own abode. At last Divine Mother comes to this world as an incarnation and She is named *Sāvitrī* who conquers Death, the main obstacle to bring Supramental power and consciousness. The Dawn indicates or suggests the arrival of Supramental consciousness in this mortal world. The poet of *Sāvitrī* stands as the maker of a new age of poetry as of life and literature. Its appearance in these days of distress and deviation brings new hope. Let us salute the Dawn, that "harmonizes with the dawns that shone out before and those that now must shine".

The king of Aśvapati who was childless performed austerities and sacrifices for a longer period of time to have a child. When his performance of sacrifices matured, the Goddess Sāvitrī appeared before him from the sacrificial fire and being pleased agreed to offer some boons. As per his boon Aśvapati was blessed with a daughter called Sāvitrī (as per the name of the goddess). In course of time Sāvitrī grew up and the king arranged her marriage with Prince Satyabān, the son of King Dyumatsen, who was living in the forest. When the parents approved this marriage, Nārada disapproved it after knowing that Satyabān, though brave, intelligent, generous, etc, was destined to die after one year. But Sāvitrī determined to marry him in spite of knowing this and ultimately the marriage took place. Just after one year or so, Satyabān wanted to go to the forest to fetch sacrificial wood. Thinking the probable danger Sāvitrī wanted to give him company, but she was not allowed after considering many things. Due to having strong will-force Sāvitrī at last accompanied him to the forest. After cutting wood, Satyabān had experienced severe pain in the head and Sāvitrī offered her lap to put his head. Within a short while Satyabān had fallen eternally asleep and Sāvitrī saw the God of Death (Yama) waiting for her husband. She found that Satyabān's soul, separated from his physical mortal frame, was taken by the God of Death. Sāvitrī had opened a dialogue with Yama and followed him until he became pleased. Ultimately the God of Death had to surrender to Sāvitrī being pleased on her devotion to her husband and argumentation with him. He committed to offer her some boons, one of which was the restoration of her husband's life. In this way Sāvitrī had won the death and came back to the hermitage with her husband Satyabān.

In *Sāvitrī* Sri Aurobindo has tried to show the symbolic presentation of an ideal woman. In this peace of literature we get an ideal image of a woman who becomes victorious on Yama, the God of Death, which symbolically suggests the victory of love over death.[8]

Sāvitrī is painted by Sri Aurobindo as a devoted wife towards her husband and she acts as per the sweet will of husband. The term "Sāvitrī" was derived from the word *savitā* meaning the Sun. The power of the Sun is called "Sāvitrī" because it protects, creates and maintains the universe. Sāvitrī is described in such a way that she is an incarnation of Divine Mother who is entrusted with liberating an individual from the clutches of Death. It suggests that the Divine Mother can transform Death to immorality. It is described in the following way:

The Mighty Mother sits in lucent calm
And holds the eternal child upon her knees,
Attending the day when he shall speak to fate.[9]

Sāvitrī is a warrior-woman who becomes glorious in encountering Death. She has destroyed Death and brought immortality for a man. It is Sāvitrī to whom a *choice is given between life and death*. She prefers to conquer Death with the help of her will-force and love. It is *a right to love and live*. Sri Aurobindo believes that it is only love, which can be a bridge between man and God. It is the force of disintegrity

[8] Mishra 1989: 4.

[9] *Sri Aurobindo Centenary Library*, Pondicherry, vol. 29, 1977, p. 661.

or a bliss of perfect union. Sāvitrī is very much brave due to having genuine love towards her husband and hence Sri Aurobindo metaphorizes her as *"The Flame"* "who can destroy even death".

It is Yama who for the first time came in contact with "Mighty Mother" who is a *claimant of Immortality* and an *embodiment of the Flaming Truth.* This is a kind of worship of the Mother Goddess even by the Lord of Death.

> Let deathless eyes look into the eyes of Death . . . transform earth's death into immortal life.[10]

On request of Yama the Divine Mother exposed herself and given him supreme enlightenment. It is described as "Eternity looked into the eyes of Death".

Sāvitrī, in fact, performs *yoga* through which she "goes" down to her heart to know her own self and finds out different levels of consciousness. In spite of knowing her husband's death within one year she marries him challenging her own fate. Because she is overconfident that she will be in a position to change her destiny. It is said:

> *My fate is what my spirits' strength can make.*
> *My fate is what my spirits' strength can bear.*[11]

The purpose of *yoga* of Sāvitrī is to know the real nature of herself. She gradually comes to know the course of evolution from Matter to Mind and the existence of psychic being. Through such meditation and concentration she knows herself and comes to know she lives in Infinity.

Sāvitrī, the conscious *Prakṛti*, conquers Yama (the King of Death) in debate, i.e. by wisdom and fearlessness and in this way she is able to bring Satyabān back to life. Satyabān has been transformed to *someone possessing the truth, which is the literal meaning of the term.* The term *aśvapaṭi* (the lord of life). The term *aśva* (horse), symbolizing life-energy. Hence Aśvapati has been painted by Sri Aurobindo as *the aspiring soul of man.*[12]

---

[10] Reddy 1989: 95-96.

[11] Ibid.: 96.

[12] Purani 1952: 203.

The *yoga* of Aśvapati has been interpreted by Sri Aurobindo as a symbol of human soul having descended on this earth from Divine heights and on the way of realizing the self and the world.[13] Aśvapati's *yoga* is for the divinization of his physical being. In Sri Aurobindo's philosophy this human body is much significant in the phenomenon of realization of the Divine. Even the mortal body can be transformed to a Divine one. Hence, his devotion to God is to divinize his physical being (*annamaya-koṣa*) at the initial stage. After this stage his soul is free from ignorance. As soon as it is free from ignorance, it becomes the substratum of a higher knowledge, power and bliss. Aśvapati has performed sacrifice to obtain a child, which is interpreted as his journey towards the occult world. This journey is only to do welfare of all people. At the end of this rigorous *sādhanā* he meets the Divine Mother and prays her to come down to this earth to save the humanity and to reduce a man's suffering.[14] Being satisfied on his austerity the Divine Mother has committed a boon to the king that she will grace the earth through her human manifestation:

> A new light shall break upon the earth, a new world shall be born, things that were promised shall be fulfilled.[15]

Sāvitrī is the Divine Mother who is *Prakṛti*. In the form of a seed she is in the form of Truth. She is the constructed bridge between man and God. Sri Aurobindo describes:

> *She is golden bridge, the wonderful fire*
> *The luminous heart of the unknown is she*
> *A power of silence in the depths of god;*
> *She is the force, the inevitable word,*
> *The magnet of our difficult ascent. . . .*[16]

The descent of Sāvitrī, the Mother Goddess, on the earth may be fruitful if there is a genuine aspiration on the part of human

---

[13] Purani 1952: 5.

[14] Mishra 1989: 20.

[15] Purani 1952: 6.

[16] *Sri Aurobindo Centenary Library*, Sri Aurobindo Ashram, Pondicherry, vol. 29, 1977, p. 661.

consciousness. Aśvapati's *yoga* is meant for his perfection. His upward journey is for the descent of Sāvitrī on this earth. From the death of Satyabān it is to be presumed that the death is inevitable in one's life and it is due to one's ignorance and suffering. The conquer over death and getting back to the life show that there is a life which is purified as well as transformed.[17]

When Truth dictates life and mind aspires for the Divinity supermind reveals. Our Matter, Mind and Life will be radically transformed when there is the manifestation of supramental consciousness. These Matter, Mind and Life will act as the vehicle of Truth and God. When mind aspires for the Divine light, the body will carry out the forces of the Divine. Ultimately a man will be able to conquer Death.

Sāvitrī in the form of a wife loyal to her husband has got power through which she snatches her husband from the cluster of Death. On the other hand, Sāvitrī in the form of Divine Mother provides immortality to a man after removing Death. In both the cases it is possible through love and devotion. Love has got an enormous power even capable of removing Death. This is the message we get from Sāvitrī.

The whole *kāvya*, i.e. *Sāvitrī*, is full of suggestion (*dhvani*) which is described as the soul of *kāvya* by the Sanskrit rhetoricians.[18] According to Ānandavardhana, *dhvani* can give a logical account of the poetic procedures to the satisfaction of the creative poet. In a successful *kāvya* there must be a prominent (*aṅgī*) *rasa*. When *rasa* is principal, it is called *dhvani*. When *rasa* is subsidiary, it should be called as *rasavādalaṁkāra*, but not *dhvani*. So, *dhvani* is the quintessence of poetry and *rasa* is the quintessence of *dhvani*.[19] In *Sāvitrī*, there is prominence of *dhvani* and hence, there is *rasa*.

Both Sri Aurobindo and the Sanskrit rhetoricians advocate that aesthetic experience (*rasa*) is impersonal, disinterested and universal delight. That is to say, a successful *kāvya* always conveys us a

---

17 S. Ghosh, *Poetry of Sri Aurobindo*, Chatuskon, p. 43.

18 *kāvyasyātmā Dhvaniriti . . .* । — *Dhyanyāloka*, p. 1

19 *vācyavācakacārututvahetūnām vividhātmanām rasādiparatā yatra sa dhvaneviṣaya mataḥ* । — *Dhyanyāloka* 2/4-5

supersensuous (*lokottara*) pleasure. From the sentences — "your enemy is dead", "your son is born", we may have some sort of pleasure which is purely this-worldly but not spiritual and hence, these sentences cannot be treated as *kāvya*. The cause of the spiritual pleasure is the object of knowledge if there is existence of suggestion followed by the presence of *guṇas* and *alaṁkāras*, and absence of defects.[20] Moreover, joy is always spiritual as it is in the nature of spirit. Every form of pleasure is the manifestation of the spirit, which is supported by Upaniṣadic statement — *ānando brahmeti vyajānāt*. The same idea has been expressed in the *Bṛhadāraṇyakopaniṣad* where Yājñavalkya said to Maitreyī that not indeed for the husband's sake the husband is dear to the wife, but for the sake of the self, the husband is dear.[21] There is a great difference between aesthetic experience and spiritual experience attained through contemplation upon the non-dual reality. Art experience cannot remain for long time and it ceases when the factors essential for this experience are withdrawn. On the other hand, the spiritual experience is permanent and hence, if it is attained, it does not cease.[22] That is why, Abhinavagupta compares this feeling (i.e. aesthetic experience) to the feeling due to the realization of Brahman.[23]

Sri Aurobindo also advocates the same view. According to him, beauty is of the Divine.

> There is a certain consciousness in which all things become full of beauty and *ānanda* — even what is painful and ugly becomes an outward play, and becomes suffused with the beauty and *ānanda* behind. It is specially the overmind consciousness of things — although it can be felt from time to time on other planes also. A

---

20 *ripuste mṛtah putrsaste jātaḥ ityādi vākyārthe jñānajanyāhlādasya na lokottaratvamiti na tatra kāvyatvaprasaktiḥ* । *yādṛśahinadan pratyarthanam kāraṇatā ca vyaṅgā vaiśiṣṭyena doṣasama-nādhikaraṇaguṇā-laṁkārasadbhāvasampāditacārutvena ca sambhavati* । — Commentary on verse 10, cu-I, *Kāvyādarśa* (K.Roy edition)

21 *na vā are patyuḥ kāmāya patiḥ priyo bhavatyātmanastu kāmāya patiḥ priyo bhavati* । — *Bṛhadāraṇyakopaniṣad* 4.4.6

22 Kane 2001: 388.

23 Jagannath Pathaka: *parabrahmasvādasabrahmacāritvam castvasya rasāsvādasya* । — Locana on *Dhvanyāloka*, p. 200; Aurobindo 1999: 135; Aurobindo 1997: 342

> great quality and the view of the Divine everywhere is necessary for this to come fully.[24]

Like Abhinavagupta, Sri Aurobindo also accepts the view that beauty belongs to Self and an object seems to be beautiful due to having the same Self within us. How can this beauty be realized? Sri Aurobindo says:

> The soul of beauty in us identifies itself with the soul of beauty in the thing created and feels in appreciation in the same divine intoxication and uplifting which the artist felt in creation.[25]

The artistic creation is capable of giving us disinterested delight and is necessarily the genius work. It comes out from something deep within which calls down the word, the vision, the light and power from a level above the normal mind (i.e. overmind). The joy of the Self cannot be realized through the mind "limited by intellectual activity, practical utility and the externals of life". The creation of beauty is poetry, as Sri Aurobindo has observed, it does not come within the purview of the reason. The beauty in poetry cannot be created through infrarational power, but it comes through suprarational power or by vision. This view of suprarational power cannot come from an ordinary mental platform, but it comes from the plane of overmind. The poetry which embodies suprarational beauty or vision and which comes from the overmind is described as *mantra*. So, we might characterize *Sāvitrī* as *mantra* in poetry, or the poetry of vision.

The derivative meaning of *mantra* also shows that reason of the infrarational stage of mind is of no use in the state of *mantra*. The derivative meaning of the term *mantra* is as follows: *mananāt trāyat iti mantraḥ* (i.e. that which saves us from making reflection is called *mantra*). *Mantra* is a kind of mental phenomenon, which, when in respect of a particular meaning of the word there is doubt as to the conflict with the other *pramāṇas*, causes knowledge in the form of *tarka* which becomes a promoter in removing that

---

24 Aurobindo, *The Future Poetry and Letters on Poetry, Literature and Art*, vol. 9, Sri Aurobindo Birth Centenary Library, Sri Aurobindo Ashram, Pondicherry, 1992, p. 495.

25 Ibid.

doubt.[26] That is to say, when a man tries to examine through his intellect that which he has known from other sources is called *mantra.* The *Sāvitrī* is a *kāvya* which does not provide a person having ordinary platform with any scope for examining it through his independent reason. As this *kāvya* is a product of suprarational mind, the poetic excellence cannot be realized through the ordinary mind and hence, the process of reflection (*manana*) is not possible so far as *Sāvitrī* is concerned. As it saves an individual from doing *manana,* it is called *mantra.*

That poetry cannot be defined in terms of ordinary human logic has been accepted by Viśvanātha, the celebrated Sanskrit rhetorician. According to him, poetry is a peculiarly unworldly phenomenon, an extraordinary creation of a supernatural, supernormal genius and hence, it cannot be governed by the rules of ordinary human intellect. In ordinary life sorrow comes from sorrow, fear follows fear, but in the world of poetry we find pleasure deriving from the painful, horrible and terrible situations.[27]

For Sri Aurobindo, poetry is the spontaneous overflow of the powerful feelings. It is not possible for a poet to give a logical account in respect of using a particular word or phrase to the critical intellect. It should be clearly borne in mind that no purpose is involved in the use of same phrase or some words repeatedly by a poet, but it is to a great extent spontaneous. A critic of *Sāvitrī* once wrote a letter to Sri Aurobindo enquiring as to why the word "great" is repeatedly used in the line about the "great unsatisfied godhead" (*Sāvitrī,* p. 19). In response to this, Sri Aurobindo says that his poetry is the spontaneous overflow of his feeling. He does not himself deliberately choose or arrange word or rhythm but only sees it as it comes in the very act of inspiration.

If there is any purpose of any kind, it also comes by and in the

---

[26] *mananam nāma śabdāvadhārite 'rthe mānāntaravirodhaśaṅkāyām tannirākuraṇānukūlatarkātmakajñānajanako mānasavyāpāraḥ* — *Vedānta-Paribhāṣā* by Swami Madhavananda, Advaita Ashram, 1970, p. 213.

[27] *hetutvam śokaharaṣādergatebhyo lokasaṁśrayāt, śokaharṣādayo loke jayantām nāma laukikāḥ, alaukikavibhāvatvam prāptebhyaḥ kāvyasaṁśrayāt* । *sukham sañjāyate tebhyaḥ sarvebhyo 'pīti kā kṣatiḥ* । — *Sāhitya-Darpaṇa* 3.6-7

> process of inspiration. . . . Thus I cannot tell you for what purpose I admitted the repetitions of the word "great". . . .[28]

The above-mentioned notion of poetry had been accepted by Ānandavardhana and Abhinavagupta also. The sorrow of the first poet at the separation of the curlew couple took the shape of a verse.[29] When Vālmīki was affected by noticing the killing of the loving curlew at the hands of the hunter, his sorrow became boundless. And it so stirred him, as to give rise to the impassioned song (*śloka*). Abhinavagupta has tried to analyse the case in the following way. The sage has no personal sorrow, but the sight of bird's sorrow stirs his aesthetic contemplation of universal sorrow which spontaneously overflows in metrical form.[30]

Poetry comes from the overmind and hence, it is described as *mantra*, having the power of vision. The poet (*kavi*) is a seer (*ṛṣi*) and can foresee Truth in the womb of the future (*krāntadarśī*). Without some kind of *yoga* a poet can neither realize, nor visualize what is going to happen in near or distant future. The yogic and poetic experience of Sri Aurobindo has been reflected in his *Sāvitrī* and hence, it becomes a successful poetry. So it is essential for a poet to rise to moments of yogic experience so that he can speak of Truth. That is why Vāmana, the Sanskrit rhetorician, prescribes *avadhāna* as a principal factor of the creation of a successful poetry. Now, let us explain the term *avadhāna*. One-pointed concentration is called *avadhāna*. It is, in other words, complete cessation of thoughts in respect of this-worldly objects. Only the concentrated mind can find the objects of description as such.[31] But Vāmana mentions clearly that our concentration will be limited to object of description alone.

---

[28] Sri Aurobindo, *Letters on Savitri*, vol. 29, pp. 839-40.

[29] *krauñcadvandvaviyogotthaḥ śoka ślokatvamāgataḥ* I — *Dhvanyāloka* 1.5

[30] *krauñcasya dvandvaviyogena sahacārihananodbhūtena sāhacarya-dhvaṁśenotthito yaḥ śokaḥ* . . . I — *Locana* on *Dhvanyāloka*, p. 86 (same edition)

[31] *cittaikāgryamavadhānam* I — *Kāvyālaṁkārasūtravṛtti* 1.3.17

vahirindriya-vyāpāra-viramān manasā vāhyārthaparoktiravadhānam I *avadhānasya prayojanamabhidhatte* I *avahitamiti* I *arthān paśyati* I *abhinavapāṭhārthānapratvandhānullikhatīyarthaḥ* I

— Commentary on *Kāvyālaṁkārasūtravṛtti*, on *sūtra* 1.3-7, ed. A. Basu, 3rd edn., Kolkata, 1971, p. 91

But Sri Aurobindo says that *yoga* is union with Supreme Being. If a poet is united with Supreme Being, he will see all future objects as such. But Vāmana is in favour of the acceptance of the phenomenon of concentration over the object of description only. All objects of description, I think, are the manifestation of Saccidānanda. If a poet has been united with the Supreme Being, all the objects of descriptions will be revealed to him as they are. So, Sri Aurobindo's view that a poet should have union with the Supreme Being is more logically intelligible.

Vision is the characteristic feature of a poet. That is, a poet must be a seer and revealer of truth. The greatest poets are endowed with a "large and powerful interpretative and intuitive vision of Nature and life and man". Homer, Shakespeare, Dante, Vālmīki and Kālidāsa are endowed with this fundamental characteristic, i.e. greatness.

The poet's vision is reflected in *Sāvitrī* and its language is the language of poetry of the Subjective Age. Therefore, *Sāvitrī* can throw a flood of light on the destiny of man.

It will have been seen by now that however intimate Sri Aurobindo's position has been with some of the leading figures of Sanskrit poetics, there are ways in which he could be said to have marked large departures. These are important in many ways. First, we may point to the fact that Sri Aurobindo's concept of poetry as *mantra* is something novel in the history of Indian poetics. Or to put the matter in other words, no philosopher in India before him brought poetry to bear upon philosophy in a measure and function of the aesthetic delight as linked by him directly to Śruti. This point has been hinted at by such thinkers as Abhinavagupta, but hardly in the overt manner as Sri Aurobindo does. Third, Sri Aurobindo has reinterpreted the concept (*rasa*) in Upaniṣadic lights, namely, that *rasa* is the taste and essence of things as they are. Accordingly, the experience of *rasa* becomes an experience of *ānanda,* though in a mortal measure. The difference, according to Sri Aurobindo, between aesthetic *rasa* and divine *ānanda,* is only a matter of degree, the one is a dwarfed image of the other. Thus poetry becomes related to Truth, and not a semblence (*sahodara*) of Truth. Hence, Sri Aurobindo has forwarded a new aesthetics based upon his concept of Reality as Consciousness-Force and delight. The notion of the planes of expression corresponds to the notion of the dimensions of the evolving mind. Thus poetry remains a cognitive affair all through. An allied point is about the role of imagination in man's spiritual or creative life. Imagination, for Sri Aurobindo, is something which is not non-intelligent, it is a sort of seeing intelligence, and it is this fashion that makes the poet a *ṛṣi*. The divine intelligence has been spoken of in the Vedas as *kavi*, and the deeper implication of this epithet has been exploited by Sri Aurobindo in such a way as never before. And lastly, he has made poetry a vehicle for communication of spiritual truths. In so doing he was a Vedic thinker of our age. This could not perhaps be said of any other thinker of Sanskrit poetics in the same sense. Sri Aurobindo would have endorsed Śaṅkara's view that art is a form of worship — *nirājandavidhiḥ* (*Saundaryalaharī*, verse 100). This is because the ideal of art, the Beautiful, is one with the Divine.

References

Aurobindo, Sri, 1995, *Sāvitrī*, Pondicherry: Sri Aurobindo Ashram.

———, 1997, *The Future Poetry*, Pondicherry: Sri Aurobindo Ashram.

———, 1999, *The Human Cycle: The Psychology of Social Development*, Pondicherry: Sri Aurobindo Ashram.

———, 2000, *Letters on Savitri*, ed. K.D. Sethna, Pondicherry: Sri Aurobindo Ashram.

Kane, P.V., 2001, *History of Sanskrit Poetics*, Delhi: Motilal Banarsidass.

Mishra, D.S., 1989, *Poetry and Philosophy in Sri Aurobindo's Savitri*, New Delhi: Harman Publishing House.

Purani, A.B., 1952, *Sri Aurobindo's Savitri: An Approach and a Study*, Pondicherry: Sri Aurobindo Karyalaya.

Reddy, V. Madhusudana, 1989, *Seven Studies in Sri Aurobindo*, Hyderabad: Institute of Human Study.

7

Sri Aurobindo's Observations on Heraclitus, an Aphoristic Philosopher*

Dilip Kumar Roy

Introduction

HERACLITUS, a Greek philosopher of Ephesus, was born, according to Diogenes,[1] around *c.* 504-01 BCE. Of this old enigmatic Ephesian we fail to determine his dates accurately. Sri Aurobindo characterizes Heraclitus as a Greek thinker having "intellectual stimulativeness" and also having "something of the antique psychic and intuitive vision and word of the older Mystics".[2] In him we find a tendency towards rationalism, but his reasoning mind does not possess that kind of "fluid clarity" which we find in the Sophists.[3]

Sri Aurobindo, while passing his observations on Heraclitus, has frequented the Veda and the Upaniṣads and also some schools of Indian philosophy like the Sāṁkhya and the Bauddha. As a result,

---

* Originally published in *Sri Aurobindo Mandir Annual* of Sri Aurobindo Pathamandir, Kolkata, in 2014.

1 Diogenes Laertius flourished in third century CE. His work is a compilation of material collected from various sources. In order to assess the historical value of Diogenes' statements we are to know, as far as possible, the particular source which he depends upon on any given occasion, and for the attainment of this knowledge we are to take up an enormous effort and a painstaking labour.

2 Sri Aurobindo Birth Centenary Library (SABCL), vol. 16: *The Supramental Manifestation*, p. 335.

3 Ibid. We may add a note on the Sophists here. The men whom we know as the Greek Sophists were not a school and shared no body of opinions: they just represented a trend or movement. They were mainly concerned with ethics and as to the relationship between laws and customs and nature. The most famous and perhaps the first Sophist was Protagoras of Abdera.

his in-depth observations have been very much challenging to the serious readers. Really speaking, Sri Aurobindo's unique presentation of the philosophy of Heraclitus rests on his intuitive vision of things, and this gives him a place of rare distinction among those famous critics and philosophers who have written about "the Word of Heraclitus".

Sri Aurobindo's writing on Heraclitus that spans seven sections comes as a ready spark produced by the discharge of the treatise of R.D. Ranade[4] on the philosophy of our Greek philosopher. Sri Aurobindo praises Ranade in great many ways, such as, Ranade's work comes to us as "a priceless gain", he "possesses in a superlative degree the rare gift of easy and yet adequate exposition", and his expression as well as his presentation have "a luminous clarity" and leave us "charmed, enlightened and satisfied".[5] But, in spite of all this, Sri Aurobindo finds *one or two difficult points* on which he does not accord with the conclusions taken up by Ranade. In a sense, we are grateful to Ranade: if he did not write such a treatise, we could have missed the rare insights — the rare gems, as it were — flashed by the intuitive vision of Sri Aurobindo regarding the aphoristic thought of Heraclitus.

Is Heraclitus a Mystic?

This is a questionable point over which many theologians, historians and philosophers opine differently. Otto Pfleiderer (1839–1908), a German Protestant theologian and religious historian, expressed his view by saying that Heraclitus was a mystic. Ramchandra Dattatreya Ranade (1886–1957), a great scholar and philosopher, rejected Pfleiderer's view totally. Heraclitus, according to Ranade, was one who stressed universal law and all-ordering Reason. Sri Aurobindo's observation on this point at issue sheds a new light on Heraclitus. He says that Pfleiderer's view might be a misconception, as stated by Ranade; but behind that misconception, says Sri Aurobindo, there is a certain truth, and the truth is that Heraclitus'

4 Ramchandra Dattatreya Ranade (1886–1957) was a scholar of great repute. He taught philosophy at Ferguson College, Poona. Later, he became Emeritus Professor of Philosophy and Vice-Chancellor of Allahabad University.

5 SABCL, vol. 16: *The Supramental Manifestation*, pp. 335-36.

derogatory criticism of Orphism[6] or the Mysteries of his time was not decisive; that is to say, Heraclitus is not ignoring the Orphic Mysticism or Mysteries of his time, but what he rebels against is "the darkness of the Dionysian ecstasy", i.e. "those aspects of obscure magic, physical ecstasy, sensual excitement which the Mysteries had put on in some at least of their final developments. . . ."[7] Thus Heraclitus, by repelling the dark side of the Mysteries, probes into "the secrets of existence" by the light of reason or with an "intuitive Apollonian inlook".[8] This does not mean that he is totally outside the mystic ring: he might be, to the utmost, "an intellectual child of the Mystics and of mysticism, although perhaps a rebel son in the house of his mother".[9]

Sri Aurobindo says that Heraclitus has something of the mystic style which we cannot overlook. And that mystic style consists in the art of what he expresses. Mostly, for expressing any philosophic idea, he takes recourse to what are called aphorism and epigram. Ranade rightly says that mere aphorism or epigram which is "usually a condensed or a pregnant effort of the intellect" is not mysticism.[10] But Ranade's description of Heraclitus' style as aphoristic and epigrammatic is not all that can be said of him; his style, as Sri

---

6 Orphism was the first known esoteric religion. It imposed the seal of the Mysteries so that the teachings given during initiation were not revealed to outsiders. Again, it gave a symbolic interpretation to existing myths such as the Theogony (the genealogy of the Greco-Roman Gods). The Orphic Mysteries were established in Greece and Southern Italy in the sixth century BCE. The symbolism of the Spiritual Marriage between God and the Soul goes back to the Orphic Mysteries; it descended from there via the Neo-Platonists into the stream of Christian tradition.

The word "Orphic" is related to the mythical poet Orpheus who was the prince of Thrace, the land to the north of Greece. His mother was Calliope, the Muse of epic poetry. Orpheus was said to have invented the Mysteries of Dionysus. "Under the Roman empire, around the time of early Christianity, there was a strong resurgence of Orphism as a mystery religion. The Orphic Hymns . . . date from this revival. Far from discarding the worship of Dionysus, Orphism now made him the very core of its doctrine" (Joscelyn Godwin, *The Golden Thread*, Quest Books, p. 49).

7 SABCL, vol. 16: *The Supramental Manifestation*, p. 336.

8 Ibid.

9 Ibid.

10 Ibid.

Aurobindo observes, in addition to what has been described by Ranade, is cryptic too. This cryptic character of his expressive thought "is enigmatic in the style of the mystics, enigmatic in the manner of their thought which sought to express the riddle of existence in the very language of the riddle".[11] Sri Aurobindo cites an example here — the example of the "ever-living Fire". As to what is to be meant by the "ever-living Fire", we should not go for its literal meaning merely, neither should we take on its metaphorical meaning. If we do so, we are sure to skip the character of Heraclitus' utterances. Thus, by "the ever-living Fire" is not to be meant "a material force of heat and flame" only, nor by it is to be meant the metaphorical sense of "eternal becoming": both of these meanings and every other thing connected with these are to be encompassed, says Sri Aurobindo, if we need to unearth its meaning hidden from us in a puzzling way. In his utterances, then, we find Heraclitus following a mystic style of hiding a truth or a thought, and to reveal that mystery we need to seek for cryptic clues instead of straightforward ones.

Now, as to the mystical language what become prominent to us are (a) its obscurity, and (b) its symbolic character. The language of Heraclitus is, undoubtedly, marked by these two. In that case, it would not be wiser enough to read him apart "from the earlier thought of the mystics".[12] Anyway, let us dwell a little, with examples, on the two above-mentioned characters that characterize the mystical language.

(a) There are many who are not inclined to conceal their activities and thoughts: for them the mystical language would seem to be obscure and meaningless; and not only that, it is verily possible that this language would prove a riddle to the generations of people who are yet to be born. Ranade finds an impossibility in understanding the meaning of the riddle involved in an utterance made by Heraclitus — *The Gods are mortals, men immortals.* Sri Aurobindo proclaims that the impossibility of making out the sense concealed in the above

[11] SABCL, vol. 16: *The Supramental Manifestation*, pp. 336-37.

[12] Ibid., p. 337.

statement is due to the fact that Heraclitus is not interpreted here from the mystic background. We are to find out the cryptic clues for understanding this riddle. Here one of the clues is the fundamental idea held by the mystics — the idea that *the immortal principle* is immanent in man, that the gods descend into *the workings of mortality*.[13] The riddle disappears from that aphoristic statement when we come to see that the "Vedic *ṛṣi* also invokes the Dawn, 'O goddess and human'; the gods in the Veda are constantly addressed as 'men'".[14] What we find in the Vedas is not anything different in the case of Heraclitus, since "the same words are traditionally applied to indicate men and immortals".[15]

The antitheses that we meet in Heraclitus' aphoristic statements are "no mere barren play upon words"; rather, they foreshadow "their reconciliation in the very terms of opposition".[16] Thus when Heraclitus says that "the name of the bow (*bio's*) is life (*bi'os*), but its work is death",[17] surely a meaning is intended, and the antithesis that we find here between life and death is not to be taken as something barren; what he intends by the word "bow" is "that principle of war . . . which makes cosmic existence an apparent process of life, but an actual process of death".[18]

(b) Heraclitus' language has a symbolic character, and hence it should not be given a literal sense more than enough, otherwise his thought would seem to be barren to us. As an example we can refer to his praise for the "dry soul" as against the "moist soul". These two phrases which are opposed to each other have symbolic meanings. "Dry soul", for him, symbolizes "the wisest and best" whereas the symbolic character of the "moist soul", says he, is that this type of soul inclines to "its natural

13 SABCL, vol. 16: *The Supramental Manifestation*, p. 337.

14 Ibid.

15 Ibid.

16 Ibid., p. 338.

17 Ibid.

18 Ibid.

delight in a sort of wine-drenched laxity".[19] What we see around are mostly "moist souls" since "it is a pleasure and satisfaction to souls to become moist". Such souls are earth-bound and pleasure-seeking. Dionysus as the wine-god inclines to what is pleasure-giving, and so he represents the "moist soul". And such "wine-drenched" life in which pleasure is sought cannot give us that sense of immortality which is found to be present amongst the wisest. Hence Dionysus, representing the "moist soul" or the "mortal" soul, is identical with Hades, the Lord of Death or the Lord of the dark underworld. Heraclitus' "dry soul" and "moist soul" are comparable to Sri Ramakrishna's "dry matchbox" and "moist matchbox". Sri Ramakrishna who represents divinity in humanity says that a person who aspires for Truth and Immortality is like a dry matchbox while one who seeks worldly pleasures is like a moist matchbox. The language of both of them, one belonging to the sixth-fifth century BCE and the other to the nineteenth century CE, was at once mystic and symbolic.

We cannot but mention here that Ranade explains Heraclitus' use of the term "dry soul" in a purely literal sense, in the sense of "the dry light of reason". Moreover, in the literal use of that term he finds enough evidence in favour of the view that Heraclitus was a rationalist and not a mystic. Further, Ranade takes the parallel expressions of the moist soul and Dionysus in a material sense: the drinking of wine cannot have ethical approbation. Ranade also says that Heraclitus' assertion that Dionysus and Hades are the same really means that wine-drinking cannot be encouraged as it is fatal to the health.

Ranade's version is not acceptable for the simple reason that Heraclitus, while speaking of the dry or the moist soul, has the soul (*psuche*), and not the intellect (*nous*), in his mind.

> *Psuche* corresponds roughly to the *cetas* or *citta* of Indian psychology, *nous* to *buddhi*; the dry soul of the Greek thinker to the purified heart-consciousness, *śuddha-citta,* of the Indian

---

[19] SABCL, vol. 16: *The Supramental Manifestation*, p. 338.

psychologists, which in their experience was the first basis for a purified intellect, *viśuddha buddhi*.[20]

And as to the moist soul we have already seen how, for Heraclitus, Dionysus, the god of the wine-born ecstasy, and Hades, the Lord of the dark underworld, are one.

Sri Aurobindo gives us a unique picture of the thought-evolution from the ancient to the modern times. In this historical procession of the human mind we cannot ignore the influence of the mystics on the intellectual thinking of the Greeks from Pythagoras to Plato. This historical thought-evolution starts with "the symbolic, intuitive, esoteric style and discipline of the Mystics, — Vedic and Vedāntic seers, Orphic secret teachers, Egyptian priests".[21] At the next turn of the thought-evolution we find how the human mind traverses "the path of a metaphysical philosophy", but this philosophy does not stand apart from the influence of the Mysteries since its aphoristic and cryptic style, its direct seizure of the Truth by intellectual vision rather than by careful ratiocination are still there, although it is intellectual in its method and aim.

The next period of the thought-evolution begins with philosophic rationalism, say, of Buddha or the Buddhists and the logical philosophers in India, of the Sophists and Socrates in Greece. But to say that the intellectual method began with them would not be an accurate statement; instead, we can say that this method remained unto itself and developed fully within its own self-horizon. "Heraclitus", says Sri Aurobindo, "belongs to the transition, not to the noontide of the reason".[22] And the result is his aphoristic thought with his cryptic style. The influence of the Mystics on Heraclitus is as certain as anything. But he is not a mystic out-and-out; he belongs to the family of the Mystics, but as "an intellectual child", as one with the tendency of being a rationalist.

The Word of Heraclitus

It might appear to us that as Heraclitus' thought has been expressed

---

20 SABCL, vol. 16: *The Supramental Manifestation*, p. 339.

21 Ibid.

22 Ibid.

in detached aphoristic statements, there is no dominant idea in his mind, — the very idea which serves as the root of those bits of aphoristic statements. But this is not really so: he has a fundamental view of existence itself which is used as the source of his aphoristic statements; naturally, such statements do not lie scattered and separated from one another; they are interrelated and interdependent. On the whole, there is a keynote of Heraclitus' thinking or there are some grand lines of his philosophy.

Heraclitus lays stress on his "Word" which we get as a translation of the Greek word *logos*. The *logos* is "an account or reality, and may also be . . . *that which is revealed by* the account. . . ."[23] That, for Heraclitus, the Reality is One becomes clear to us from his saying:

> It is wise to hearken, not to me, but to my Word, and to confess that all things are one.[24]

We shall see how the Reality has been visualized by Heraclitus.

As in Indian, so in Greek mind the problem that first appeared in the form of a question or a set of questions was the problem of the One and the Many. This is an important problem since "our conception of God, of existence, of the world and of human life and destiny"[25] would depend upon how we deal with the problem in question. The world we experience everyday is a world of multiplicity: this is a fact which defies denial. Now, the question that crops up here is: is the multiplicity of things and beings real or only phenomenal? Does unity exist at all? If so, what is the nature of that unity? Is it a oneness of totality or a oneness of nature or a oneness of essence? Or, if both unity and multiplicity, the One and the Many are real, what are the relations between them? Are they parallel to each other? Or, are they coexisting aspects of what is transcendental to them, i.e. of the Absolute? These are no barren logical questions, nor are they metaphysical abstractions which cloud the mind and make it opaque. These questions are such that if they go unanswered, we shall be at a loss as to the original contribution

23 A.C. Grayling (ed.), 1995, *Philosophy: A Guide Through the Subject*, Oxford University Press, p. 343.

24 *Fragments of Heraclitus*, 50.

25 SABCL, vol. 16: *The Supramental Manifestation*, p. 341.

of Heraclitus to philosophy; also, we shall be deprived of having what he thinks of existence or of the Real itself.

Regarding the One and the Many Heraclitus' view "arose from his strong concrete intuition of things, his acute sense of universal realities".[26] For him both unity and multiplicity are real and coexistent. If that be so, then existence cannot but be eternally one as well as eternally many. Taking Matter as the principle of oneness, we can say that there is one Matter, but there is a multiplicity of bodies. In this way we can say, there is one Mind, but there are many mental beings. Thus, whatever we fix on as the principle of oneness, corresponding to that we get the many or the multiplicity: there is eternal coexistence between the one and the many. Heraclitus takes hold of this truth, and all the rest of his philosophy develops from that. The philosophy of Heraclitus corresponds much more to the idea of the concrete universal, the One existing in the many, Identity in Difference.

It has been said that there is One eternal. But the question is: what is that One eternal? That One eternal, according to Heraclitus, is "the ever-living Fire" which is the substrate or "stuff" (*Urstoff*) of the universe. Sri Aurobindo observes that Fire does not merely suggest a physical substance or energy: "Heraclitus has clearly an idea of something more" "in his concept of ever-living Fire".[27] And that "something more" is that Fire is "the physical aspect, as it were, of a great burning creative, formative and destructive force", and the totality of these processes is "a constant and unceasing change"; behind this constant change (the change of the One into Many and of the Many into One) what works unceasingly is "a sort of substantial Will-to-become" which acts as "the foundation of Heraclitus' philosophy".[28]

Ranade tells us that Heraclitus denies Being and affirms Becoming only – like Nietzsche and the Buddhists. But, Heraclitus, observes Sri Aurobindo, does not exclude Being from his view of things. "Being is an eternal becoming and yet the Becoming resolves

---

[26] SABCL, vol. 16: *The Supramental Manifestation*, p. 342.

[27] Ibid., p. 343.

[28] Ibid., pp. 343-44.

itself into eternal being."[29] Being and Becoming are simultaneously true — true in each other; they are the two aspects of the ever-living Fire.

Now, the question is: why did Heraclitus choose Fire as the *Urstoff* of the universe? Certainly, his choice of Fire as the essential nature of Reality is not simply due to the sudden change of his mind, nor due to the sheer necessity of showing that he is something different from his predecessors. There is a positive reason behind this choice of his, and that reason is bound up with his main philosophic thought. In the process of Fire, Heraclitus distinguished two paths — the downward and the upward paths, or a downward and upward movement. "That process he sees as a constant change and a changing back, an exchange and an interchange in a constant whole."[30] The cosmos comes into being in virtue of this tension.

> When fire is condensed it becomes moist, and under compression it turns to water; water being congealed is turned to earth, and this he calls the downward path. And, again, the earth is itself liquefied and from it water comes, and from that everything else; for he refers almost everything to the evaporation from the sea. This is the upward path.[31]

We cannot avoid one question: if all things are fire and are, as a consequence, in a constant state of flux, how will the stable nature of things in the world be explained? Heraclitus offers explanation in terms of measure: the world is "an ever-living Fire, with measures of it kindling and measures going out".[32] There is "an exchange and an interchange in a constant whole" — "all things are an exchange for Fire, and Fire for all things, even as wares for gold and gold for wares".[33] Thus, while the substance of each kind of matter thrives always on change, the aggregate quantity of that kind of matter remains the same, as has been illustrated by modern science in its "law of conservation of energy".

---

29 SABCL, vol. 16: *The Supramental Manifestation*, p. 344.

30 Ibid.

31 Diogenes Laertius, 9, 8-9.

32 *Fragments of Heraclitus*, 30.

33 Ibid., 90.

We, then, come to see that constant change and relative stability of things — both remain in the universe. We also see that a relative stability of things is due to the different measures of Fire, kindling or going out in more or less equal proportions. What Heraclitus calls the "hidden attunement of the Universe" is constituted by the fact of this measure, of the balance of the upward and downward paths.

Two Apophthegms of Heraclitus

The whole of Heraclitus' thinking begins from his two apophthegms: (i) "All things are one", and (ii) "One out of all and all out of One". These are terse sayings embodying a general truth. To unfasten what is locked in these pithy sayings, we need to discuss whether Ranade's assessment of Heraclitus' philosophy as the philosophy of Becoming is acceptable or not.

Ranade seems to think that Heraclitus denies Being and affirms Becoming only. Here Sri Aurobindo makes a comment by saying that Ranade has taken Heraclitus' theory of perceptual change too much by itself. Sri Aurobindo continues that if Becoming is the all of Heraclitus' philosophy, we fail to understand as to why our Greek philosopher should seek for an "original and eternal principle, the ever-living Fire"; moreover, it is difficult for us to admit with Ranade that Heraclitus held the theory of a cosmic conflagration and if we concede what Ranade asserts, it will be difficult "to imagine what could be the result of such a cosmic catastrophe".[34] To bring all becoming into Nothingness? Not at all; Heraclitus' aphoristic thought is direct opposite to the Buddhists' speculative Nihilism. An absolute conflagration, if there be at all, can reduce all existing things into the ever-living Fire, the eternal principle of being.

> . . . something that can be imaged as Fire which, if an ever-active force, is yet a substance or at least a substantial force and not merely an abstract Will-to-become, — something out of which all cosmic becoming arises and into which it returns. . . .[35]

And this "something" is nothing but eternal Being which Sri

[34] SABCL, vol. 16: *The Supramental Manifestation*, p. 346.

[35] Ibid.

Aurobindo, by his analytic observation as well as by his probing insight, comes to find out in Heraclitus' philosophic thought. Indeed, Heraclitus cannot deny "an eternal basis" which is Being, while speaking of the cosmos as eternal becoming.

The first apophthegm of Heraclitus which has been already referred to is "All things are one". This apophthegm is explained in terms of Being and Becoming. In one aphorism Heraclitus says, "we do and we do not enter into the same waters, we are and we are not". This aphoristic statement clearly indicates that "there is an identity in things, in all existences, *sarvabhūtāni*, as well as a constant changing".[36] To say that there is a Being as well as a Becoming is to say that we have an eternal and real existence as well as a temporary and apparent existence. Along with "a constant mutation" or change there is "a constant identical existence". Due to this constant identical existence we can verily say that all things are one, say, Day and Night are one, Death and Life are one, Good and Evil are one and so on.

Heraclitus' formula, "All things are one", states an account of "the eternal truth of the cosmos", while his another formula, "One out of all and all out of One", exhibits an account of "the process of the cosmos".[37] The first formula has been explained; the eternal truth of the cosmos lies in the fact that all things are one in the sense that there is something in the motion and change of all things "which insists on stability", "which assures unity, which triumphs into eternity".[38] That something which is the eternal oneness of all things is the ever-living Fire.

As to the second formula, "One out of all and all out of One", what is to be said is that this signifies the cosmic process of evolution and involution, the movement of life and the harmony of existence. We shall see how Sri Aurobindo's intuitive mind gets hold of them and undoes them from the depth of this apophthegm.

In the process of the cosmos One is continually becoming all

---

36 SABCL, vol. 16: *The Supramental Manifestation*, p. 347.

37 Ibid., p. 351.

38 Ibid., p. 350.

things every moment, and this is to be termed as "the eternal flux of things"; but all things again are continually returning to their source, to their principle of oneness — the principle of the ever-living Fire. Because of the eternal becoming of One into many and of the eternal going back of many to One, the unity of the cosmos, the stability of measures is maintained. The one ever-living Fire, which is "at once the one substance and the one force", has been expressed by Heraclitus "as the upward and downward road".[39] The one eternal principle of Fire, following its downward path, creates the world of multiplicity which it dissolves into itself, while following the upward path: there seems to be no end to this simultaneous upward and downward motion of things. The question that crops up at this point is: does Heraclitus hold the theory of conflagration (*pralaya*)? His account of the process of cosmos makes us convinced of the fact that he does not exclude the theory of conflagration from his system of thought. What comes to the focus of our attention is the fact of a spectacular coincidence of Heraclitus' thought with the Indian notions such as the Purāṇic conflagration of the world and the Vedāntic theory of the eternal cycles of manifestation and withdrawal from manifestation.

We come to find that both the early Greek and the Indian systems hold the theory that the creation of the world takes place through some kind of evolutionary change out of some original substance or energy. This original substance, according to the Sāṁkhya system in India, is *pradhāna* or *mūla-prakṛti*, and the creation starts from this original substance or root-energy through the evolutionary process. Fire, according to the Sāṁkhya, is not the primal substance, but this Indian system gives to the principle of fire the function of creating all forms; similarly, in the Veda Agni has been pronounced as the great builder of the worlds, and here at least we find how Heraclitus' thought echoes the Indian thought. Of course, the early Greek and the Indian systems may disagree as to the nature of the creative energy, the *phusis* of the Greeks. What distinguishes Heraclitus among the early Greek thinkers is his conception of the upward and downward road — the road up and

---

39 SABCL, vol. 16: *The Supramental Manifestation*, p. 352.

down being one and the same. Sri Aurobindo observes that this conception of Heraclitus

> corresponds to the Indian idea of *nivṛtti* and *pravṛtti*, the double movement of the Soul and Nature — *pravṛtti*, the moving out and forward, *nivṛtti*, the moving back and in.[40]

Misconceptions may arise regarding Heraclitus' theory of a periodic conflagration. Heraclitus has not simply affirmed that the One is always Many and the Many always One, he has also stated, "One out of all and all out of One". Plato has phrased the thought of Heraclitus thus:

> the reality is both many and one and in its division it is always being brought together.[41]

By it, it is meant "a constant current and back-current of change". It may be presumed that as the One by downward change turns fully into the All in the descending process, so the All by upward change may fall back completely on the One: in the former case the oneness of the ever-living Fire is not affected, rather it remains eternally, while in the latter case the All, though dissolved into the One, may essentially exist, since it can repeat the downward movement and thus manifest as the many. Sri Aurobindo's observation here is:

> All difficulty disappears if we remember that what is implied is a process of evolution and involution, — so too the Indian word for creation, *sṛṣṭi*, means a release or bringing forth of what is held in, latent, — and that the conflagration destroys existing forms, but not the principle of multiplicity.[42]

Taken in this sense, observes Sri Aurobindo, Heraclitus' theory of a periodic conflagration will not be charged with any inconsistency; rather, his theory reveals a "complete logic of his system".[43]

---

40 SABCL, vol. 16: *The Supramental Manifestation*, p. 353.

41 Ibid., p. 354.

42 Ibid.

43 Ibid.

The Law of Relativity: The Logical Result of Heraclitus' Philosophical Concepts

The logical outcome of Heraclitus' philosophical concepts is what is called "the law of relativity". The word "relative" is to be followed in terms of the word "absolute". That Heraclitus has dispensed with the absolute reality is a misconception. "Since all is one in its being and many in its becoming, it follows that everything must be one in its essence".[44] This means that there is an absolute reality. The same absolute reality is in each of its different aspects. Good and evil, for example, are not just opposites to, and different from, each other; rather, they are the different aspects of the same absolute reality. Good and evil are one, because they are essentially the One, and the distinctions we make between them remain no more, when looked at from the divine or absolute point of view. "To God all things are good and just, but men hold some things to be good, others unjust."[45] Thus Heraclitus attributes relativity to man, not to God.

Heraclitus says that the first principle is willing and not willing to be called by the name of Zeus. On the basis of this aphoristic saying, an objection is made against Heraclitus: he attributes relativity to God. But this objection is based on misunderstanding. The name Zeus is the relative human idea of the Godhead. Thus while the One accepts the name Zeus, that does not mean that the One is bound by it: herein lies the significance of "not willing".

> Brahman is willing to be called Viṣṇu, and yet he is not willing, because he is also Brahmā and Maheśvara . . . and yet not any of these things, *neti, neti*.[46]

Thus, we come to see that the divine, for Heraclitus, "is at once one and many, an absolute and a relative"; all the relativities are "the relations of the many" which "persist by that in them which is absolute".[47]

---

[44] SABCL, vol. 16: *The Supramental Manifestation*, p. 359.

[45] Ibid., p. 360.

[46] Ibid.

[47] Ibid., p. 361.

The Practical Bearing of Heraclitus' Philosophy on Human Life

Actually speaking, Heraclitus' philosophical or metaphysical ideas have no practical effect on human life. In the words of Sri Aurobindo,

> But when we seek among Heraclitus' sayings for the human application of his great fundamental thoughts, we are disappointed.[48]

Indeed, we get little direct guidance from him. He, however, leaves the packed opulence of his first ideas behind, so that we can draw from it the required ideas for our own benefit.

We come to see that Heraclitus possesses an aristocratic view of life which is based on what is called "Power". Philosophically, he conceives this Power as the nature of the original principle of ever-living Fire. He gives prime importance to the power of knowledge and/or the power of character which need to be cultivated in human life:

> Power and excellence generally are the things that prevail in human life and are supremely valuable, and these things in their high and pure degree are rare among men, they are the difficult attainment of the few.[49]

We get other sayings of Heraclitus which are quite interesting because of the fact that these refer to the divine element in human laws. One such saying is: "Fed are all human laws by one, the divine".

Heraclitus' denunciation of animal sacrifice is interesting in the sense that

> the ancient system of sacrifice in Greece and in India . . . had a psychological significance, purification of the soul as well as propitiation of higher and helpful powers, and was therefore in all probability mystic and symbolical.[50]

One of the master ideas of the ancient Mysteries was purification.

---

[48] SABCL, vol. 16: *The Supramental Manifestation*, p. 363.

[49] Ibid.

[50] Ibid., p. 364.

In the *Gītā* and in the development of Judaism the prophets, the psychological idea of sacrifice was retained.

It is true that Heraclitus presents a melancholy image of human transiency, but this melancholy image is not what finally determines the human life. Against this image we have one cryptic sentence: "the gods are mortals, men immortals". The literal meaning of this sentence is that the gods are powers which perish, while the soul of man is immortal, but this cryptic sentence must at least mean that there is an immortal spirit in man although outwardly he cannot overcome his transiency. In another saying of Heraclitus we find, "thou canst not find the limits of the soul"; and the profoundest of all utterances made by him is "the kingdom is of the child". If man be an infinite and immortal spirit, there is no reason why he should not awaken to a higher and nobler kind of life, why he should not aspire for the realization of his own self.

The Concluding Observation

Sri Aurobindo finally observes that Heraclitus, with his "deep divining eye", foresaw many "largest and profoundest generalizations of Science and Philosophy", but "there is one great gap and defect whether in his knowledge of things or his knowledge of the self of man".[51]

Heraclitus, says Sri Aurobindo, saw two aspects of the Self — the aspect of the universal reason and the aspect of the universal force; but he did not see what the eye of Indian thought saw, namely, the aspect of the universal delight. For the knowledge of the truth of things all the three aspects mentioned above are necessary: these are universal reason or consciousness active in divine knowledge, universal force active in divine will and universal delight active in divine love and joy. Heraclitus' knowledge of things falls short of the third aspect. The third aspect is "a deeper secret" behind the first two aspects — force and reason; this, by taking up the other two, "can establish something higher than justice, better than harmony, truer than reason, — unity and bliss, the ecstasy of our fulfilled existence".[52]

---

51 SABCL, vol. 16: *The Supramental Manifestation*, p. 369.

52 Ibid., p. 370.

This divine ecstasy Heraclitus might have seen if he had taken his vision a little farther. He did not see that from exchange "the highest possible idea of interchange, a mutual dependency of self-giving as the hidden secret of life" can be reached; and also he did not see that from a mutual dependency of self-giving can be developed "the power of Love replacing strife and exceeding the cold balance of reason".[53] Heraclitus could not see the gate of this divine ecstasy, although his one saying about the kingdom of the child almost touches the heart of the secret.

---

[53] SABCL, vol. 16: *The Supramental Manifestation,* p. 371.

8

Sri Aurobindo and Spiritual Humanism

Bijayananda Kar

SRI Aurobindo (hereafter Aurobindo) (1872–1950) was one of the foremost leaders of the Indian renaissance movement. During that period, some noted Indians with the background of both classical Indian tradition and its foreign counterpart developed a new trend with some reformative measures and tried to impress upon others their own national identity by exposing as well as formulating the modern (the then) concept of Indianness in general. Such an emphasis is not necessarily a mark of sentimental upheaval; but, on the other hand, it was quite important to check the blind imitation of foreign elements and, at the same time, appreciating and inculcating the noble and practical elements in foreign source and absorbing those into their own. Such a move was seminal and was remarkably successful in forming the cultural, intellectual and socio-political distinctness. It is, no doubt, in tune with the then demand of pre-independent India.

Aurobindo's contribution is no exception to this general trend. Since his early days he had the access of coming in close contact with foreign (specially European) intellectual tradition in its different facets and, after coming to India, he tried to assimilate the dominant classical Indian tradition with the modern intellectual/cultural climate in such a manner so that, according to him, a novel life-view/life-world can be brought out without any imposition from outside. To put in one word, his appeal for divine life, spiritual religion of humanity can be held as the outcome of his long sustained reflective pursuit.

I

In this context, his repeated reference to "two negations" comes to the limelight. He was critical about "refusal of the ascetic" and "materialistic denial" as well. The long-rooted life-world, fully neglecting the phenomenal practical needs and requirements which, to a considerable extent, present in classical Indian perspective, did not convince him. He was sharply critical about its ascetic and virtually life-denying character. He was, in this regard, opposed to the rigid ceremonial rites and rituals. The other standpoint "materialistic denial" (which is sometimes treated as dominant in the foreign Western sphere) is bent upon, according to Aurobindo, totally rejecting the finer spiritual element in the life-world, is equally untenable. For, it reduces man to sheer matter. The undue emphasis on mechanization in all spheres of human living is rather unwholesome and ruptures the very sense of nobility and humanity. On the contrary, Aurobindo prescribed for a blending of spirituality and materiality to which he termed as spiritual humanity and that he professed to be the only hope for future.

Of course, he had dearly never spelt out his preference for humanism. Reason for this is quite obvious. The established account of humanism during his time was only confined to the interest of man and his welfare, least caring about anything else. Humanism, in that sense, is simply against the acceptance of any form of superhuman attainment of divinity, mostly propagated in the religio-theological source. The anti-religious formulation of humanism is found to be quite close to secularism (definitely in one of its established senses). It is notable, in this context, to hear from J.S. Mill (a prominent secular-cum-humanist) that whatsover is secular is anti-religious and whatever is religious is anti-secular. It is obvious that Aurobindo's scheme cannot favour such an account of humanism. He had definitely a soft corner for religious outlook. His approach to philosophy, in this regard, is distinctly close to religion in general. He held:

> Philosophy "is the intellectual search for the fundamental truth of things" and "religion is the attempt to make truth dynamic in the soul of man".[1]

This shows that his overall reflective tone is to adopt a complementary stand to both philosophy and religion unlike the

[1] Aurobindo 1971: 314.

radical form of humanism. Nevertheless, a softer account of humanism (which is already in use as a matter of fact) takes a tolerant approach to religion within the humanistic framework. According to that, human interest and welfare can be the goal and it can move along with a religious temper as long as it does not have any conflict or discord with the other. To that extent, there is scope for the formation of, what may be called as, religious humanism and that seems to be the undertone of Aurobindo's expression "spiritual religion of humanity". The spiritual basis is not to hamper but to boost up and accelerate the humanitarian goal and, in that way, it is to safeguard the objective of human welfare and well-being. This seems to facilitate in designing the stand of Aurobindo as favouring a form of spiritual humanism. His view, in this regard, that "we are not only ourselves, but all others" is quite pertinent. His sense of life divine is not to be construed as something transcendental to life but is an expression of the fulfilment of life itself. His humanism is not opposed to religion. The essence of man, in his view, is not the individual, not mere mind, not mere body but the universal spirit. There seems to be an appeal for the transformation of attitude to life. Proper significance of human unity can be realized, to Aurobindo, by means of deep sense of spiritual oneness.

> Philosophy is not simply intellectual and "a play of dialectical subtlety" or mere "pursuit of metaphysical truth" but the discovery "of the basic truths of all existence which ought to become the guiding principles of our own existence".[2]

II

Now, let there be a probe into the various persuasive recommendations; he puts forward in order to establish his viewpoint. Before evaluating his recommendation about "spiritual religion of humanity as the only hope for future", it would not perhaps be futile to assess his conception about both philosophy and religion which are like two formidable pillars for the formation of his viewpoint as a whole.

He held philosophy to be the intellectual search for the

---

[2] Aurobindo 1970: 369.

fundamental truth of things. No doubt, this view of philosophy, as a matter of fact, is not in frequent use. But, for that, Aurobindo's stand need not be set aside. The recommendation is to be assessed on its own strength. Well, what is the significance of fundamental truth of things? The artist's view about flower and the botanist's view about it are never same. Accordingly what is, if at all, treated as fundamental to one is not same to the other. Moreover, what is claimed by the saying: fundamental truth of things? Are all things that one comes across must be rooted on one fundamental truth? The word "all" becomes perfectly intelligible in a limited context like "all students in the class have passed in the test". Its use is descriptive of the concerned fact. But, the other expressions like "all things (of the universe) are fundamentally or basically one" is not found to be descriptive. It is rather a sweeping generalization based on a kind of conceptual plunge, as it were. It is on the presupposition that things must be essentially one and that is the fundamental truth. In such a case, neither its fundamentality nor its truth is established. It is only believed to be true or existing, before it is proved to be true. It thus turns out to be conjectural and least factual. Being presupposition, its acceptance is not mandatory and its rational cogency is quite bleak.

Aurobindo held religion to make truth dynamic in the soul of man and it is to express the philosophic truth. It is not clear as to why philosophic truth is to be expressed by religion and that makes religious truth dynamic in the soul of man. Religions have different theories of their own and each of them has certain fixed, determinate and distinct marks for its identity and these do not change unless the theory is fully given up to something else and thereby it giving rise to a different religion altogether. This is, of course, different from other modifications in a particular religion and those are only reformative within the system. It means that any religion is somewhat static in its core and dynamism in that sense does not have any scope.

Further, Aurobindo's view on religion is neither noticeable in any lexical source nor is in use in any standard religious practices. It is markedly personal, being confined to Aurobindo and his followers. Well, that itself does not necessarily undermine its worth, if there is any. But before to make any remark, perhaps the issue is not pointless to be clear about what this view stands for. What is the implication of the saying that truth is to be dynamic in the soul of man. It seems to pre-assume that there is a soul (self/spirit) of man and truth is to be made dynamic there. Ordinarily, truth stands for any judgement which is either designated as true or as false. Truth is thus a predicative expression. Things that exist or happen are not by themselves either true or false. The judgemental expression about the existence or occurrence by way of formulating a knowledge-claim is either true or false. Mere existence or mere occurrence as such, in this sense, remains beyond truth and falsity. Only when something becomes specified about existence of something and is described accordingly, then such description becomes true or otherwise it is false, as the case may be. Existence is the state or fact of being there (real/living).

It is, of course, the case that existence is said to be real and non-existence unreal. So to maintain that snake perceived at a place and time is unreal and the rope later on perceived in the same place is real, becomes definitely in order. But, from this, it does not follow that rope that is said to be real is ever to be construed as pemanently or eternally real; unless one is bent upon presupposing that something which is real in the perfect sense must be eternally real. "Real" must be, according to such prescriptive stand, absolute real or the only reality. Such peculiar meaning of the term: real/existence is not only uncommon but it also seems to be resting upon one arbitrary stipulation for which neither there is any factual evidence nor there is any plausible justified ground.

Aurobindo's demand that religion is to express the philosophic truth does not appear to be precise. First of all, can there be something as the philosophic truth which is mandatory to each and everybody or to any philosophical standpoint? Of course, validity or invalidity of a particular philosophical stand lies on the context on which it is presented. Never does it thereby hold that the yonder stand is the perfect and only applicable to any situation whatsoever. Moreover, it is found that a philosophical stand is formulated on any affair without being necessarily confined to religion. It is not necessary that a religious stand has to be made free from obscurity and superstition only if it is tied up with philosophic truth; unless, one is to woo the presupposition that philosophic truth, whatsover, has a pervasive feature to engulf the religious framework compulsorily.

With this background of analysis, let there be a move for an appraisal of spiritual religion of humanity or spiritual humanism, as touched upon before. Initially the expression: spiritual religion requires clarification. Is religion bound to be spiritual? If so, in what sense? Does spiritual mean that spirit/soul/self (in any form) as an entity/being must find place in any religious set-up? As a matter of fact, it is found not necessary. Religious sense is preached and practised with or even without the acceptance of spirit as stated before. The acceptance of soul in the religious framework is never mandatory. However, as per simple common sense, "spirit" is used in the empirical level (quite legitimately) referring to the strength, energy and vigour of an individual, in a situation or context. There is a legitimate use for such expressions like "why are you not spirited to play the game, in which you are interested before?", "His dealings with the guests are not cold and dull but full of spirit and energy". And, such kind of use of "spirit" is very much present in any kind of reflective enquiry, not simply being limited to religion. But, in that case, the adjectival qualification of spiritual to religion does not appear to be precise and pinpointed.

Now, let there be a pause about the concerned use of "humanity". It is mostly used to the state of a person being friendly and generous to people and animals in a reasonable way without any pre-acceptance of any superhuman being or God. Another meaning sometimes attributed to it (like humanity only referring to people rather than God and one animal or a machine) is ignored here on account of its being too radical and somewhat missing the core point of emphasizing on human cause by way of completely neglecting the required human concern towards other things and animals of nature. The former sense of humanity is not simply a mark of kindness and good gesture or mark of goodwill, but it is also accompanied with some amount of considerate understanding. In that way, humanity is acceptable to a humanist framework in general.

Considering this to be encouraging, some have moved on to impress upon the element of honesty and sobriety in the concept of humanity. And, in that way, they seem to have opted for a spiritual meaning (of their choice) of the conception, i.e. religious or spiritual humanism. Perhaps, Aurobindo's suggestion that philosophical framework has to be dynamized with the religious spirit has the undertonal approval for such reformulation.

Despite the strenuous attempt of forming a close meeting point between philosophy and religion, it is to be marked, with all fairness, that throughout the ages, manifold form of philosophizing, in the established sense, has been made possible without being necessarily related with religion. As already said, philosophical investigation is fruitfully carried with or without being tied up with religion. So also the spirit of humanism or humanity is grown in people's general outlook with or without the religious boosting. It is argued in certain dominant circle, that religious sense for humanitarian move upsets the independent, distinct goal or objective (at least from the moral angle which is inbuilt in the very connotation of the term: humanism, viz. "it emphasises the fact that the basic nature of human beings is good",[3] As per the Aurobindite stand, humanist effort becomes rather subservient to the demand of certain religious belief/faith. But that is actually never warranted. Morality is not spirituality. So also the goal of humanism can be well determined independent of any sort of spiritual/religious background.

In this connection, Aurobindo's suggestion that philosophy being the discovery of the basic truths of all existence becomes the guiding principle of all existence seems puzzling. Because, in one of his own writings, he held philosophy as the intellectual search for the fundamental *truth* of things (as already stated) and in another writing he held philosophy as the discovery of basic *truths* of all existence. Which one, then, is to be accepted — the truth or truths? If there is one fundamental truth of (all) things, then obviously there cannot be any room for basic truths of all existence. Now, leaving aside such imprecise expressions, another difficulty is well pointed out as to how basic truth/truths of all existence ought to be a guiding

---

[3] Vide *Oxford Advanced Learner's Dictionary*, p. 586.

principle.[4] If something is stated to be basic, then it is what is the case. The issue of its being a guiding principle for existence does not arise. For, if something is what it is, then it is on its own right. To follow it as a guiding principle or as valuable that ought to be accepted is not logically indispensable. The point of following it either as guidance or not is another issue. Both are not of the same type. They may go together to some; but there is no logical necessity for that.

III

A prophetic tone seems to be there in Aurobindo's suggestion that spiritual religion of humanity as the only hope for future. There is, no doubt, his being definite about it. It may not be outrightly rejected as due to any dogmatic prejudice or blind belief. There is deep conviction in his saying and he seems to have advanced some reason for it. The validity of the expression lies on its being uniquely experienced and such experience is not purely a private or personal affair. It is one yogic spiritual experience often advocated by the mystics. For that the yogic procedure is wide open and if a person wants to go into that, there is no bar. It is said to be experiential and anybody, if he/she becomes sincerely keen, then it can be attained accordingly. It is not all proper to remark that Aurobindo's or any such mystic's experience is totally private and can never be open to others interested. Nevertheless, if there is attempt to have any intellectual understanding of such experience, then Aurobindo repeatedly warned that to be a failure. To him "intellect is incapable of knowing" the supreme spiritual experience. That may be ordinarily mystical, but that does not at all rub out its reality. Aurobindo, his followers and other like-minded mystics seem to be one in defending the reality of such experience. If this is accepted, then there seems to be no palpable difficulty in accommodating his visionary expression about the future as something revealing.

Well, the issue is not that simple as it prima facie appears. True, at the intellectual level, there is nothing wrong to concede of such unique experience as real. One need not be sceptical about

[4] Prasad 1991: 1.

somebody's having such experience. That such experience does occur to somebody cannot be seriously challenged. But, all the same, there is another important issue which needs here to be well noted. From the fact that somebody has certain experience and his experience is real, it does not follow that the content of such experience must be real in itself. There is a gap between what is experienced and what is there. One may raise an objection here saying that, in that case, one can be endlessly sceptical. Because, whatever we claim as a piece of knowledge is gained directly or indirectly through experience. There is no other way of determining the objectivity or reality of that experience.

True, experience of some form always remains as the foundation of knowledge. But even then, a point here need not be missed. When someone claims experience of certain thing then usually there are several criteria to determine that, through the testing and verification of other required experiences. And, this process is taken privately by individual person and publicly by sharing that with others as well. In that way, certain objects or phenomena which are not known through ordinary simple observation become a matter of discovery by means of technical scientific tests and experiments. It becomes later confirmed by sharing with other competent ones.

But such cases are found to be different from mystic experience. The experience is narrated by the mystic in a very unusual manner. To Aurobindo, finally the spiritiual experience is the acme of yogic experience. "To reach the spiritual consciousness and the divine is the ultimate goal."[5] It is also said to be infinite, absolute and divine light or the supreme experience of God that is very much present, not being transcendent but immanent to human consciousness (of course, in the extraordinary sense).

Now, apart from raising sceptical question about the content of such typically experienced phenomenon, there are a number of conceptual difficulties in comprehending such account of experience, as advocated. How can such divine, infinite supreme consciousness be articulated? To have the experience of infinite is to limit it to a particular context and then it turns out to be finite. The very logical

---

[5] Prasad 1991: 1.

dichotomy between the two becomes thereby obliterated the demand that such experience cannot be unreal and is infallible or inviolable seems to be uncritically pre-assumed without any minimum sense of rational validity. The inculcation of spiritual humanism with humanitarian sense of well-being both in theory and practice is actually made possible by a proper utilization of intellectually regulated socio-moral set-up without any transempirical, mystical union of individual and the divine consciousness.

Whatever it may be, this is to be unquestionably acknowledged that Aurobindo's extensive reflective contribution, besides other important contemporaries, has made a good impact on the then Indian mind for arousing the required sense of self-identity in the international platform.

References

Aurobindo, Sri, 1970, *The Synthesis of Yoga*, Pondicherry: Sri Aurobindo Ashram.

———, 1971, *The Supramental Manifestation and Other Writings*, Pondicherry: Sri Aurobindo Ashram.

Kar, Bijayananda, 1985, *Sri Aurobindo and Spiritualistic Humanism*.

Oxford Advanced Learner's Dictionary, 6th edn., Oxford: Oxford University Press, 2001.

Prasad, Rajendra, 1991, "Aurobindo on Reality and Value", *Journal of the Indian Council of Philosophical Research*, IX(1).

9

Political Philosophy of Sri Aurobindo
A Critical Appreciation

Asok Kumar Mukhopadhyay

Introduction

Aurobindo Ghosh (1872–1950), widely known as Sri Aurobindo,[1] was educated in St. Pauls School (London) and Cambridge University, as his father wanted him to be a perfect Anglophile. He also qualified for the ICS. It was only after his father started changing his views about the British rule in India that Aurobindo got influenced and determined to drive the Britishers out of India. He refused to accept B.A. (Cantab) degree and got himself disqualified in the ICS by not appearing at the compulsory training in horse-riding. In his Cambridge days he was instrumental in forming a secret society named "Lotus and Dagger" and took the solemn vow to dedicate his future for the cause of liberation of his motherland. He felt that he had better things to do for India, the world and humanity. He came back to India in February 1893 and devoted himself to the task of freeing his motherland whose blood was being sucked by the British imperialists. On reaching India, he served the Princely State of Baroda, first in the Treasury and then as a Professor, Vice-Principal and Principal of Baroda Raj College. He found the people of India in the early 1890s suffering from a cultural amnesia and having forgotten the glory of ancient and medieval Indian heritage and culture. He firmly resolved to end this amnesia of his imitative countrymen. He derived inspiration from the writings of

[1] The name "Sri Aurobindo" was first used by his colleague and devotee Motilal Roy. Aurobindo came to be widely known as "Sri Aurobindo" since 1926 when he attained *siddhi* (perfection) in his Pondicherry Ashram.

Bankim Chandra Chatterjee and Swami Vivekananda and received high tributes from Rabindranath Tagore in course of time.

Background

Aurobindo began a new life at Boroda, which had its culmination in Bengal between 1905 and 1910. It flourished in four different aspects of his social and political thought, viz.

(a) heritage of classical Indian literature,

(b) creative writing which he had started in his Cambridge days,

(c) keen interest in politics to give it a radical and new turn keeping to the Indian tradition of justice, Vedānta, freedom and spirituality, and

(d) practising *yoga* as a mental exercise to achieve his ends and get acquainted with the Indian culture and tradition.

He started visiting Bengal intermittently since he married 14-year-old Mrinalini in 1901 as per Hindu custom and decided to wait till she reached adulthood as otherwise marriage at minor age, he thought, would be a torture and exploitation. In Bengal he established contact with a band of young trusted lieutenants with the help of his younger brother Barindra.

Aurobindo developed a strong dislike for the timid political approach of the leaders of the Indian National Congress, which never went beyond the moves of prayer and petition to the colonial rulers. He openly started criticizing the colonialists in a series of famous articles titled "New Lamps for Old" in the columns of *Induprakash* published from Bombay. In these articles he boldly voiced the aspiration of the Indian people and observed that the spirit of the moderate Congressmen was never a spirit of truth, sincerity and wholeheartedness, and India would not have independence by following the Moderates' method of constitutional agitation. In these articles he bitterly attacked the policies of the first generation of Indian liberals, not only their policy of mendicancy but also their preference for individualism, materialism and liberal democracy. This series of articles annoyed the British rulers as well as the Congress leaders, who applied pressure on the editor of *Induprakash* to stop publishing Aurobindo's articles.

In the meantime, Aurobindo was fed up with Baroda's life and decided to shift his base to Calcutta. He came in contact with Bengal's affluent and enlightened patriot-zaminder Raja Subodh Chandra Mullick who persuaded him to accept the post of Principal of the newly-founded National Council of Education, Bengal, which later blossomed into Jadavpur University. Aurobindo permanently came to Calcutta in 1905 when the elites of the city had already started protesting vigorously against Viceroy Curzon's administrative measure of dividing the Bengal province by creating a new province by merging eastern Bengal with Assam. Aurobindo enthusiastically jumped into this anti-British movement and came to a position of ideological leadership.

When Barindra Kumar Ghosh, in collaboration with Bhupendranath Dutta, younger brother of Swami Vivekananda, launched a weekly newspaper named *Yugantar* in 1906 and began preaching the ideals of freedom and jingoistic aspiration, Aurobindo joined this group and started preaching aggressive nationalism to fulfil his mission of flogging a race which appeared dead because of decades of colonial torture and exploitation. Almost simultaneously, he joined with the revolutionary nationalist Bipin Chandra Pal and launched a new English newspaper named *Bande Mataram*. Aurobindo, however, always preferred to work behind the curtains while contributing for *Bande Mataram*. The British rulers were flummoxed about the author of the fiery nationalistic articles, who showed boldness of attitude and high level of philosophical thought in powerful and chaste diction, scorching sarcasm and refined sense of intellectual wit. The educated middle-class people soon began boiling against the British colonial rule. S.K. Ratcliffe, the editor of *The Statesman*, recollected later how the leading articles as well as special articles of *Bande Mataram*, written in English with brilliant arguments and pungent comments, expressed the most effective voice of nationalist extremism. A powerful and mystified spell overtook the reading public in India and waves of revolutionary nationalism flooded the general public opinion to heightened spirit of revolutionary nationalism.

Soon the British government decided to prosecute the newspaper *Bande Mataram*, but the prosecution failed to prove that Aurobindo was the editor. Aurobindo attended the Surat session (1907) of the Indian National Congress. Here he, in cooperation with Bal Gangadhar Tilak, the Pune-based propagator of extremist nationalism, organized the Congress delegates to launch a frontal challenge to the moderate leadership over issues of the goal and programmes of INC. The session ended in pandemonium and open split in the ranks of INC. Aurobindo usually avoided taking active part in the din and turmoil, and remained emotionally unmoved.

Aurobindo was arrested in Calcutta in 1908 for his alleged involvement in the anti-government conspiracy of bomb-making and confined in jail for a full one-year. Aurobindo was supported by the leading barrister Chittaranjan Das during trial. The government failed to prove Aurobindo's active involvement in violence and conspiracy against the state. Das, while concluding his arguments in this case, hailed Aurobindo as "the poet of patriotism, the prophet of nationalism and the lover of humanity". Bankim Chandra Chatterjee had coined the word "Bande Mataram" (salute to Mother) in 1881 in his novel *Anandamath*, but it was Aurobindo, through his writings during the Swadeshi movement in Bengal, transformed this emotional phrase into a *mantra* for the national revolutionaries all over India.

In a real historical sense, Aurobindo gave the finishing touch to Swami Vivekananda's initiation of spiritual nationalism in India. Aurobindo's sole aim was to end the cultural amnesia of the Indian people. He was the first Indian thinker to clearly understand that the umbilical cord of Indian nationalism does not distinctly lie in imitating the West and adopting the European style of management of political affairs but is deeply rooted in India's spiritual tradition and experience of spirituality. He endeavoured to use spiritual nationalism as a weapon to whip up the moribund Indian race. It has been rightly noted by some commentators that Aurobindo cooked the synthetic mixture of matter and spirituality and transcreated it through intellectualism of the West and spirituality of the East. The net product of his intellectual efforts has been the dynamic interaction between ancient India and the development of a new civilization of the Occident. He selected the emerging religious and reformative sects like the Brahmo Samāj, Arya Samāj, the

Ramakrishna–Vivekananda order, neo-Vaiṣṇavism and even Islamic renaissance to carry on his message of human evolution. He had come back from England as an atheist, as confessed by himself in a letter to his brother Barindra,[2] but he took to spirituality and other languages of India's traditional idealism as part of a master strategy to flog the dying Indian race.

After he was released from Alipore Jail (May 1909), he decided to retire from active politics, because he found that meanwhile new leadership had arrived with new programmes and his basic job of imparting dynamism in Indian nationalism was already achieved. Sister Nivedita had earlier warned him that the British rulers would not allow him to do what he intended to do and had been planning re-arresting him and deporting him, because at the highest level of British administration he had already been marked as "the most dangerous man that British India has to reckon with."[3] As he was not interested in grabbing power and political office, he secretly left Calcutta and took refuge in the French colony Pondicherry in April 1910. While in Pondicherry, Aurobindo however remained a sharp critic of British colonialism and imperialism, and sustained his interest in the developments in Indian politics. On his own admission, he was essentially a poet and a political philosopher, a revolutionary of a non-conventional type and a visionary of organic unity of humanity.

Nation–State and Nationalism

As a student of classical literature in Cambridge University, Aurobindo was intellectually trained to understand the character of every idea and phenomenon by tracing its origins. He traced the growth of nationalism in the Greek concept of city state, the Semetic or the Mongolian monarchy, the Celtic clan and the Aryan *kula* or *jāti*. He found nationalism as a mixture of all these institutions. In the historical process of formation of the "nation", he emphasized three factors: (a) role of strong kingship, (b) role of fixed social hierarchy, and (c) foreign domination. He advanced historical facts

[2] Sri Aurobindo to Barindra Kumar Ghosh in April 1920.

[3] Viceroy Lord Minto to Secretary of State for India Lord Morley, India Office Records, London.

and anecdotes in support of his argument, but his concept of "nation" was his own. Aurobindo dwelt on the fundamental principles of community life as revealed in Indian nationalism. He considered "nation" as an essential step because different people are entitled to achieve freedom in their own diverse fashions. He argued that the history of human civilization is the history of national cultures, each bringing to light one particular aspect of cosmic reality, which did not receive acceptance by conventional sociologists and political scientists, as he who viewed the birth of nationalism as an all-comprehensive process of human political evolution.

Aurobindo went through the histories of Russia, England, Spain, the Turks, Romans and the Goths to conclude that the concept of nation state was one of domination and supremacy. He also referred to the process of the West's domination over Japan and China, Egypt and the Arab world, through repression and power. He distinguished between the empire-building cycle in ancient time and the nation-building cycle in modern time, and noted three differences. First, in the ancient cycle a local unit overshoots the regional and national unit to become an imperial body, while in modern cycle it heads towards a larger unification of society and humanity. Second, the metro cities like London and Paris were only offshoots of over centralization of power through disharmony and development of kingly authorities, and feudalism provided justification towards the balancing of centripetal and centrifugal forces within the society but building of the political will somewhat destroyed the individual's freedom of thought and action by foisting the will of the rulers. On this point, Sri Aurobindo comes very near the Marxist position that the ruling ideas of each age were only the ideas of the ruling class. Third, while the modern nation-building process in Europe is marked by a process of revolt, resistance and rebellion against authoritarianism, in the ancient world this was not possible.

Sri Aurobindo has drawn a theoretical distinction between people and nation. He felt even Asiatic civilizations in their most flourishing political periods had been dominated by social, religious and cultural ethos of the people and not by the ruling class. In Sri Aurobindo's perception, nationalism is a living force and has a soul of its own. In his *The Human Cycle*, he has endeavoured to discover the living force of nationalism and observes:

> The nation or society, like the individual, has a body, an organic life, a moral and aesthetic temperament, a developing mind, and a soul behind all these signs . . . it essentially is a soul rather than has one; it is a group-soul. . . .[4]

He saw the genesis and growth of Indian nationalism being primarily motivated by the reaction against the West. Like many other Indian intellectuals, Aurobindo also found the symbol of mother–son relation between the individual and the nation. In this connection he comes to his favourite theme of "Sanātan Dharma" not only in the case of India but of world human community at large. For him, "Sanātan Dharma" was both nationalism as well as internationalism.

Aurobindo found a historical generalization and an awakened consciousness of a cultural unity through India's art, culture, literature, mysticism and religion. By propounding the idea of "Sanātan Dharma", Aurobindo appeared a spiritual mystic and deliberately crossed his rational borders of thought and felt that the unity or harmony could be found in the non-physical aspect of thinking above material needs, even in the case of one's love for one's country and commitment towards humanity. His political thinking was primarily motivated by, and spiritually based on, the concept of clan and tribe. He had been consistent in resolving issues that were unresolved in the ancient period by trying to find roots. He thought that the feeling of a nationality mostly rested on geographical unity, common past and powerful common interest. To him, homogeneity of race, religion or language was not an indispensable element in the formation of nationality and growth of nationalism. He put emphasis on the psychological foundation of nationalism, which enabled individuals to think in terms of a nationality as a part of humanity. The concept, though novel and ideal, could in reality only be a utopia. It could be that Aurobindo had taken up this stand as a part of his efforts of flogging the

---

4 Sri Aurobindo, *The Human Cycle*, chap. IV titled "The Discovery of the Nation-Soul".

colonized Indian people to fight the British imperialism through a rejuvenation of their mind. He never approved national egoism or aggressiveness. Nationalism could also be analysed as an emergence of concealed emotion of man and attitude constellation. But, at the same time, common interests and passions do converge in creating nationalistic principles and help a man shake off his apparent weakness and wavering attitude by imagining him as a part of an organic unity in the form of a nation. Aurobindo condemned modern capitalism and imperialism because instead of nourishing the legitimate interests of the people these systems support personal aggrandizement, insolence and chauvinism.

Sanātan Dharma

After Aurobindo came out of his solitary confinement in Alipore Jail in 1909, he refined his concept of nationalism making it expansive and global-oriented. To him, "Sanātan Dharma" was an all-embracing religion and an extended form of Hinduism, and yet the religion of all conventional religions. He consciously turned down the offer from B.S. Munje and G.K. Gokhale for supporting the cause of Hinduism in the early 1920s. To Aurobindo, the expression "Hindu supremacy" had no meaning because, according to him, there were no Muslims in India; the Indian Muslims in the twentieth century were the descendants of Hindus who were forced by circumstances to abandon their religion. In fact, Aurobindo considered institutionalized religion as an illusion but it did have a therapeutic value. Therefore he conceived of "Sanātan Dharma" for creating a bigger and better human society. He used this new concept for theorizing on state, politics, nationalism and philosophy.

To Aurobindo, "Sanātan Dharma" was no dogmatic orthodox church. It had profound influence of ideas taken from the Vedas, Upaniṣads and *Gītā*, Yoga and even Tantra. It contained the eternal principles of human life mixing with the Cosmos.[5] Aurobindo used this concept as an instrument to cross the trans-cultural barriers and move towards the concept of world humanity for sustaining a balanced human cycle. It was far from his mind that "Sanātan

---

[5] V.P. Varma, *Political Philosophy of Sri Aurobindo* (1960); also Sri Aurobindo, *On Himself* (1972).

Dharma" would be confined within the boundaries of India's geographical borders. During his revolutionary days in a letter to his wife, Aurobindo confessed to have a kind of "madness" to consider India as his living mother who would show the world humanity the way to freedom, happiness, love, brotherhood and an eternal journey.[6] By equating nationalism with "Sanātan Dharma", which was not a creed or religion or faith, he modified the conventional character of Indian nationalism as having something of *sattvika* (pure) character. He found this concept a useful ideological weapon which could be used with full zeal and aggression to fight the imperial rulers. Coming out of jail confinement in 1909, he started spiritualizing the entire model of nationalism in order to get the Indian people out of their frustration at the failure of violent revolutionary politics. He was then indeed looking for something greater and all-encompassing. In his two brilliant essays, "Political Will and Testament" and "To My Countrymen" written sometime in December 1909, he had already indicated his own frustration in a subtle tone to suggest that he indeed had found some worthwhile and life-sustaining concept which could make himself and the humanity happy.

The new concept of "Sanātan Dharma" had two sociological aspects, viz.

(a) it was a powerful message of religious revival, and

(b) it was strongly fused with messianic elements.

Sri Aurobindo wanted to revive the past glory of India and make it modern so that it could be used in a way that would not put ferric notions over it. This very concept indicates that Aurobindo's political thought was universal, oriental and international at the same time. As a philosopher, he felt that there are three essential issues in life, viz.

(a) fixed and permanent spirit which can never be changed but only become obscure and lost;

(b) developing a constant soul which should not be meddled with; and

[6] Sri Aurobindo's letter to his wife Mrinalini.

(c) the brittle mutable body is only the play of the infinite mind.

The concept of "Sanātan Dharma" was the permanent spirit conceived as "spiritual nationalism" which, he believed, might help the Indians come out of their defeatism and gain in intellectual maturity, moral strength and self-confidence. By this concept, he wanted to rid the concept of nation–state and nationalism from messianism. It would serve as collective effort expressing the complete and supreme divinity in man. To him, the aim of the Indian nationalist movement was the expansion of the Indian civilization and he never wanted it to be confined to demands for political autonomy and independence only.

That is why, Sri Aurobindo refused to address to the world over All-India Radio on behalf of the Indian people when India gained independence on 15 August 1947. Instead, he obliged by writing a brief message reflecting his concept of "Sanātan Dharma", in which he mentioned his five dreams,[7] viz:

(a) unity among Hindus and Muslims,

(b) the role that Asia needs to play towards liberating humanity,

(c) world unity for protecting humanity,

(d) India's spiritual gift to the world, and

(e) evolving global consciousness and human unity.

He specifically pointed out in his message that "India has indeed achieved freedom but not unity"; that means, for him, India's freedom would not be fruitful without Hindu–Muslim unity. This essential unity would be possible through "Sanātan Dharma".

Sri Aurobindo believed in what may be called "Political Vedānta" which symbolizes one of the most influential and profound thoughts of Indian spiritual philosophical system. Obviously he had adopted and elaborated the system left behind by Swami Vivekananda's "practical Vedānta". He had admitted this point in his essay "On Himself". There is the difficulty with Aurobindo's thought that it is

[7] Sri Aurobindo's written message was read out on Tuticorin Radio Station on 14 August 1947 on the eve of India gaining independence. For details, see Nirmalya Mukhopadhyay's unpublished PhD thesis "Sri Aurobindo and Politics", University of Calcutta, 2015.

mostly ethereal and beyond the intellectual capacity of average intelligent persons. Even on a theme like "secularism", he moved into the world of non-physical elements of thinking. Defining secularism, he said:

> To me, it means the use and interpretation of spiritual notions for material purposes and not the negation of spiritual and absolutist ideas.[8]

Similarly, he shaped Vedānta in his own way to suit the needs of the Indian people in particular and humanity in general. To him, the world is not an illusion (*māyā*), it is real, and people will have to achieve salvation and renunciation. The new form of Orientalism that Aurobindo tried to build up was his ideational instrument for confronting the West. So he based his theory of passive resistance modelled, to some extent, on the philosophy of Practical Vedānta and Buddhism.

Doctrine of Passive Resistance

Aurobindo's doctrine of passive resistance is a great instance of his syncretic political philosophy. He followed Aristotle's theory of "golden mean" and tried to synthesize a mean between passive and aggressive resistance. Being greatly influenced by Irish philosopher and revolutionary Parnell, he mostly based his theory of passive resistance. He vehemently opposed the opposition-cooperation-opposition strategy followed by the Congress liberal leaders like G.K. Gokhale, Pheroze Shah Mehta and Surendranath Banerjee. Aurobindo was quite sure this kind of intellectuals will never succeed in achieving India's freedom because their method of agitation was based on appeasement of the British rulers just to avoid any major repression by the ruling class. They, according to Aurobindo, only displayed a spirit of moral and sentimental enthusiasm and inoffensive philanthropic patriotism. By contrast, the school of politics Aurobindo belonged to was not based on abstractions, formulae or dogmas but on the practical necessities and the teaching of political experience, common sense and world history. Aurobindo never allowed himself to come under the spell

[8] Sri Aurobindo, *On Himself* (1972).

of jingoistic and unreasonable love for the motherland. To him, it was a matter of political strategy to speak in strong and aggressive terms to turn the popular tide against the liberal "Moderates". In his days of political activism, he was no less a power theorist as he silently witnessed and enjoyed the ransacking of the Congress platform by the "extremist" delegates at the Surat session (1907). His equivocal attitude to many issues of practical politics painted him as unattached yet deeply involved in all forms of political activity.

On his own admission, Sri Aurobindo was essentially "a poet and politician", although he never understood "politics" in the conventional party-oriented language.[9] He always sought to find a spiritual overtone in his political thinking. He outlined three essential conditions for national progress through actualization of Swaraj:

(a) an unhindered intellectual growth and independent motion and action that would stand for an anti-thesis of passive thoughts, fatal dependence and helpless condition of the people of India;

(b) the necessity of organizing a national Will as a strong central authority; and

(c) the most vital but subtle issue of organized resistance.

But he was never explicit on the third condition. He understood that India was overtly a spiritual and religious nation and the people, because of economic exploitation, would only take up arms in the name of God and religio-spiritual culture. So, for him, it was more than the cultural issues embodied in the writings of *Rāmāyaṇa*, *Mahābhārata* and *Gītā*, as he understood that the people influenced by the Vedānta could be utilized for a fight against the British with arms. He felt that in India attack on religion, culture, social order, heritage and spirituality would be better resisted than talking about the uprising of exploited peasants and workers. He found that legitimization of protests and armed revolts could be better managed through religion and spirituality instead of theoretical analysis of socio-economic exploitation of peasants and workers.

Aurobindo defined his doctrine of passive resistance on the basis

---

[9] Sri Aurobindo, *On Himself* (1972).

of three premises, viz.:

(a) endure punishment to fight for what is just and right,
(b) non-cooperation with the ruler or oppressor, and
(c) self-suffering.

These principles he derived from the Upaniṣads and *Gītā*, which talk of tolerance, perseverance, sacrifice and suffering to attain salvation (*mokṣa*) or the *summum bonum* of life.

Aurobindo enunciated three canons of passive resistance, viz.:

(a) to violate an unjust law is not only justifiable but is also a duty under given circumstances;
(b) to resist an unjust executive order or coercive interference is also a duty; and
(c) to practise social boycott and excommunication of traitors and other collaborators of the unjust ruler who are engaged in treason against the nation is also a duty.

Passive resistance, to Aurobindo, was the negative measure and self-help, the positive programme to obtain an explicit and dynamic realization of national consciousness. The Nationalist Party, then led by Gokhale and Aurobindo, adopted the programme of resisting the industrial and commercial activities of the British and promoted the positive programme of "Swadeshi" which was practised only in Bengal between 1905 and 1907.

While suggesting boycott by way of resistance to the unjust rule of the British Raj, Aurobindo put forward Hampden's refusal to pay taxes to the Stuart monarchy and endorsed Tilak's call to farmers to stop paying taxes when famine struck western India in 1896. But Aurobindo himself did not call the farmers in Bengal because of his fear that refusal to pay taxes to the British government might have released maximum chaos in society. While experimenting with his political agitations over racial discrimination between the whites and the blacks in South Africa, M.K. Gandhi in 1896 had used the technique of non-violent *satyāgraha* and referred to non-violence as the highest creed to him. But it was Aurobindo who wrote in *Bande Mataram* in 1907 the first extensive public statement on his doctrine of passive resistance. Before him, no one had clearly outlined its objective, methods and limitations. Unlike Gandhi, Aurobindo never considered active resistance to foreign rule and oppression by violent methods a morally inferior method. He argued that the method of resistance, active or passive, would depend on the nature and extent of repression. By passive resistance, Aurobindo meant refraining from those methods which would, in any way, help the foreign oppressive government. He, even, did not rule out open armed revolt as the last resort for a subjugated nation struggling against oppression and exploitation by an imperialist power. Passive resistance, Aurobindo thought, would be advisable only so long as the oppressive and exploitative administration confines itself within the boundaries of constitutional and peaceful governance. Passive resistance would turn into active resistance the moment the government resorts to violent repression. That is, where the government depends on the people for running its administration, refusal to help the government by way of boycotting, and non-cooperating with, the government establishment would be most preferable. Aurobindo was conscious that passive resistance would be a negative approach only, hence he supplemented it with the positive programme of "Swadeshi" in social, economic, cultural and political fields.

Sri Aurobindo promoted the moral side of passive resistance. He identified three types of revolution, viz.:

(a) material revolution which produces immediate results which are powerful and dynamic;

(b) moral and intellectual revolution which has the maximum amount of intensity; and

(c) spiritual revolution which is the most comprehensive but hardest to achieve; such revolutions normally take long years.

The alleged *ādeśa* (command) of Lord Vāsudeva (Kṛṣṇa) to him in Alipore Jail to leave active politics could be Aurobindo's attempt towards spiritualizing Indian politics on the basis of India's culture and heritage. The rationalists argue that given the social conditions in the country that Aurobindo found after being released from the jail in 1909, he could have felt totally depressed to find the movement he had set in during 1905-07 was almost dead. He might have received popular ovation on his release but he had lost control over the Indian politics as the Moderate liberals like Gokhale and Surendranath had openly and eagerly welcomed the Morley–Minto reforms and the voice of the national revolutionaries was not heard at all effectively in 1909. Aurobindo wanted to overcome his depression by deciding to go back to his old passion to follow the *jñāna-mārga* (path of knowledge) for the pursuit of truth. In fact, Aurobindo started his preparation to go out of the reach of the British police and intelligence officers and decided to leave Bengal immediately and secretly in order to reach the capital city of the French colony. He definitely decided to shun active politics in search for his new passion for world consciousness and humanity. Henceforth Aurobindo's ideas of both politics and philosophy were all geared towards his grand ideal of Human Unity.

Concept of Freedom

To Sri Aurobindo, freedom means unhindered ability to obey the law of personality development, to grow to man's natural self-fulfilment, to find out naturally and freely man's harmony with the environment.[10] Perfect freedom, according to him, is inner freedom which is fulfilled in the freedom of the human soul. Freedom then means, as he understands, power to expand and grow towards perfection by the law of one's *dharma,* meaning inherent nature. In this sense, self-determination is the effective principle of liberty, which gives free opportunity for the soul (the inner being) of its self-fulfilment. This concept of freedom seeks to synthesize the individual and the society. In an ideally harmonized society, the respect for individual liberty and free growth of the personal being is harmonized with respect for needs, efficiency, solidarity and natural growth of the social life. If a real and spiritual unity were effected, free individuals would be *compelled by themselves,* by their own needs, to accommodate perfectly their own growth with the growth of their fellows, as they would not feel themselves complete except in the free growth of others. This stand of Aurobindo may remind one of Rousseau's concept of the sovereignty of General

---

[10] V.P. Varma, op. cit. See also V.R. Mehta, *Foundations of Indian Political Thought* (1999), chap. 9.

Will and the paradox of his concept of freedom that the erring individual (i.e. one who cannot agree with the General Will) would be "forced to be free". Rousseau implied that the individual himself would ultimately see reason in the General Will. But Rousseau's position still remains a paradox. Sri Aurobindo's argument is different, as he holds that any imposed order, when carried too far, inhibits the principle of natural growth. He argues that "dwarfed or robbed of elasticity, the devitalized individuality, even while it seems outwardly fair and symmetrical, perishes from within". The law for humanity is to pursue its upward evolution towards the divine, taking full advantage of the free development and gains of all individuals and groups and nations. The fulcrum of all the wholes, however, is the individual, because everything in Nature is meant for the individual to develop his potentiality. Similarly, free development of community or nation from within is the best condition for the growth of perfection of mankind. The law for the individual to perfect the individuality by free development from within implies respect for the same free development in others. This law is to harmonize one's life with the life of other social aggregates. Similarly the law for community or nation to perfect its corporate existence implies a free development from within, with full respect for, and to aid and be aided by, the same free development of other communities or nations. The conditions which are necessary for the development of individual potentialities from within are also necessary for the development of the world. Aurobindo stressed that both liberty and equality are external attributes of the spirit. The union of these two can only be achieved by the power of human brotherhood and spiritual freedom. He, however, never explained what kind of social, economic and political freedom must be secured in order to enjoy spiritual freedom. Nowhere has he explained how to reconcile the doctrine of *svadharma* (i.e. working for development of one's inherent nature) with the doctrine of *loka-saṁgraha* (i.e. working for the organization and welfare of the people). Aurobindo's diagnosis of the ills of the modern age is profound and full of possibilities but he has not identified any concrete line of action.

Sri Aurobindo considered the state an organized force, not

comparable to any organism, which works like a machine, without tact, taste, delicacy of intention. Hence he totally disapproved the idea of state interference in education, religion and culture as "an absurd monstrosity". He prescribed the state's main duty to "secure for man a just and equal chance of self-development and satisfaction to the extent of (his) powers and in the line of his nature. The basis of his ideal state would be a deep faith in the value of the individual personality and dignity.

He presented a vision of community life which is far different from both the individualist and the collectivist vision of socio-economic and political reconstruction. He has resolutely refused to allow either the individual to destroy society by his greed and cupidity or the organized state to crush the individual and destroy the society. By defining the state as merely an institution of "social will", Aurobindo indicated the urgency of safeguards against misuse of governmental powers. But he stopped short of suggesting the institutional framework which would ensure a harmonizing state power. He rejected parliamentary or presidential form of democracy but did not provide any suitable organizational alternative system of democratic governance.

Human Unity

While in Pondicherry, Sri Aurobindo's thought centred around the concept of unity of mankind. His two books — *The Human Cycle* (1918) and *The Ideal of Human Unity* (1919) — serve as the bridge between his earlier thinking on nationalism and his later metaphysical thinking revealed in his immortal treatise *The Life Divine* (1950). In *The Human Cycle*, a major philosophical treatise on politics, Aurobindo explained the cosmic process in terms of the rich differentiated totality of its civilizational forms, institutions and ways of life, and clarified its message for the individual–community relation. Here he suggested the best solution to the problem of realizing human unity in the twentieth century. He believed that a nation, like the individual, has a body, an organic life, an aesthetic temperament, a developing and group soul. In *The Ideal of Karmayogin* (1909) he looked forward to the emergence of India as a great nation, which would make its timely contribution towards the spiritual development of mankind. There is the need of awakening the soul of India, not by imitating Europe but by cultivating *tapasyā* (creative discipline), *buddhi* (harmonized intellect) and *śakti* (divine strength).

Sri Aurobindo's integral philosophy of creative evolution and human unity acknowledges the basic impulse of change and destruction of dated institutions. While his political ideas attached supreme importance to the ideal of the nation–state and simultaneously considered the nation–state as a necessary stage in development towards human unity. Aurobindo's political philosophy is thus neither conservative in the sense of blind adherence to the past, nor revolutionary in the sense of total rupture with the past. His political philosophy is a political synthesis of the two.

He lashed out the liberal politicians, the revivalists, and the socialists. His argument was that the liberals did not want to destroy British imperialism and always begged for some concessions, they neglected economic equality and encouraged commercial instinct, their individualism was false as the individual as a social being was considered as part of utilitarian values; the revivalists wanted to restore the villages as isolated republics; and the socialists neglected the individual and the socialist state eventually became totalitarian. He sought an alternative to the liberal, rationalistic creed of English utilitarians.

Sri Aurobindo viewed reason as an extension or a vehicle of intuition and integral vision of life. He preferred to explain the central reality of life in terms of logical connection between intuition, reason and experience. In the light of this view of reality, he sought to provide a new perspective in understanding the problems of life and politics.

Sri Aurobindo was convinced that the unity of mankind is evidently a part of Nature's eventual scheme which must be achieved. He believed that human society needs some common workable order of harmony and conciliation. The soul of man discovers its spiritual character and effects an upward transformation of life from inertia (*tamas*) to purity (*sattva*). The unity of mankind, he argued, could be achieved neither by administrative nor by economic unity through some kind of financial globalization as it developed towards the close of the twentieth century. It can only be secured by an enduring foundation, a new religion of humanity springing from the inner law of human development. He argued that it is the law of Nature that everything should move towards larger and larger aggregations and, therefore, the ideal of human unity should be the culmination of the process. But every development in Nature takes place slowly and does not happen at one point of time. Human civilizations, rich and strong, have evolved one after another, but they all declined and faded out for some reason or other. In the current phase of human history two forces are at work with equal strength. First, a force of interrelation and interaction between the units of human race leading to clashes and wars, demands for liberty and equality, and demands for mitigating the ruinous consequences of the process; and second, a force of common uniting elements, smaller units merging to larger unity secured by external forces or common sentiments. In course of time, the religion of humanity will weld the human race because of the compulsion of choosing either growing unity or lingering suicide. He rejected the conventional versions of a "world government". Rather he preferred a sort of loose federation of the national governments, in which the people of each nation would retain their powers to pursue the values of their own culture, civilization and spiritualism in their own ways, thereby facilitating human unity. The evolution of humanity, in his view, has always been of an involuted nature.

Aurobindo himself said in 1909: "one good thing that I got because of British wrath was that I found God".[11] At the end of an analysis of his activities and views on politics and culture, this statement could be deconstructed that his God is no personified deity, it is Humanity and World Consciousness with a feeling of fraternity.

References

Documents from Sri Aurobindo Ashram, Pondicherry.

Mehta, V.R., 1999, *Foundation of Indian Political Thought*, New Delhi: Manohar.

[11] Sri Aurobindo, *Tales of Prison Life* (originally *Karakahini* in Bengali, 1909), Sri Aurobindo Ashram, Pondicherry, 1997.

Sri Aurobindo, 1997, *On Himself*, Pondicherry: Sri Aurobindo Ashram Trust.

———, 2006, *Autobiographical Notes and Other Writings of Historical Interest*, volume 36 of *The Complete Works of Sri Aurobindo*, Pondicherry: Sri Aurobindo Ashram.

———, 1999, *The Human Cycle*, Pondicherry: Sri Aurobindo Ashram.

———, 1977, *The Life Divine*, Pondicherry: Sri Aurobindo Ashram.

———, 1998, *The Ideal of Human Unity*, Pondicherry: Sri Aurobindo Ashram Trust.

———, 1997, *War and Self Determination*, Pondicherry: Sri Aurobindo Ashram Trust.

———, 2003, *The Complete Works of Sri Aurobindo*, Pondicherry: Sri Aurobindo Ashram.

Varma, V.P., 1960, *The Political Philosophy of Sri Aurobindo*, Bombay: Asia Publishing House.

10

A Perspective on Inter-Personal Relation
A Journey from Jean-Paul Sartre to Sri Aurobindo

Susmita Bhattacharya

RABINDRANATH Tagore has made a significant statement in his *Religion of Man*, "Relationship in the fundamental truth of this world of appearance".[1] When man starts his journey in the evolutionary process he has in him two distinct primary impulses — one is individualistic and another is collective or social. Thus, every man has his own personal life and a social life. Accordingly he also follows a personal motive of conduct and also a social motive of conduct. But why does one accept the other's existence in his own orbit? Though one has a social or collective impulse, history of human civilization is not always based on peaceful coexistence of man only. From the early stage of civilization one can find a crudity, conflict in human relationship. So conflict, tension, violence, cruelty — everything is there in human relation.

Jean-Paul Sartre has discussed these things in detail in his famous book *Being and Nothingness* (1943). Sartre has pictured man as alone, insecure and somewhere a separated being from everything in his surroundings. Sartre has shown that whenever man tries to make a relation with other person invariably he fails. In *Being and Nothingness* Sartre has posited a very strong belief that whenever two persons get related with each other, after some time they discover that their relation absolutely fails to make them satisfied. Two persons then merely exist, there is a sense of bewilderment between them always. Slowly the relation turns into a void, a total disappointment.

---

[1] Rabindranath Tagore, 1963, *Religion of Man*, London: Unwin Books.

According to Sartre, all the human relation at last turns into a subject–object relation, i.e. a man is at the same time a subject to oneself and object to another man. And this dichotomy also exists for the other person, so Sartre has maintained that the relation between two men is the relation of endless conflict. This conflict, Sartre believed, grows out of a dense insecurity of an individual. Due to this insecurity man is always afraid of losing his own belonging or anything else in the presence of another. If one can uncover the veil from this Sartrean thought one can reveal a simple truth that basically when a man is suffering from insecurity in this world, he is always looking for something which can be his own, exclusively his own property. He is always afraid of losing his possession, etc. It does not mean that possession means always a material possession — a relation, an association of someone with whom one likes to share his thoughts, love or many things; most of the time that man was possessed by the other and the reverse of this picture bears the same truth. Everyone likes to be free, secured within his own limit. At the same time he also cannot tolerate the other's existence or presence since he is always suffering from a fear of losing his own freedom. Then he wants to enjoy his freedom fully but at the same time wants to be related with somebody since he realizes that "other" is an inevitable part of his world. So, here arises a tension between two individual beings which has made Sartre say that man is a useless passion. In 1960 Sartre wrote another important book *Critique of Dialectical Reason.* The picture of human relationship depicted in this book is quite different from *Being and Nothingness*. In *Critique* Sartre confessed that the relation between two individuals does not always end with conflict. Gradually in *Critique* Sartre surpassed this notion of conflict which he once believed. In *Critique* he had to create another picture of human relationship. He showed that first of all a few people came too close to each other at the beginning of human civilization. Gradually these groups turned into a collective unit, i.e. a society was formed by unification of many small groups. But these small groups had the tendency to collide with each other. Sartre commented that this conflict was due to the scarcity of natural resoures and many other things. And due to this scarcity which persists even today, a conflict or collision is inevitable between two groups of men.

In 1945 Sartre had given a lecture on "Existentialism and Humanism" in Paris. This lecture was fundamentally a defence of existentialism as humanism. In this lecture Sartre tried to give another dimension of human relation as well as humanity. Sartre stated that the conflict or confrontation is not the last word of an individual's life. But an individual also has to try to overcome this conflict, rather he has to keep a keen urge of going beyond this conflict. Rabindranath Tagore in his *Religion of Man* said:

> From the time when men became conscious of his own self he also became conscious of a mysterious spirit of unity which found its manifestation through him in his society. It is a subtle medium of relationship between individuals, which is not for any utilitarian purpose but for its own ultimate truth, not a sum of arithmetic but a value of life".[2]

In 1980 Sartre in his "Last Dialogue" with Beni Levi, confessed that he had not understood human relation properly. Since the ultimate truth is not the conflict of two persons or groups, but beyond this conflict there must be "something" which one has to find out. So what is that "something" for which a man can surpass his own religion, belief, all presupposed ideas and discover his truer or real identity? To answer this sort of question Sartre referred to the concept of myth of the primitive men. Each primitive group had its own myth, totem, etc. Through their very own myth, totem, the members of the group could discover their mutual relation with each other. Actually these myths and totems according to Sartre helped to establish a sense of solidarity within a group. They were a total unit, different from another. This sense of unity helped them survive unitedly. Sartre mentioned in his dialogue that they (primitive men) invented an animal as a totem (they adopted it as an emblem), they believed that this totem was the genetic source of a particular group. So they started to believe themselves as brothers. But why did this totem make them think so? Sartre answered — a sense of brotherhood developed at that early stage through this concept. So the concept of brotherhood got another dimension by the invention of totem. But Sartre also mentioned that this invention is not the actual meaning of brotherhood.

---

[2] Rabindranath Tagore, 1972, *Religion of Man*, Delhi: Macmillan.

But one may object that Sartre practically tried to avoid the problem by inventing the concept of myth. One may suggest that Sartre adopted the Socratic method, i.e. whenever there was any difficulty or problem, concept of myth was then surely invoked for a solution. But what Sartre tried to stress was that brotherhood is the relation of human beings within the same clan. Sartre emphasized on a major point that the "birth" of two men must have got an equal importance. Thus when they talked to each other they seemed like the children of the same "mother". So the members of the same clan are nothing but the biological offspring of the same father and mother. Therefore, Sartre stressed on the point that "brotherhood" is nothing but the realization that all men are the children of the same mother.

But a question may be raised here: one can accept the concept of brotherhood theoretically but in real life when one is struggling through a critical situation for one's own survival, how can one be considered as brother to the other? So is there any interrelation between the concept of brotherhood and morality? In his "Last Dialogue" Sartre said that brotherhood is the mutual relation between man and man. Considering the human civilization one can say that men are emotionally and actively related with each other. Men have a future which will be based on their action. There will also be crisis in socio-economic sphere, i.e. primarily of scarcity. But there must be mutual cooperation with each other. Thus the future of humanity lies in the mutual sharing of two men. This relation will be developed on the truth that whatever "I" have is "yours" and whatever "you" have is "mine". And moreover, we can share our own resources: whenever the other one of us is in crisis.

Sartre in his "Last Dialogue" denied the so-called "production relation" of man propounded by Karl Marx. Sartre asserted that the deepest relation between two men is the relation which exceeds any sort of "production relation". Since they are not merely "producer" or "produced", they are something more than this relation. Their truer identity is that they are human beings. So according to Sartre, today we have to rethink or review the concept of humanity once again.

Sartre wanted to say in his "Last Dialogue" the "secret solidarity" between human beings. But what is the rudimentary source of this secret solidarity? Sartre cannot satisfactorily answer this question. We cannot get any stable human relation if we accept the concept of myth or totem. "Concepts" are of no use to get any permanent solution in the crisis of human relation. Rabindranath Tagore once said in his *Sādhanā*:

> Man must realize the wholeness of his existence, his place in the infinite; he must know that hard as he may strive he can never create his honey within the cells of his own hive, for the perennial supply of his life food is outside their walls.[3]

Sri Aurobindo in his *Essays on the Gītā* has discussed the same thing with a new dimension. So let us have a look at Sri Aurobindo's vision as reflected in this book:

> . . . the individual being begins with ignorance and persists long in ignorance. Actually conscious of himself he sees the ego as the cause and whole meaning of life and not the Divine. He sees himself on the doer of works and does not see that all the workings of existence including his own internal and external activities are the workings of one universal Nature and nothing else. . . . Because of this ignorance whose seal is egoism, the creature ignores the law of sacrifice and seeks to take all he can for himself and gives only what Nature by her internal and external compulsion forces him to give. . . . He misses the true meaning of life and, since he does not use life and works for the enlargement and elevation of his being through sacrifice, he lives in vain.
>
> Only when the individual being begins to perceive and acknowledge in his acts the value of the self in others as well as the power and needs of his own ego, begins to perceive universal Nature behind his own workings and through the cosmic godheads gets some glimpse of the One and the Infinite, is he on his way to the transcendence of his limitation by the ego and the discovery of his soul. He begins to discover a law other than that of his desires, to which his desires must be more and more subordinated and subjected; he develops the purely egoistic into the understanding and ethical being. He begins to give more value

[3] Rabindranath Tagore, 2005, *Sādhanā*, New Delhi: Rupa & Co.

> to the claims of the self in others and less to the claims of his ego; he admits the strife between egoism and altruism and by the increase of his altruistic tendencies he prepares the enlargement of his own consciousness and being. . . .
>
> But this is only a long intermediate stage. It is still subject to the law of desire, to the centrality of all things in the conceptions and needs of his ego and to the control of his being as well as his works by nature, though it is a regulated and governed desire, or clarified ego and a Nature more and more subtilized and enlightened by the sattwic, the highest natural principle. All this is still within the domain, though the very much enlarged domain, of the mutable, finite and personal. The real self-knowledge . . . can only come when he perceives that the self in him and the self in others are one being and this self is something higher than the ego, an infinite, an impersonal, a universal existence in whom all move and have their being, ...[4]

So, an individual according to Sri Aurobindo starts his journey with sheer egoistic or self-centred attitude. Then he understands that he has to come to terms with other's existence, he has to take help from others. But the other remains the other still. He suffers from insecurity, disharmony and precarious value. In this stage also, relationship depends on mutuality of interests. It is not true unity. Relation with other is not based on an inner realization of oneness. Coming to next stage, a man finds his own self in others. Only in the life of his fellow being is his life complete because he finds his own self in others. It does not depend on any external or material satisfaction. His existence is not complete without other's existence. Thus other is no longer the other. Other is an extension of his own self. This is the "supreme oneness". Out of this "supreme oneness", supreme value will one day emerge. In Sartrean language this "supreme value" can be expressed as "identification with other" — this identification will help a man to find his own inner value. This value can be based on Sri Aurobindo's terminology "an inner relation of oneness". Thus man is always keen to be associated with another man. An individual has at the same time his own needs, impulses, desires and also an urge to be associated with another human being.

---

4 Sri Aurobindo, 1955, *Essays on the Gītā*, Pondicherry: Sri Aurobindo Ashram.

One has to feel that this existence will not be meaningful unless the other exists. So, there must be a conflict between two opposite desires, interests, motive of conducts, etc. But how could this problem be resolved — by constructing some moral/ethical standards or criteria or something else? Does ethics play a necessary role in resolving this problem? In order to make reconciliation between two conflicting instincts, a third principle must come in.

According to Sri Aurobindo, there are four main standards of human conduct that make an ascending scale. The first is personal need, preference and desire; the second is the law and good of the collectivity; the third is an ideal ethic; necessity the last is the highest divine law of the nature. So the satisfaction of personal idea and feeling, need and desire, propensity and habit has to be constantly subordinated, by the necessity of the situation created by the society as a whole. According to Sri Aurobindo, "This social need is the obscure matrix of morality and of man's ethical impulse."[5]

British philosopher John Stuart Mill discussed this issue in his well-known book *On Liberty* which definitely claims another separate discussion. Here some of his major arguments will be discussed in the context of individual and collective relation. According to Mill,

> Though society is not founded on a contract, and though no good purpose is answered by inventing a contract in order to deduce social obligations from it, every one who receives the protection of society owes a return for the benefit, and the fact of living in society renders it indispensable that each should be bound to observe a certain line of conduct towards the rest. The conduct consists first, in not injuring the interests of one another; or rather certain interests . . . Secondly, in each person's bearing his share (to be fixed on some equitable principle) of the labours and sacrifices incurred for defending the society or its members from injury and molestation.[6]

He further said:

> As soon as any part of a person's conduct affects prejudicially the interests of others, society has jurisdiction over it, and the question

[5] Sri Aurobindo, *Synthesis of Yoga*, Pondicherry: Sri Aurobindo Ashram.

[6] John Stuart Mill, 1946, *On Liberty*, London: Oxford University Press.

> whether the general welfare will or will not be promoted by interfering with it becomes open to discussion.[7]

But one cannot always draw a clear demarcation between an individual and the society like Mill. There are so many facts where one could not determine who is perfect — individual or society? For example, when an individual takes a decision of his own, he may think that his decision will not affect the society, but on the other hand, society may demand that one's personal decision will not only affect his/her own life but also affect simultaneously the collective lives of the society. Mill did not suggest any solution to these borderline cases. Individual freedom or strict individualism is not the last word of the relation of individual and community.

Besides this there is still one more question. Mill gave immense importance to individual's freedom. The concept of freedom can be conceived in both ways: intrinsic and instrumental. Though Mill gave very much importance to the freedom of an individual, a question may still be raised: how can a person use his freedom in a right way? Here, some kind of inner "compass" is necessary. So the question is: what sort of compass can be the guide in an individual's life? These questions are not always answered very distinctly in Mill's philosophy. But on the other hand, Sartre also asserted that individual freedom is a must for one's own becoming or development. But this freedom cannot go farther alone, since freedom is also a multidimensional concept. A man having his own freedom is also responsible for others. One may ignore the other exclusively by limiting oneself to only one's freedom, desire and action — but in practice one cannot always do that. Why? Because the collective existence is also necessary for his very own existence. Indeed, the relation between an individual and a society is not static but rather dynamic. So space should be needed for their mutual growth. Sri Aurobindo discusses the same thing in *The Human Cycle* and shows that every individual being has two aspects — individual and collective. Sri Aurobindo stated very firmly and distinctly:

> Every time the society crushes or effaces the individual, it is inflicting a wound on itself and depriving its own life of priceless

7 John Stuart Mill, 1946, *On Liberty*, London: Oxford University Press.

> sources of stimulation and growth. The individual too cannot flourish by himself; for the universal, the unity and collectivity of his fellow beings, is his present source and stock; it is the thing whose possibilities he individually expresses, even when he transcends its immediate level, and of which in his phenomenal being he is one result. . . . This is what true subjectivism teaches us first, that we are a higher self than our ego or our members, secondly, that we are in our life and being not only ourselves but all others; for there is a secret solidarity which our egoism may kick at and strive against, but from which we cannot escape.[8]

Thus in man we find two distinct master impulses, the individualistic and the social. The possibility of their opposition and the attempt to find their equation lie at the very roots of human civilization and persists in their figures when he has passed beyond the vital animal into a highly individualized mental and spiritual progress. The existence of a social law external to the individual is at different times a considerable advantage and disadvantage to the development of the highest truth in man. It is an advantage at first when man is crude and incapable of self-control and self-finding. So it is necessary to moderate man's demands, to discipline its irrational and often violent movements and even to lose itself sometimes in a larger and less personal egoism. But the same social law becomes a disadvantage for the human being when he/she is ready to transcend the human formula or any external social standard which seeks to impose itself on him/her from outside. The condition of the perfection of this sort of individual being is that he/she shall grow from within and in an increasing freedom he/she will transcend the limited concept of perfection, training and discipline of any social order.

Therefore, though Sri Aurobindo admits the importance of social order for the growth of an individual, he emphasizes the need of a certain freedom of the individual for the same purpose:

> No state or legislator or reformer can cut him rigorously into a perfect pattern; no church or priest can give him a mechanical salvation; no order, no class life or ideal, no nation, no civilization

---

8 Sri Aurobindo, 1997, *The Human Cycle*, Pondicherry: Sri Aurobindo Ashram.

> or creed or ethical, social or religious Śāstra can be allowed to say him permanently, "In this way of mine and thus for shall thou act and grow and in no other way and no further shall thy growth be permitted." These things may help him temporarily or they may curb and he grows in proportion as he can use them and then exceed them, train and teach his individuality by them, . . . Always he is the traveller of the cycles and his road is forward.[9]

Sri Aurobindo in this context also mentioned,

> It is the old Indian discovery that our real "I" is a Supreme Being which is our true self and which it is our business to discover and consciously become and, secondly, that that Being is one in all, expressed in the individual and in the collectivity, and only by admitting and realising our unity with other can we entirely fulfil our true self-being.[10]

The central theme of all these experiences is that an individual first has to discover his own true self, then he makes his society more harmonious, beautiful and complete with his own inner potentialities. An individual will be utterly incomplete in its truest sense unless and until he exceeds his own limited self.

---

9 Sri Aurobindo, 1997, *The Human Cycle*, Pondicherry: Sri Aurobindo Ashram.

10 Ibid.

11

An Educationist in a Princely State
Sri Aurobindo and His Early Thoughts on Education

Anirban Ganguly

Introduction

IT is interesting to note that education was one of the constants in Sri Aurobindo's life. Starting from his early years in India from 1893 when he returned after a completely occidental education in England to his last days in Pondicherry — now Puducherry — the field of education remained a constant in Sri Aurobindo's life.

The thought of how education in India could be remoulded and restated in a new light, in a new dimension which would reflect the civilizational and cultural identity of the people and would be responsive to the traditions of the land while rejuvenating the ancient knowledge systems was something that pre-occupied Sri Aurobindo throughout his life. While in service of the princely state of Baroda in western India, he had the occasion of closely associating with the education system, during his political action in Bengal in the early years of the last century Sri Aurobindo actively associated with the movement for a national education for India; in fact he was one of the principal advocates and articulators in the educational debate of that epoch. In his retirement at Puducherry, Sri Aurobindo's focus on education continued albeit in a limited manner.

It was in Puducherry, nearly a century ago, that he wrote his ideas on a national system of education for India and enunciated his now well-known principles of education. In 1946, about four years before his passing away Sri Aurobindo again referred to the need for evolving a national system of education and before that in

1943 he had endorsed the efforts of the Mother, his spiritual collaborator, to inaugurate a school for the children of those who had joined his Ashram. Sri Aurobindo saw this school as a nucleus that would one day lead to a greater educational manifestation and expression by establishing a new approach to education.

In this paper I have essentially looked at Sri Aurobindo's educational involvement during his stay in Baroda between 1893 and 1906. Interestingly it was during this phase, while he observed the colonial Indian system of education in India, that Sri Aurobindo articulated many of his fundamental thoughts on education. These were to evolve over the years into more crystallized articulations and positions. A study of this phase provides an insight into Sri Aurobindo's early insights into education and enables us to trace the evolution of his educational thinking. I have attempted to read some of his writings of the epoch, to examine some of his articulations and educational activities, and through these trace his thinking and approach to the educational problems in India. Sri Aurobindo's essential role in the princely state of Baroda was that of an educationist and this first role defined his lifelong connection and link with education turning him into one of the pre-eminent educational thinkers of our age.

Exploring and Restating Self-identity through Education

A major line of action that Sri Aurobindo had supported for national resurgence and reconstruction, during his days as the leader of the advanced nationalist group, fighting for India's independence from the British, was the task of setting up an edifice of National Education.

Along with *Swaraj* (self-rule), *Swadeshi* (indigenous industrial production) and Boycott, National Education became a principal plank in the nationalist group's platform. The demand for establishing a system of national education was not a mere agitational programme but was one which attempted to bring about a decisive systemic change in the educational framework of India. The earnestness was evident when a serious attempt was made to open a national college in Calcutta in August 1906 and to systematically set up a chain of national schools and colleges all over Bengal and other parts of the country to try and provide a viable alternative for those who felt the colonial academic set-up to be mind-stunting and deracinating. Sri Aurobindo himself along with Lokmanya Tilak and other leaders of the nationalist bloc toured parts of India in order to elicit support for the cause of national education.[1]

Dictating a general note on his political life sometime around 1946, necessitated in order to rectify misconceptions about his stand and policies while in politics, Sri Aurobindo stated:

> . . . national education was another item [of the political action] to which he [i.e. Sri Aurobindo] attached much importance. He had been disgusted with the education given by the British system in the schools and colleges and universities, a system of which as a professor in the Baroda College he had full experience. He felt that it tended to dull and impoverish and tie up the naturally quick and brilliant and supple Indian intelligence, to teach it bad intellectual habits and spoil by narrow information and mechanical instruction its original productivity.[2]

It was essentially these challenges to the Indian mind and to Indian education that Sri Aurobindo sought to address through his writings, speeches and educational activism, first, during the revolutionary phase and even later when he retired from active politics. The emphasis was on the preservation of self-identity and also on the fact that loss of the inherent psychological and intellectual prowess of the Indian mind would eventually lead to the loss of a distinct national identity.

What concerns us in this discussion is the early phase, especially the phase when Sri Aurobindo came back to India and enlisted himself in the service of the Baroda state, it was a period when Sri Aurobindo himself worked to explore and articulate his civilizational self-identity.

---

1 See e.g. R.C. Majumdar, 1997, *History of the Freedom Movement in India,* vol. 2, repr., pp. 82-85; Haridas and Uma Mukherjee, 2000, *The Origins of the National Education Movement,* repr., pp. 126-34; Sri Aurobindo, 2005, *Speeches on Indian Politics and National Education* (1922), pp. 11-18, 62-65.

2 Sri Aurobindo, 2006, *Autobiographical Notes and Other Writings of Historical Interest,* p. 58.

In Baroda, Sri Aurobindo's chief roles were that of an educationist, an administrator and a student of the Indian classical scriptures. He undertook a wide and meticulous study of the Indian classics and scriptures. He recalled that period and his efforts at educating himself in assimilating the "spirit of Indian civilization":

> In England he [Sri Aurobindo] had received, according to his father's express instructions, an entirely occidental education without any contact with the culture of India and the East [it gave him though a wide exposure and introduction to the culture of ancient, mediaeval and modern Europe]. At Baroda he made up the deficiency, learned Sanskrit and several modern Indian languages, assimilated the spirit of Indian civilisation and its forms past and present.[3]

In order to try and assess how Sri Aurobindo worked on himself it would be interesting to take a look at his study of Indian languages and classics. Among other things, he worked at translating *Mahābhārata*. Dinendra Kumar Roy (1869–1943), a Bengali littérateur and author, who had been engaged "to help [Sri Aurobindo] to correct and perfect his knowledge of the language and to accustom him to conversation in Bengali"[4] observed that Sri Aurobindo was engaged in translating *Mahābhārata* and that he understood Sanskrit *Rāmāyaṇa* and *Mahābhārata* quite well and that he wrote poems based on some episodes of the *Mahābhārata*, "occasionally he used to read out poems to me", recalled Dinendra Kumar Roy and "[H]e would open *Rāmāyaṇa* and *Mahābhārata* and read out the original words to verify whether his rendering had been faithful."[5]

Interestingly from his own observations it appears that Sri Aurobindo learnt both Bengali and Sanskrit on his own – regarding the learning of Bengali he commented, that "before engaging [a] teacher [he] already knew enough of the language to appreciate the novels of Bankim and the poetry of Madhusudan".[6]

Around 1899 Romesh Chandra Dutt (1848–1909), historian,

---

[3] *Sri Aurobindo Birth Centenary Library*, vol. 30, Index & Glossary, p. 1, 1976.

[4] Sri Aurobindo, 2006, *Autobiographical Notes*, op. cit., pp. 43-44.

[5] Dinendra Kumar Roy, 2006, *With Aurobindo in Baroda*, p. 18 (tr. Maurice Shukla).

[6] Sri Aurobindo, 2006, *Autobiographical Notes*, op. cit., p. 44.

littérateur and administrator, whose poetic translations of parts of *Rāmāyaṇa* and *Mahābhārata* had just been released and had received high acclaim in England had come to Baroda, and on hearing that:

> Aurobindo had translated certain parts of *Rāmāyaṇa* and *Mahābhārata*, he expressed an eagerness to see the translations. . . . Mr. Dutt, discerning as he was in literary matters [said] "Seeing your poems, I regret all the trouble I went to trying to translate the *Rāmāyaṇa* and the *Mahābhārata*!"[7]

This meeting must have taken place sometime during 1898 and 1901, the period when Dinendra Kumar lived in Baroda and from whose description it is clear "that Dutt's reaction to Aravind's translation was positive".[8]

For a while — 1900 and 1901 — Sri Aurobindo developed the habit of noting down the books he was studying and also the number of pages read everyday, a closer look at these notes give an insight into the system he followed while reading the classics and also give an idea of what he read and the time he took to cover the subject:

> In September 1900 Sri Aurobindo studied a Sanskrit text of the *Mahābhārata*. On the fourth of September, besides correcting his class's examination papers, he read the 63 *ślokas* of *sūktas* 53 and 54 of the Virāṭaparva. He had read up to this point (i.e. *sūktas* containing 1,533 *ślokas*) in just eight days. In three more days he read twice over the whole first part ("Pūrvamegha") of Kālidāsa's famous *Meghadūta* or Cloud-Messenger.[9]

A further delving into extracts from Sri Aurobindo's notebooks gives an idea of the range he covered during this period, and it is useful to examine this aspect of his stay in Baroda in order to understand his involvement with education — first for himself, when as a student of classic he immersed himself in self-culture, self-study and then in the form of his academic duties as an educationist and education administrator. The extract from the notebooks point to

7 Dinendra Kumar Roy, 2006, op. cit., pp. 28-29.

8 For a description of this encounter between Dutt and "Aravind" see, e.g. Meenkashi Mukherjee, 2009, *An Indian for All Seasons: The Many Lives of R.C. Dutt*, pp. 250-53.

9 Roshan and Apurva, 1993, *Sri Aurobindo in Baroda*, pp. 101-02.

the following:

> On Thursday 3rd January 1901 he began the study of another of Kālidāsa's poem the *Raghuvaṁśa* — Canto I. 95 *śloka*s read with reference to Mallinātha's *Ṭīkā* [commentary]; understood; a number of words unknown, a few *śloka*s baffling till commentary consulted.
>
> Fri. Jan. 4th: *Raghuvaṁśa*. Canto I re-read with dictionary; meaning of unknown and imperfectly known words ascertained. Wealth and success *śloka*s of the *Hitopadeśa* entered in Collection. Tennyson's Coming of Arthur read with notes; also the whole introduction.
>
> Sat. Jan. 5th: *Raghuvaṁśa*. Canto II. 75 *śloka*s read with Mallinātha's Commentary. As Canto I. Freytag's Die Journalisten [A German play written in 1852 by the German playwright and novelist Gustav Freytag (1816-95)], a page and a half. Fate *ślokas* of *Hitopadeśa* entered in Collection.
>
> Sun. Jan. 6th: Raghuvaṁśa. Canto II re-read with dictionary. Die Journalisten 16 pages, i.e. to end of scene I.[10]

"Aurobindo's library", recalled Dinendra Kumar Roy, contained:

> piles of books in various European languages, all sorts of books in French, German, Russian, English, Greek, Latin, Hebrew. . . . His collection contained works by all the English poets from Chaucer to Swinburne . . . Homer's *Illiad*, Dante's great epic, our *Rāmāyaṇa* and *Mahābhārata*, books by Kālidāsa and other such poets were all there in his library.[11]

Can it be surmised from the above that Sri Aurobindo's habits and method of self-study which enabled him to successfully master subjects of which he had no exposure prior to his arrival in India, engendered in him a disgust for the mechanical "snippet"-oriented education that he found being encouraged by the official colonial machinery?

Handling and Observing Education in India

Ever since his return to India from England in 1893 Sri Aurobindo was associated with the imparting and organizing of education in

---

[10] Roshan and Apurva, 1993, op. cit., pp. 101-02.

[11] Dinendra Kumar Roy, 2006, op. cit., p. 36.

some capacity or the other. At Baroda, among other duties, he taught French in 1897 as a part-time lecturer at the Baroda College and then taught English as a permanent professor from 1900 onwards.

In 1904 he was appointed Vice-Principal of the College and became the Acting-Principal from March 1905 to February 1906 and in 1905 he became temporary "Minister-in-Charge of Education" of the Baroda State. These various stints must have given Sri Aurobindo an opportunity to observe at close quarters the colonial educational structure and its effect on the Indian students' mind and life.

His association thus with the education system of this country began since his return and, as he himself admits, this close and active association with the colonial academic world made him contemplate on the current nature and future possibilities of education. Sri Aurobindo's quest for evolving "a true education", it may be argued, began from this period onwards.

Recalling later his teaching experience at Baroda, Sri Aurobindo once observed that what had surprised him then "was that students used to take down everything verbatim and mug it up by heart". This sort of a thing, he felt, would never have happened in England.[12] Since the age of seven when he was taken to England, Sri Aurobindo had a thorough exposure to the British and European system of education and was deeply conversant with it and back in India he witnessed first-hand the application of a colonial system of education and quickly discerned its drawbacks. Commenting on methods followed by the students in the Baroda College, for example, Sri Aurobindo noted that

> the students besides taking my notes used to get notes of some professor from Bombay. . . . Once I was giving a lecture on Southey's Life of Nelson. My lecture was not in agreement with the notes. So the students remarked that it was not at all like what was found in the notes. . . .[13]

---

12 K.R. Srinivas Iyengar, 2006, *Sri Aurobindo: A Biography and a History*, p. 52, Sri Aurobindo International Centre of Education, 5th edn., Pondicherry.

13 Roshan and Apurva, 1993, op. cit., p. 78.

It may have been such experiences, which one finds in evidence even in the contemporary educational system and his keen observation of the human mind that, presumably, compelled Sri Aurobindo to critically examine the system.

Writing during this period (1893–1906) on the degradation of the faculties of the Indian mind brought about by the misapplication of educational principles, Sri Aurobindo observed rather scathingly, that the "university system" threatened and had initiated the process of irretrievable degradation leading to a final extinction of whatever was left of the "intellectual alertness", "quickness and originality of the Indian mind".[14]

"The first fundamental mistake" therefore of the educational approach, wrote Sri Aurobindo, in an early incomplete piece on education, was to "confine ourselves to the training of the storing faculty memory and the storage of facts and to neglect the training of the three great manipulating faculties, viz. the power of reasoning, the power of comparison and differentiation, and the power of expression", these faculties, he argued, exist "to a certain extent in all men" but they "demand cultivation, they demand that bringing out of natural abilities which is the real essence of education".

Sri Aurobindo's warning was that if this "fundamental mistake" was perpetuated and the three mental powers were not cultivated at the appropriate stage of the growth of the human mind it would lead to an eventual and general intellectual degeneration of an entire people.[15] For Sri Aurobindo the "easy assumption" that the primary and perhaps sole duty of education was to simply supply the mind with information and facts expecting the rest to develop on its own was an erroneous assumption.

> Amount of knowledge is in itself not of the first importance but to make the best use of what we know. The easy assumption of our educationists that we have only to supply the mind with a smattering of facts in each department of knowledge and the mind

---

[14] *Complete Works of Sri Aurobindo (CWSA)*, vol. 1, pp. 359-60, Sri Aurobindo Ashram, Pondicherry, 2003.

[15] Ibid.

> can be trusted to develop itself and take its own suitable road, is contrary to science, contrary to human experience and contrary to the universal opinion of civilized countries.[16]

This position which argued that the gathering of knowledge was not the primary but one of the duties of education and that what was of a more fundamental importance was the development of faculties that would assist in making right and cogent use of that knowledge is a position that remained constant in Sri Aurobindo's articulations and arguments on education, formulated over the decades.

Commenting on such a reductionist way of perceiving education — that it is merely for information gathering — Sri Aurobindo argued rather graphically in the same piece:

> To give the student knowledge is necessary, but it is still more necessary to build up in him the power of using his knowledge. It would hardly be a good technical education for a carpenter to be taught how to fell trees so as to provide himself with wood and never to learn how to prepare tables, chairs and cabinets or even what tools were necessary for his craft. Yet this is precisely what our system of education does. It trains the memory and provides the student with a store of facts and secondhand ideas. The memory is the woodcutter's axe and the store he acquires is the wood he has cut down in his course of tree felling. When he has done this, the University says to him "We now declare you a Bachelor of Carpentry; we have given you a good and sharp axe and a fair nucleus of wood to begin with. Go on, my son, the world is full of forests and provided the Forest Officer does not object you can cut down trees and provide yourself with wood to your heart's content." Now the student who goes forth thus equipped, may become a great timber-merchant but unless he is an exceptional genius he will never be even a moderate carpenter.[17]

In the same article Sri Aurobindo also argued that teachers ought to:

> Devote nine-tenths of their energies to the education of the active

[16] *Complete Works of Sri Aurobindo (CWSA)*, vol. 1, p. 360.

[17] Ibid., p. 359.

> mental faculties, [viz. the power of reasoning, the power of comparison and differentiation and the power of expression], while the passive retaining faculty [which he calls memory], should occupy a recognized and well-defined but subordinate place. . . .

Sri Aurobindo's perception or his continuing argument in the article was that a mere rearranging of the curriculum could not bring about such an approach and he enumerates that various subjects, if approached with an altered attitude — that is devoid of the usual mechanical information-providing approach — could be of help in developing these faculties:

> It is true that certain subjects are more apt to develop certain faculties than others; the power of accurate reasoning is powerfully assisted by Geometry, Logic and Political Economy; one of the most important results of languages is to refine and train the power of expression, and nothing more enlarges the power of comparison and differentiation than an intelligent study of history. But no particular subject except language is essential, still less exclusively appropriated, to any given faculty. There are types of intellect, for instance, which are constitutionally incapable of dealing with geometrical problems or even with the formal machinery of Logic, and are yet profound, brilliant and correct reasoners in other intellectual spheres. There is in fact hardly any subject, the sciences of calculation excepted, which in the hands of a capable teacher does not give room for the development of all the general faculties of the mind. . . . [18]

In the Baroda College Sri Aurobindo did not limit himself only to taking classes and to self-study but actively participated in various recreational activities. His acceptance of the Chairmanship of the Baroda College Union and Debating Society, brought him in closer contact with a larger number of students and gave him a greater opportunity to not only observe the effect that the education imparted had on them but to also share some of his views with them. His task as Chairman of the debating society was to mainly introduce visiting lecturers to the Union and "to regulate the course of the debate in such a way that the best in the students came out

---

[18] *Complete Works of Sri Aurobindo (CWSA)*, vol. 1, pp. 360-61.

and they didn't miss the spirit of intellectual inquiry in the excitement of the moment".[19]

Sri Aurobindo seized the opportunity of such occasions to project his ideas of what Indian educational institutions ought to strive to achieve in order to reach not only a certain degree of academic excellence but also to be able to create an atmosphere which would be congenial to an all-round personality development of the learner. A reading of some of the details of his only recorded talk of this period allows us to delve into Sri Aurobindo's early thinking on education.

In a talk that he delivered on 22 July 1899 before the College Social Gathering Oxford and Cambridge and what Indian universities ought to learn from them, Sri Aurobindo described the changes that the atmosphere of these ancient European seats of knowledge brought about in the character and outlook of a pupil who had spent three years within their precincts:

> He goes up from the restricted life of his home and school and finds himself in surroundings which with astonishing rapidity expand his intellect, strengthen his character, develop his social faculties, force out all his abilities and turn him in three years from a boy into a man. His mind ripens in the contact with minds which meet from all parts of the country and have been brought up in many various kinds of trainings, his unwholesome eccentricities wear away and the unsocial, egoistic elements of character are to a large extent discouraged. He moves among ancient and venerable buildings, the mere age and beauty of which are in themselves an education. He has the Union which has trained so many great orators and debaters, has been the first trial ground of so many renowned intellects. He has, too, the athletics clubs organized with a perfection unparalleled elsewhere, in which, if he has the physique and the desire for them he may find pursuits which are also in themselves an education. The result is that he who entered the university a raw student, comes out of it a man and a gentleman, accustomed to think of great affairs and fit to move in cultivated society, and he remembers his college and university with affection, and in after days if he meets with those who have

[19] Roshan and Apurva, 2006, op. cit., p. 87.

> studied with him he feels attracted towards them as to men with whom he has a natural brotherhood. This is the social effect I should like the colleges and universities of India also to exercise, to educate by social influences as well as those which are merely academical and to create the feeling among their pupils that they belong to the community, that they are children of one mother.[20]

Sri Aurobindo essentially covered here the aspects of intellectual training and character training — learners having come in contact with others expand their mental horizon, develop a certain degree of reciprocity and their idiosyncrasies of character and conduct hitherto based on the thought of self-first give way to a larger sense of accommodation and assimilation. The emphasis on physical training and the social influence Sri Aurobindo saw as developing a sense of brotherhood, companionship which brings about a greater social integration and equality. These, he felt, were the results of education in a premier educational institution in the West and which could, according to him, be implemented in India.

As a note of warning to those who thought that education was complete once one successfully completed the university course Sri Aurobindo argued that the university merely equips the pupil to continue his onward journey of self-development:

> There is too much of a tendency in this country to regard education as a mere episode, finished when once the degree is obtained. But the university cannot and does not pretend to complete a man's education; it merely gives some materials to his hand or points out certain paths he may tread, and it says to him, — "Here are the materials I have given into your hands, it is for you to make of them what you can"; or — "These are the paths I have equipped you to travel; it is yours to tread them to the end, and by your success in them justify me before the world.[21]

It is in such utterances and positions that one discerns a hint of another of his fundamental position on education, that education is an ongoing process in life and does not halt with the end of academics.

---

20 *CWSA*, vol. 1, p. 354.

21 Ibid., p. 355.

Early Public Expressions of the Educational Malaise: Analysing the Contemporaneity of Bankim Chandra Chatterjee's Education

During his stay at Baroda, as I have argued, Sri Aurobindo witnessed first-hand the application of the university system in India. It is evident from his own remarks that the situation as he found it and its adverse effects on the Indian mind had disturbed him much.

Though he formulated his educational regeneration framework during his active political phase in Bengal, he had started highlighting the defects and deficiencies of the system much earlier. We have analysed his address on education at the Baroda College Union gathering in 1899 but it would be interesting to observe that as early 1894 Sri Aurobindo had started publicly attacking the colonial educational system again in the pages of the Bombay Marathi–English weekly *Indu Prakash*. The subject was not education directly but was instead a seven-part article written between 16 July and 27 August 1894 on the iconic bard of Bengal, Bankim Chandra Chatterjee, who had just passed away. In the series Sri Aurobindo made some very bold and perceptive observations on the education then imparted in India, these observations were the first expressions, in seed form, of his later political programme and philosophy of education.

Sri Aurobindo discussed in this series the various facets of Bankim's life and work, giving a background of the society he lived and worked in, of his literary output, of his contributions to Bengal and to the Bengali people, of his hand in creating a national consciousness, in short, Sri Aurobindo analysed Bankim's contributions towards creating "a language, a literature and a nation".

In analysing "His Youth and College Life" Sri Aurobindo revealed how Bankim's genius was already self-expressing and that he was fortunate to be saved [i.e. to preserve and nurture that genius] by being unconventional in his approach to the education system then prevalent. Describing the situation thus Sri Aurobindo wrote:

> He [Bankim] ascended the school by leaps and bounds; so

> abnormal was his swiftness that it put his masters in fear for him. They grew nervous lest they spoil by over-instruction the delicate fibre of his originality, and with a wise caution they obstructed his entrance into the highest class. . . .[22]

That over-instruction at the formative stage impedes the natural growth of the child and blocks the surfacing of her/his latent qualities and talents is an idea that is found in these words, such a position Sri Aurobindo would reiterate even later. In preventing Bankim from being promoted and thus being over-instructed with non-essentials his masters, Sri Aurobindo argued, did him a very good turn and assisted in the growth of his genius.

Sri Aurobindo's discussion of Bankim's education evolution looked in the same detail at his higher education:

> Bankim had always an extraordinary luck. Just as at school his fine promise was saved by the prudence of its guardians from the altar of High Education, the Moloch to whom we stupidly sacrifice India's most hopeful sons, so it was saved at Hugly College by his own distaste for hard work. . . . [23]

Sri Aurobindo saw higher education in the country as impediment to the emergence of essential qualities of the student. He considered it to be more of a routine drudgery to be indulged in, in order to attain a position in the job market of the colonial administrative set-up. Bankim, Sri Aurobindo argued, refused to do that, he refused to undergo the grinding hard work of cramming and regurgitation. Instead what did Bankim do, he initiated himself in the process of *svādhyāya* (self-study) having won easily laurels within the existing system without, one would say much effort, he indulged himself in his "caprices", and "conceived at this time", observed Sri Aurobindo, "a passion for Sanskrit and read with great perseverance at a *paṇḍit*'s *tol* [indigenous school]".

In a single year Bankim had studied and absorbed the major Sanskrit works — both grammar and literary. "Advancing at this pace," pointed out Sri Aurobindo, "he managed in something under

---

22 *CWSA*, vol. 1, op. cit., Bankim Chandra Chatterji, 2003, *His Youth & College Life*, p. 91, Sri Aurobindo Ashram, Pondicherry.

23 Ibid.

four years to get a sense of mastery in the ancient tongue and a feeling for its literary secrets which gave him immense leverage in his work of creating a new prose. . . . "

Keeping in line with Sri Aurobindo's broader educational point it can be argued that it was in the classes which he attended in a *tol* system that Bankim succeeded in extracting the essence that these systems had to offer and having thoroughly imbibed them could give an altogether original direction to the language that he began expressing himself in. In Sri Aurobindo's perception Bankim could do this because, first, he decided to break away from the routine of an artificial instruction and second, because he had the urge to pursue his interest, it was this urge — his *svabhāva* (his innate propensity for a perfect self-expression) which gradually led him to his *svadharma* (his unique duty in life).

The next unnatural — for the period — step was his cutting short "his attendance at Hugly College" at the age of seventeen because, as Sri Aurobindo analysed:

> His spirit needed larger bounds than a school routine could give it, and refused, as every free mind does, to cripple itself and lose its natural suppleness. It was his constant habit, a habit which grew on him with the lapse of time, to hide himself in a nook of the College Library and indulge his wandering appetite in all sorts of reading. At the eleventh hour and with an examination impending, he would catch up his prescribed books, hurry through them at a canter, win a few prizes, and go back to his lotus-eating.[24]

This, Sri Aurobindo argued, was the case with brilliant minds in "all countries", and its positive side was that, "it save[d] [these minds] from the sterilizing effects of over instruction; . . . "[25] Through a discussion of this aspect of Bankim's educational evolution, Sri Aurobindo articulated the principal which argued that learners, in course of their instruction, must be allowed to participate in some creative activity, which is after their hearts, their inclinations and interests. It is such an approach that, Sri Aurobindo felt, contributed immensely to the moulding of character, outlook and personality

---

[24] *CWSA*, vol. 1, op. cit., Bankim Chandra Chatterji, 2003, op. cit., p. 91.

[25] Ibid.

and in unfolding the latent genius in the individual.

This idea, stretched across a spectrum of half a century, was put into practice when the International Centre of Education was founded in Sri Aurobindo's name at Puducherry in 1951. The realization that every child was unique and had the capacity to express that uniqueness if provided with a balanced educational atmosphere and framework and with the right environment was one of the dominant ideas that shaped the Centre of Education. Over the years it refused to tie itself up in a routine of instruction and examination and instead facilitated innate talents the learners to manifest their by providing scope for a variety of activities that could attract the interest of the growing mind and develop their varied interests and capacities.

A continued reading of Sri Aurobindo's series on Bankim reveals his early educational ideas in a micro form. Discussing briefly Bankim's sojourn at the Presidency College at Calcutta, Sri Aurobindo pointed out that he was preparing himself for law with the intention of qualifying as a High Court pleader but, "at the right moment for literature the Calcutta University came into being and Bankim took literary honours instead of legal. The court [thus] lost a distinguished pleader and India gained a great man."

Though Bankim found time from "hard official drudgery and larger literary toil to appear with his usual distinguished success for the B.L.", it is to be observed that finally it was in his area of interest that he could alone make a lasting and original contribution acquiring for himself an exalted place in the psyche and imagination of the nation and its people.[26]

Through these series Sri Aurobindo has essentially tried to analyse how the colonial education system denied the deeper dimensions of education which reflected in the capacity of identifying one's area of interest in which one could deeply train oneself, widely excel and eventually discover a deeper fulfilment and evolve a finer excellence.

This series on Bankim, is perhaps, among the few writings of

---

26 *CWSA*, vol. 1, op. cit., Bankim Chandra Chatterji, 2003, op. cit., pp. 92-93.

Sri Aurobindo which contains many such expressions of his early educational thought. A further exploration of its other sections provides further insight into his early educational thought.

Terming Indians as a scholastic people Sri Aurobindo, very interestingly and strikingly argued that the Indian mind in the field of education was obsessed with the passing of examinations and the acquiring of academic degrees. He saw this as the *summum bonum* of the educational system then. "We are a scholastic people," he commented, "and in our life examinations and degrees fill up half the book. But examinations and degrees are a minor episode in the history of a mind."[27]

Such a position would eventually evolve into another fundamental principle of Sri Aurobindo's education thought. This principle essentially argued that the education which had as its principle objective the successful passing of examinations and the earning of a degree was not the true kind of education because it did not develop fully the faculties and powers of the mind, and focused rather on unthinking retention.

The Centre of Education at Puducherry where the role of examinations and degrees, as understood in the conventional sense, is non-existent or at the most negligible put into practice this fundamental principle.

Such an educational course may appear impractical or of no value to those accustomed to the pace of an exam oriented education but this was the approach of the Centre of Education right from its inception. It would be necessary at some point to look at the concept of competition and examination in context of Integral Education, since both these terms seem to be largely driving educational goals today and are at the root of much societal discord and dissatisfaction. Such an approach which is dominated by a sense of competition appears to seed young minds with the growth of artificial needs, the concept of excelling at any cost and prevents a spontaneous growth of qualities of empathy, compassion and brotherhood.

The lack of this growth in young minds — or rather the

27 *CWSA*, vol. 1, op. cit., Bankim Chandra Chatterji, 2003, op. cit., p. 93.

prevention of this growth, for all of these uniting qualities are present in the individual — contributes towards an imbalance in collective life. Like Tagore's early stand at Visva-Bharati, examinations in the Centre of Education at Puducherry too were never given primacy and did not emerge as the base of the educational system.[28]

The seed of his first principle of teaching that nothing can be essentially taught is also found in Sri Aurobindo next observation in the piece. ". . . [N]othing which is worth knowing can be taught" argued Sri Aurobindo while evolving another pillar principle of his education thought:

> Not what man learns, but what he observes for himself in life and literature is the formative agency in his existence, and the actual shape it will take is much determined by the sort of social air he

[28] The Visva-Bharati prospectus stated: "The system of examination will have no place whatsoever in the Viswabharati, nor is there any conferring of degree." Vide Abhik Kumar De, *Rabindranath O Charu Chandra Dutt: Kayekti Prasanger Prekhite* [Beng] in *Chaturanga,* vol. 67, no. 1 for Tagore's letters on the subject. Writing to Charu Chandra Dutt [C.C. Dutt I.C.S. (1876–1952), a close revolutionary associate of Sri Aurobindo, an important financier of the revolutionary movement, one of the first historians of the Indian National Congress, he was given charge of writing it in the 1928 session of the Congress, associated with Tagore at Visva-Bharati between 1931-38 out of which he held the post of Vice-Chancellor for five years and later joined Sri Aurobindo Ashram at Puducherry in 1946 where, till his passing in 1953, he was actively involved in the educational experiment of the Ashram] on 7 January 1936 Tagore expressd his anguish at having to institutionally bow down before the examination structure of the Calcutta University because there was a demand/clamour for it. Such a compromise Tagore felt was gradually narrowing the manifestations of his educational ideal. The article contains some revealing letters on this aspect and gives an insight into Tagore's own thinking on the issue. The prospectus of Sri Aurobindo International Centre of Education contains the following words printed in bold, "the Centre of Education awards no degrees or diplomas" and states one of its objects as providing "an atmosphere where knowledge is sought for the sake of knowledge and for the building up of the character". In its note on the higher courses of the Centre of Education the prospectus states that, "there is no system of conventional examinations or tests and the system of continuous assessment and evaluation of the student is continued". Vide, handbook brought out by the Centre of Education on its system of education and its aims and objectives. Thus the parallel between the two regarding the examination system and awarding of degrees is evident, the difference being that Tagore's experiment was perhaps on a wider scale.

> happens to breathe at that critical moment when the mind is choosing its road. All else is mere dead material useless without the breath of a vivifying culture. If examinations and degrees are the skeleton of university life, these are its soul and life-blood, and where they exist poorly or not at all, education, except for the one or two self-sufficing intellects becomes mere wind and dust.[29]

This, it may be argued, is the essence of Sri Aurobindo's early critique of the education system. The idea that examinations and degrees are just a part of the whole system and that the real formative acquisitions are those that the individual observes and absorbs from his surrounding and that the environment has an influence on the growth of the mind is articulated in these observations.

In continuation Sri Aurobindo discussed the environment in which Bankim grew and developed his faculties. Raising the issue of language, Sri Aurobindo argued that when the Indian students' mind is "tenderest and needs the most careful rearing" it is then subjected to "the wicked and wantonly cruel strain of instruction through a foreign tongue"; and an "enormous academic labour"[30] in mastering this language pushed them towards a premature exhaustion and decline.

Discussing the positive contribution of the environment Sri Aurobindo pointed out that whatever Bankim lost, being exposed to a rigid and unresponsive academic system, he made up through "his youthful surroundings" from which he gained much "emotional experience and great flexibility of mind". Bankim's exceptional talent, argued Sri Aurobindo, was nurtured and saved because of its environment:

> . . . With a limited creature like man, the power of the environment is immense, Genius it is true exists independently of environment and by much reading and observation may attain to self-expression but it is environment that makes self-expression easy and natural; that provides sureness, verve, stimulus. Here lies the importance to the mind in its early stage of self-culture of fine social surroundings; — that sort of surroundings which our

---

[29] *CWSA*, vol. 1, Bankim Chandra Chatterji, 2003, op. cit., p. 93.

[30] Ibid., p. 97.

> universities do nothing and ought to have done everything to create.[31]

This is another cardinal pillar of Sri Aurobindo's educational philosophy, the importance of the environment in moulding the individual. The then prevailing education system, Sri Aurobindo felt, did not provide the opportunity for young minds to consciously imbibe from their surroundings.

Sri Aurobindo reiterated in his later articulation on a philosophy of national education this dimension of the environment as the medium. It became a cornerstone of his third educational principle, which argued for the need to work from "the near to the far, from that which is to that which shall be".

"The basis of a man's nature," Sri Aurobindo argued in his famous principle, "is almost always, in addition to his soul's past, his heredity, his surroundings, his nationality, his country, the soil from which he draws sustenance, the air which he breathes, the sights, sounds, habits to which he is accustomed. They mould him not the less powerfully because insensibly, and from that then we must begin".[32]

On the language used for instruction Sri Aurobindo agued much in the same manner in later writings:

> The mother-tongue is the proper medium of education and therefore the first energies of the child should be directed to the thorough mastering of the medium.

Interestingly on the language issue Sri Aurobindo supported the learning and mastery of a variety of languages but only when

> When the mental instruments are sufficiently developed to acquire a language easily and swiftly, that is the time to introduce him [the child] to many languages easily and swiftly.[33]

The system of exposing the learner to many subjects at a time and to burden the mind with over-instruction was a degenerative

---

31 *CWSA*, vol. 1, Bankim Chandra Chatterji, 2003, op. cit., p. 98.

32 Ibid., pp. 384-85.

33 *CWSA*, vol. 1, Bankim Chandra Chatterji, 2003, op. cit., p. 394.

approach according to Sri Aurobindo. "To find your vocation and keep to it," Sri Aurobindo argued:

> . . . is not indeed a showy, but it is a simple and solid rule of life. We forget that the mind is as mortal and as much subject to wear and tear as any perishable thing, forgetting that specialism is one condition of the highest accomplishment, forgetting that our stock of energy is limited and that what we expend in one direction, we lose in another. We insist on burning the candle at both ends. This spirit appears in our system of public instruction, the most ingeniously complete machine for murder that human stupidity ever invented, and murder not only of a man's body but of a man's soul, of that sacred fire of individuality in him. . . .[34]

This thought seems to have stuck and later when writing exclusively on the subject of a national education, Sri Aurobindo reiterated this point of trying to teach a number of subjects all at once, by giving an imperfect little of each, he called it the method of teaching by "snippets":

> A subject is taught a little at a time, in conjunction with a host of others, with the result that what might be well learnt in a single year is badly learned in seven and the boy goes out ill-equipped, served with imperfect parcels of knowledge, master of none of the great departments of human knowledge. . . . The old system was to teach one or two subjects well and thoroughly and then proceed to others. . . .[35]

Sri Aurobindo brought up the issue of instruction in the mothertongue once more in the pages of the article and argued that Bankim's mastery of his mother tongue gave him the capability of producing such a rich and unique literary output. Talking of learning a foreign language and using it as a medium of expression Sri Aurobindo observed that, "in a language [one has learnt], [one] may write graciously, correctly, pleasingly, but [one] will never attain to the full stature of [one's] genius". Bankim was fortunate, he argued, because he "wrote in his own beautiful mother tongue and could therefore unravel himself near completely".

---

34 *CWSA,* vol. 1, Bankim Chandra Chatterji, 2003, op. cit., p. 105.

35 *CWSA,* vol. 1: *On Education: Simultaneous & Successive Teaching,* p. 393.

Bankim's originality, Sri Aurobindo observed, "Would in any case have forced its way out" and if he had only worked "single-heartedly in the field of his rich harvests" and did not have to undergo the strains of a daily official drudgery would his output have been far greater than is otherwise available.[36]

Sri Aurobindo saw Bankim making Bengali the principal language of public expression for the Bengali, "Bankim's influence has been far-reaching," Sri Aurobindo observed, concluding the assessment,

> Perhaps it may very roughly be summed up thus. When a Maratha or Gujarati has anything important to say, he says it in English; when a Bengali, he says it in Bengali. That is, I think, the fact which is most full of meaning for us in Bengal. It means besides other things less germane to literature, that, except in politics and journalism which is the handmaid of politics, English is steadily driven out of the field. Soon it will only remain to weed it out of our conversation.[37]

While elaborating on the discussion of language Sri Aurobindo referred to the work of Kali Prasanna Ghosh[38] who had, Sri Aurobindo felt, already given shoulder to the wheel that would

---

[36] *Bankim Chandra Chatterji: His Versatility,* op. cit., p. 105.

[37] Ibid.

[38] Kali Prasanna Ghosh (1843–1910): Bengali scholar and littérateur, learnt Persian, Sanskrit and Bengali in childhood and learnt English at the age of ten in the Dacca Collegiate School. Studied the *Mugdhabodh, Raghuvaṁśa, Meghadūtam* at the entrance level and then studied English literature, history, psychology, logic, theology, etc. at Calcutta. In 1870 he became the editor of *Subhasini,* a journal of Brahmo youth, and in 1874, edited the journal *Bandhab.* While working as the principal officer of the Raja of Bhawal he established the Sahitya Samalochana Sabha (literary discussion society), equally dexterous in speaking English, Kali Prasanna became a distinguished member of the Bangiya Sahitya Parishad, later became its vice-president, and became the president of the Sahitya Sammelan. (Source: *Bangali Charitabidhan,* vol. 1, 2nd edn., 2002, Kolkata.) Kali Prasanna followed a Sankritized Bengali style and it resembled that of the early writings of Vidyasagar. He was conferred the honorific of Vidyasagar by the *paṇḍit*'s of Dacca, and came to be known popularly as the Vidyasagar of East Bengal. The reflective essays collected in his *Prabhatchinta* (Morning Thoughts, 1877) and *Nisithachinta* (Midnight Thoughts, 1896) enjoyed a vogue for a long time as school textbooks. Source: Sukumar Sen, 2002, "Essays and Essay Writers (1850–1914)", in *Studies in Bengal Renaissance,* 3rd rev. edn., NCE, Kolkata.

finally drive out the usage of English in the public domain. "Not long ago," wrote Sri Aurobindo:

> Anyone moving in that province of the mind which Babu Kali Prasanna has annexed, would have held it beneath the dignity of his subject to write in any medium but English. Work like Babu Kali Prasanna's marks an important stage in the great revolution of sentiment which our literary class has set going, the revolution of sentiments which promises to make the Bengalis a nation. . . . Young Bengal gets its ideas, feelings and culture not from schools and colleges, but from Bankim's novels and Rabindranath Tagore's poems; so true is it that language is the life of a nation.[39]

If "a renaissance creates a new mind, brings about a reawakening"[40] then it certainly did that in Bankim, it presented him as a new mind which brought about a new awakening. It was this "revolution of sentiments" that nurtured Bankim and he in turn gave his energies into making a nation through the power of his language and imagination.

A detailed reading of this piece on Bankim was thus necessitated as it contained a number of key ideas on education that Sri Aurobindo developed later, ideas that indicated a way towards a future national education philosophy. Some key ideas, such as the principle that nothing can be truly taught, that the environment had a deep impact on the formative mind, that one should have the leisure to follow one's own inclinations and develop oneself in ones chosen field of interest and thereby make one's unique contribution to one's national life, the importance of the vernacular in expressing oneself and in forming one's identity, the importance of not dissipating oneself in a maze of subjects and thus prevent the mind from developing the capacity of delving deep into a subject, etc. can be discerned in this piece. These are the earliest known public formulation of Sri Aurobindo's educational ideas, formulation which would gradually find greater articulation and credence in course of the evolution of the national education movement.

---

39 *Bankim Chandra Chatterji: What He Did for Bengal & Our Hope in the Future*, op. cit., pp. 115, 118.

40 R.K. Dasgupta's Introduction to the 3rd edn. of *Studies in the Bengal Renaissance*.

Early Suggestions for Reform in Education

For a brief period in 1905 Sri Aurobindo was Minister-in-Charge of Education in the Baroda state and held simultaneously the post of the acting Principal of the Baroda College. While carrying out this dual responsibility, he wrote a minute on a "Proposed Examination for Teachers" dated 9 August 1905 for the consideration of "The Minister of Education" — Baroda.

> The minute contained some of his early opinions on the examination system. "I have gone very carefully," wrote "A.A.G. Ag. Principal, Baroda College", "through the scheme of the proposed examination for teachers . . . [&] I do not quite see the object of introducing this severe and stringent examination into our State. Our schools are working quite well enough on the whole for the purpose of education as given in this country. I do not myself think very highly either of the principle or methods or results of that education but, being subject to the Bombay University, we have to take things as they are and cannot attempt anything ideal. . . .[41]

Sri Aurobindo's dissatisfaction with the then prevailing university system in India expressed itself through the minute. But as an official of the Baroda state, Sri Aurobindo could not demand a radical disaffiliation with the official system. The examinations, Sri Aurobindo had then suggested, could be modified by "a mild test" because, as he observed:

> The sort of examination here proposed is such as might be prescribed in an European country where the science and art of education are really advanced. Here it is likely to degenerate into a formality harassing the teachers but useless to the State. . . . Undoubtedly the teachers will cram up the subjects learning by rote as is the habit in this country and percentage of them will pass, but there it will end; a few of the brighter and smarter young men may understand and make the attempt to apply the principles they learn, but that will be all. . . .[42]

---

[41] *CWSA*, vol. 1, op. cit., Opinions Written as Acting Principal, Baroda College: 1905, pp. 745-54.

[42] Ibid.

Looking at the discussion on the "Junior Examination" in Part II of the minute, one briefly comes across Sri Aurobindo's reflections on the method:

> Instead of the elaborate affair [proposed system of examinations] it will be enough to see whether the teacher can make the boys understand the lesson, explain a subject correctly and command their attention. . . .[43]

One also finds a detailed note on the necessity of a "Head Assistant for the High School"; where Sri Aurobindo discussed, in some detail, the workings of the Baroda High School revealing the fact that he did have first-hand experience and knowledge of the administrative aspects of the colonial education system and the running of schools under it.

Sri Aurobindo was not only concerned with creating a new philosophy of education but he also realized that the whole structure of education would have to be reconstituted if national education had to really play the role of nation making. Interestingly, in one of his last articles on education, while in Bengal, in January 1910, Sri Aurobindo articulated the demand for setting up a wholly new teacher's training courses that would train teachers, keeping in mind the national requirement and temperament.[44] It was this aspect that was missing from the national education experiment initiated by the National Council of Education. He realized that the teachers' coming out of training colleges instituted by the colonial education department would be incapable of imparting a radically new educational direction to the country.

---

[43] *CWSA*, vol. 1, op. cit., Opinions Written as Acting Principal, Baroda College: 1905, pp. 745-54.

[44] In his article on National Education in the *Karmayogin* of 1 January 1910, Sri Aurobindo pointed to the problem of inadequacy of trained teachers, he pointed out that the necessity of "providing a regular and plentiful supply of teachers trained in an entirely new system of instruction" [as he had hoped the national education system would eventually evolve] still remained because the Council, he observed "has systematically ignored [it], and not even the elementary steps of establishing a Teacher's Training Class in Calcutta and issuing a series of suitable books in the vernacular has been attempted. [*CWSA*, vol. 8, *Karmayogin*, p. 388, Sri Aurobindo Ashram, Pondicherry, 1997.]

Perhaps the following words, meant for public delivery, best illustrates Sri Aurobindo's position and thinking on the demand for national education, its use as an instrument for self-determination. Drafted in 1902, this incomplete speech contains some more educational thoughts, it would be useful thus to cast a brief look at it:

> The subject on which I wish to address you this evening . . . is Education. Some of you may ask yourselves, why this subject rather than another? It is not a new subject but rather quite a threadbare one; you have already heard and read much about it and probably listened to much better lectures on the subject than any I can give you; it has besides been handled by a great many men in high places of authority; most of all, it has been taken up by no less a person than Lord Curzon himself and measures are to be formulated and perhaps carried into execution for the reform of what is defective in the present system. "What more do you want," you will perhaps ask, "or why should we trouble ourselves about it? The Government of India will in its own good time reform the whole business and of course when their new system is in force the Baroda Schools and Colleges will assimilate themselves to it. Meanwhile it is quite superfluous for us to bother our heads about the matter." Now in answer to that attitude I have to say this that the Government of India is in the first place not the fit body to formulate the necessary improvements and in the second place not the fit instrument to put them into force. It is no fit to formulate them because it cannot realize and feel as we do where the shoe pinches us and therefore in mending it. . . .[45]

The early formulations of an uncompromising critic of the colonial educational system had begun. Sri Aurobindo's early articulations through his essays, notes, minutes and speeches contain his early ideas and thoughts on education; a reading reveals the fascinating contemporaneity of these thoughts and the possibility of their dynamic application to the ongoing quest for evolving a national education policy for India. The educational points articulated by an educationist in an Indian princely state, more than a century ago, remains as relevant today as when they were first articulated.

---

45 *CWSA*, vol. 1, *On Education*, op. cit., p. 357.

References

Aurobindo, Sri, 1976, *Birth Centenary Library*, vol. 30: *Index & Glossary*, Puducherry: Sri Aurobindo Ashram.

———, 1997, *Complete Works*, vol. 8, Pondicherry: Sri Aurobindo Ashram.

———, 2003, *Complete Works*, vol. 1, Pondicherry: Sri Aurobindo Ashram.

———, 2005, *Speeches on Indian Politics and National Education*, (1922), Pondicherry: Sri Aurobindo Ashram.

———, 2006, *Autobiographical Notes & Other Writings of Historical Interest*, Pondicherry: Sri Aurobindo Ashram.

De, Abhik Kumar, "Rabindranath O Charu Chandra Dutt: Kayekti Prasanger Prekhite" [Beng] in *Chaturanga*, 67(1), Kolkata.

Iyengar, K.R. Srinivas, 2006, *Sri Aurobindo: A Biography & A History*, Pondicherry: Sri Aurobindo International Centre of Education, 5th edn.

Majumdar, R.C., 1997, *History of the Freedom Movement in India*, vol. 2, Kolkata: Firma KLM, repr.

Mukherjee, Haridas & Uma, 2000, *The Origins of the National Education Movement*, Kolkata: National Council of Education, Bengal, repr.

Mukherjee, Meenkashi, 2009, *An Indian for All Seasons: The Many Lives of R.C. Dutt*, New Delhi: Penguin.

Roshan & Apurva, 1993, *Sri Aurobindo in Baroda*, Puducherry: Sri Aurobindo Ashram.

Roy, Dinendra Kumar, 2006, *With Aurobindo in Baroda* (tr. Maurice Shukla), Puducherry: Sri Aurobindo Ashram.

Sengupta, Subodh Chandra and Anjali Bose (eds.), 2002, *Bangali Charitabidhan*, vol. 1, Kolkata: Sahitya Samsad, 2nd edn.

Studies in Bengal Renaissance, Kolkata: National Council of Education, Bengal, 3rd rev. edn., 2002.

Contributors

Dr Susmita **Bhattacharya** is Assistant Professor of Philosophy in a government college of West Bengal. Her areas of interest are Phenomenology, Existentialism, Postmodernism, Recent Indian Philosophy, especially the philosophy of Sri Aurobindo. She has completed her PhD in Human Existence: Crisis and Beyond – Visions of Sri Aurobindo and Soren Kierkegaard.

Professor S.E. **Bhelke** is the Former Professor and Head, Department of Philosophy, University of Pune. Presently he is the Director of the Centre for Studies in Jainism,Vidyavihar, Mumbai. His areas of interest are Western and Indian Logic, Epistemology, Metaphysics, Aesthetics, Ethics, Classical Philosophy, Kashmiri Saivism, Ayurveda and Indian Psychology. He has written and edited several books in Marathi, Hindi and English.

Dr Anirban **Ganguly** is the Director of Dr Syama Prasad Mookerjee Research Foundation, New Delhi. He is the member of the Central Advisory Board of Education (CABE). Dr Ganguly had his early education at Sri Aurobindo International Centre of Education, Puducherry and successfully obtained his doctoral thesis from Jadavpur University, Kolkata on "The Early Nationalist Education Movement in India". He has jointly edited the book *Education: Philosophy & Practice*. Ganguly is the author of the books *Debating Culture* and *Swami Vivekananda: Buddha & Buddhism – A Mystic Link.*

Professor Raghunath **Ghosh** is the Professor of Philosophy and Ex-Dean, Faculty of Arts, Commerce & Law, University of North Bengal. He has published fourteen books on Nyāya, Aesthetics, Buddhism, Modern Indian Thought and many scholarly papers in renowned journals. He was UGC Visiting Fellow and ICPR Visiting Professor to many universities.

Professor Bijayananda **Kar** is the former Professor of Philosophy, Utkal University. As a British Council Fellow he has acted as Visiting Professor in London, Oxford, Manchester and Edinburg universities. He was invited as a Visiting Fellow to Greece and Paris. He has written many scholarly books like *Indian Theories of Error; Analytical Indian Philosophy; Value Perspective in Indian Philosophy* and *The Philosophy of Lokāyata.*

Professor Ulrich **Mohrhoff**, a scholar in Physics joined the Sri Aurobindo International Centre of Education (SAICE) in Pondicherry in 1972, where he studied Physics, Sanskrit and Indian Philosophy. He is the author of *The World According to Quantum Mechanics: Why the Laws of Physics Make Perfect Sense After All.* He has written several papers in renowned journals like *Foundations of Physics; Journal of Consciousness Studies; International Journal of Quantum Information; Quantum Studies: Mathematics and Foundations* and *American Journal of Physics* and was the editor of *Anti Matters,* a quarterly open-access e-journal addressing issues in science and the humanities from non-materialistic perspectives.

Professor Asok Kumar **Mukhopadhyay** is the Former Netaji Subhas Chandra Bose Professor of Political Science, Calcutta University and Former UGC Emeritus Fellow in Political Science. He has written many scholarly papers and books like *Bharatiyo Rashtrocinta Parichoy* (ed.); *Politics of Water Supply: The Case of Victorian London* and *Panchayat Administration in West Bengal.*

Professor Stephen **Phillips**, the scholar from Harvard University, is the Professor of Philosophy and Asian Studies at the University of Texas at Austin. He has written several books and scholarly papers. *Yoga, Karma, and Rebirth* and *Classical Indian Epistemology: The Knowledge Sources of the Nyāya School* are his books. His book *Yoga, Karma, and Rebirth* has received the recognition of "Outstanding Academic Title" by *Choice* in 2010. He was the Visiting Professor at The Centre for Sri Aurobindo Studies, Department of Philosophy, Jadavpur University in 2008.

Professor Ramesh Chandra **Pradhan**, Former Professor of Philosophy, University of Hyderabad, was the Common Wealth Academic Staff Fellow at Oxford University. His areas of specialization are Philosophy of Language, Wittgenstein, Analytic Philosophy. He is the author of many books among which we can name *Recent Development in Analytic Philosophy; Great Mirror: An Essay on Wittgenstein's Tractatus, Truth;* and *Meaning and Understanding.*

Dr Dilip Kumar **Roy** was a Reader in Philosophy of the erstwhile Presidency College, Kolkata. He later joined the Educational Service of the Government of West Bengal. He has published several books, viz. *The Philosophy of George Santayana; The Comparative Study of Religions; The Dynamic Absolute – A Preface to Sri Aurobindo's Integral Advaita* and *Upaniṣad Prasange Sri Aurobindo.* Dr Roy received Sri Aurobindo Puraskar from Sri Aurobindo Samiti of Sri Aurobindo Bhavan, Shakespeare Sarani, Kolkata for his contribution to the field of Sri Aurobindo's Yoga and Philosophy.

Professor Indrani **Sanyal**, Professor of Philosophy, Jadavpur University, is the founder member of the Centre for Sri Aurobindo Studies, Jadavpur University. She was the coordinator of the Centre from its inception. She is an eminent scholar and is comfortable in all branches of Philosophy, especially in Metaphysics, Ethics and Modern Indian Thought. From her special interest in the philosophy of Sri Aurobindo she has edited with others *Sri Aurobindo and His Contemporary Thinkers; Education: Philosophy and Practice;* and *Understanding Thoughts of Sri Aurobindo.* She has also edited *Sri Aurobindo: The Poet, Yogi and Philosopher: A Collection of Essays* by Arabinda Basu.

Index